MARKIEVICZ

Lindie Naughton is a Dublin-based journalist and writer. Her books include *Markievicz: A Most Outrageous Rebel*; *Lady Icarus: The Life of Irish Aviator Lady Mary Heath*; *Faster, Higher, Stronger: A History of Ireland's Olympians*, written with Johnny Watterson; *Let's Run: A Handbook for Irish Runners*; and *How to Mow the Lawn: Gardening for Beginners*.

MARKIEVICZ
Prison Letters and Rebel Writings

EDITED BY
LINDIE NAUGHTON

MERRION
PRESS

First published in 2018 by
Merrion Press
An imprint of Irish Academic Press
10 George's Street
Newbridge
Co. Kildare
Ireland
www.merrionpress.ie

9781785371615 (Paper)
9781785371622 (Kindle)
9781785371639 (Epub)
9781785372094 (PDF)

British Library Cataloguing in Publication Data
An entry can be found on request

Library of Congress Cataloging in Publication Data
An entry can be found on request

Interior design by www.jminfotechindia.com
Typeset in Minion Pro 11.5/14

Cover design by www.phoenix-graphicdesign.com

Contents

Introduction   1

The Letters

    Paris, 1900   8

    Ireland, 1901–1916   14

    Easter Rising, 1916   22

    Mountjoy and Aylesbury Prisons, August 1916–July 1917   32

    Free Again, July 1917–June 1918   62

    Holloway Prison, June 1918–March 1919   67

    'On the Run', March–June 1919   102

    Cork Jail, June–October 1919   106

    'On the Run', October 1919–September 1920   153

    Mountjoy Prison, September 1920–July 1921   164

    After the Truce, July 1921–March 1922   197

    American Tour, April–June 1922   202

    Civil War and Final Arrest, Mid-1922–December 1923   210

    Final Years, 1924–1927   217

Dramatis Personae   239

Acknowledgements   260

Index   261

Introduction

Constance Georgine Gore-Booth was born in London on 4 February 1868, the eldest of five children born to Robert Gore-Booth (an Anglo-Irish landlord) and his English wife Georgina; the family lived at Lissadell House outside Sligo.

In later years, she would abhor the drop of black English blood in her veins, but she owed much to her background. With the Great Famine of the 1840s seared in the collective memory, all five children were given a strong sense of their social obligations from an early age. It was no accident that her brother Josslyn became a strong supporter of the co-operative movement, sister Eva a poet and tireless fighter for the rights of women and workers in England, and Constance herself a staunch nationalist and socialist. While Josslyn and Constance lived all their lives in Ireland, Eva ended up living in England as did Mabel and Mordaunt, the youngest of the children.

Times were changing not just in Ireland but all over the world, with women demanding their rights, landlords forced to give their land over to their tenants and revolution in the air. Constance was determined to escape the stifling conformity of Irish rural life and, with the reluctant agreement of her family, trained as an artist first in London and later in Paris. It was in Paris that she met Casimir Markievicz and when his first wife died they became engaged to marry, with Constance taking on Markievicz's son, Stanislas, known as Staskou. The pair were well-suited – both artistic, both fun-loving and generous and both very tall. Constance was 32 when they married in September 1900; their daughter Maeve (later rendered Irish-style as Medhbh by Constance) was born at Lissadell House in 1901.

The couple's original plan was to remain in Paris but on a return visit to Ireland they met the writer and artist George Russell, who admired their dynamism and persuaded them to move to Dublin. Installed in a house called St Mary's in Rathgar, they quickly became part of Dublin social life then dominated by the 'Irish Irelanders' who, inspired by Douglas Hyde and the Gaelic League, wanted Ireland to return to its Celtic roots and reject the shallowness of English culture. Like many other rebels of the time, they became involved in the theatre, with Constance taking parts in numerous plays and Casimir writing and producing. Politically, the Home Rule movement was gaining momentum, although, in the background, the Irish Republican Brotherhood, unconvinced by Home Rule proposals, was keeping a close watch on political matters.

By 1908, Constance, now aged 40, was bored by the Dublin social scene. She joined Inghinidhe na hÉireann, the revolutionary women's movement founded by Maud Gonne, and Sinn Féin. In 1909, incensed by the foundation of the Boy Scouts, she set up a more militaristic Irish version called Na Fianna. Without Na Fianna, the 1916 Rising could not have happened, Patrick Pearse would later say.

In the filthy, overcrowded tenements of inner-city Dublin, James Larkin and James Connolly were fighting for workers' rights and preaching the gospel of socialism. The lockout of 1913 radicalised many and Constance was firmly on the side of the workers, spending long days in the soup kitchen established by Connolly at Liberty Hall (the headquarters of the Irish Transport and General Workers' Union). Many saw it as her finest hour.

Not everyone supported the Home Rule movement and in 1913 came the foundation of the Ulster Volunteers to protect Ulster's status within the United Kingdom of Great Britain. In response, the Irish Volunteers and the Irish Citizen Army began recruiting members within days of each other in Dublin. Women were welcomed as equals in the Irish Citizen Army, set up by James Connolly to protect workers in the tense days after the lockout; women in sympathy with the Irish Volunteers set up a separate organisation called Cumann na mBan. Constance was one of a number of women to join the Irish Citizen Army, and Connolly, who was then resident in Belfast, made her Rathmines home his Dublin base.

When the final preparations for the 1916 Rising were made, Constance was named third in command in the Irish Citizen Army behind Connolly and ex-British army soldier Michael Mallin. Her original responsibility during the Rising was to move between the various rebel outposts in Dublin, using Dr Kathleen Lynn's car. When she arrived at St Stephen's Green around noon on Easter Monday, Mallin asked her to remain, which she did.

With last-minute changes of plan and too few volunteers to call on, the rebellion was always doomed to be little more than a symbolic gesture. The small group of Irish Citizen Army rebels lasted less than a day in St Stephen's Green quickly retreating inside the solid walls of the Royal College of Surgeons. From there they surrendered the following Sunday.

Markievicz famously kissed her gun before handing it over – a display of bravado some argue was designed to distract attention from Mallin, who, with a wife and four children and another on the way, had hoped to escape execution.

Both were condemned to death but in Constance's case the sentence was commuted 'purely on the grounds of her sex'. She would spend eighteen months in Aylesbury prison in England, living with prostitutes, child murderers and pickpockets in horrific conditions.

When released from prison in 1917, she arrived back in Dublin to a rousing welcome as one of the few 1916 leaders to have escaped the firing squad. By mid-1918 she was back in jail, this time interned in Holloway Prison, along with Maud Gonne and Kathleen Clarke, after a botched attempt by the British to impose conscription on Ireland in the dying days of the Great War.

On 11 November 1918, World War I ended and an election was called for 14 December. For the first time, women over 30 were given the vote and the right to stand for election. Constance, still interned in Holloway, was selected as the Sinn Féin candidate in the St Patrick's Ward of Dublin. She won by a landslide, becoming the first woman to be elected an MP to the House of Commons.

As a Sinn Féin member, she did not take up her seat, but, once released, she became part of the first Dáil Éireann, or Irish parliament, established in January 1919. The Dáil leader Éamon de Valera gave her the position of Minister for Labour, making her only the second woman in Europe to take up a ministerial position. Since the Dáil was rapidly declared illegal by the affronted British, she spent much of the next few years either in jail or on the run.

She still managed to work hard at her job, becoming a skilled negotiator in labour disputes. Older and wiser, she appealed repeatedly to Irish men and women to unite, rather than squabbling among themselves, as was so often the case.

In December 1921, after the ending of the War of Independence and the signing of the Anglo-Irish Treaty, came the most disastrous falling out. Like many republican women, Constance opposed the Treaty, believing that it was a betrayal of the 1916 Proclamation, which aimed to establish an Ireland of equal opportunity for all: men and women, rich and poor. The pro-Treaty faction saw the Treaty as a first step to that idea; Markievicz correctly foresaw a continuation of the same style of conservative administration, with little changing apart from the names.

After the horrors of the ensuing civil war, with Irishman killing Irishman, a profoundly disillusioned Constance supported de Valera as the only politician she felt could unite the warring factions of republicanism. Despite her suspicion of all leaders, she presided over the inaugural meeting of the Fianna Fáil party and was elected to the Dáil as a Fianna Fáil deputy in 1927.

Just over a month later, she was dead, officially from complications following an operation for peritonitis. Her funeral was one of the largest ever seen in Ireland, with the streets lined by an estimated 300,000 Dubliners. They adored their 'Madame', recognising her as one of the few who had fought their cause. Five years later, the right-wing and authoritarian de Valera was in power and the rights of women, for which Constance and others had fought so hard, were swiftly eroded.

Most of the letters in this book were written while Constance was in jail – from May 1916 to July 1917 in Mountjoy and Aylesbury, June 1918 to March 1919 in Holloway, June to October 1919 in Cork, September 1920 to July 1921 in Mountjoy and November to December 1923 in the North Dublin Union.

She admitted to her sister Eva, recipient of most of the letters, that she hadn't been the best of correspondents before her incarceration. 'I was always a rotten correspondent and hated writing and now it is such a joy,' she wrote in a letter from Aylesbury dated September 1916.

Her letters to Eva from prison were first gathered together and published in book form as *The Prison Letters of Countess Markievicz* by Esther Roper, Eva's companion. She prefaced them with a long biographical sketch written with the help of Hanna Sheehy Skeffington, who was a co-executor of Constance's will. Helping edit the letters was the writer and historian Dorothy Macardle, whose monumental work *The Irish Republic* was first published in 1937.

Quite who inherited the originals of the letters when Roper died in 1938 is not clear; what is certain is that the letters written from prison and while Constance was 'on the run' were donated to the National Library of Ireland by Dorothy Macardle in 1951, seven years before her death. Transcriptions made by Roper of all Eva's letters to Constance ended up in the Public Records Office of Northern Ireland in Belfast as part of the Lissadell archive. The originals of many, notably the long letters to Eva from her US trip, are lost. In 1986, Virago reissued *The Prison Letters of Countess Markievicz* with a new introduction by Amanda Sebestyen, and some minor corrections to the letters.

Consulting the originals in the National Library of Ireland makes it obvious that the published versions of the prison letters skirted around some sensitive issues and blanked out the names of people who quite possibly were still alive at the time of the original publication.

This edition of the letters attempts to present them as they were; errors of fact and punctuation have been tidied up but little else. They breathe life into the story of one of Irish history's most fascinating characters, with all her foibles and enthusiasms. Ever conscious of the prison censor's peering eyes, she signs herself extravagantly as Constance de Markievicz, with the initials I.R.A., I.C.A., M.P. and T.D. variously tacked on to the name. She attempts to organise her life outside the prison with the help of Eva, her brother Josslyn, Jennie Wyse Power, Hanna Sheehy Skeffington, Susan Mitchell and others. She describes her dreams, the books she has been reading and the paintings she is working on; in Aylesbury she worries about Michael Mallin's widow and about Bessie and Bridie, who worked for her in Surrey House and were also staunch republicans.

In Holloway, her concerns are for her companions Maud Gonne and Kathleen Clarke, who didn't always welcome the attention. She keeps up with the news on a bewildering number of family members and friends, not always identifiable, and shows a keen interest in the juicier scandals of the day, as well as reading voraciously. She grows plants and manages to make gardens wherever she goes. In her letters, every inch of paper is covered not just with words but occasionally with small sketches. Some 'unofficial' letters are written on toilet paper; she uses what she can.

Included in this edition are other letters to family members and friends, including her beloved stepson Staskou, her brother Josslyn and her mother, known to the family as Gaga; the occasional reply is included to give context, as are letters about her sent between family members and friends. A few letters originally in public libraries and quoted in full by Anne Marreco in her 1967 biography of Markievicz are included; these have since disappeared.

Constance wasn't perfect; she could be overbearing and bossy, as is obvious from these letters. When it came to politics, she grew wiser and more sceptical with age, as is also clear. What endeared her to so many was her generosity, her open-mindedness and her huge heart.

As her daughter Maeve put it, whatever you may have thought of her politics, her character 'was really a very nice one'. That certainly comes across in this exceptional collection of letters.

THE LETTERS

Paris, 1900

In 1899, Constance Gore-Booth, by then past her thirtieth birthday, left a life of horse riding, amateur dramatics and jolly japes at Lissadell House, Sligo, to study art at the Académie Julian in Paris. While there, she would meet her future husband Count Casimir Markievicz. In January 1900, her beloved father Henry Gore-Booth died in Switzerland; he had travelled there with his wife because of his ailing health. Constance had spent Christmas with them.

To Josslyn Gore-Booth   *[Early 1900].*

My dear Joss,

I am engaged to be married and I hope you all won't mind because it's a foreigner, but I am awfully fond of him and he is not like a French man, much more like a fellow countryman. Mama and Mabel know him. I love him very much and am very happy but I wish he was English because of you all though I don't mind for myself but I'm so afraid of it putting a barrier between me and you all and making you think of me as an alien and a stranger.

He is an artist and very clever and has had two big pictures accepted to the big exhibition. I feel so bewildered that I really don't know what to tell or where to begin. We have known each other a year and seen a great deal of each other and I waited a long time to be quite sure and to know him well and the more I know him, the more sure I am that we have every chance of being happy.

We are such good comrades and have every interest in common besides loving each other so much. We both paint for the love of it, and we both like the same sort of amusements after our work.

Do write to me soon, for I'm so fussed and anxious and want so dreadfully to hear what you will say. If you only knew him, you couldn't help liking him in spite of his being a foreigner.

Good bye,

Yrs,
Con

To Josslyn Gore-Booth   *[Early 1900].*

My dear Joss,

Many thanks for your kind letter. There was no good saying anything before I had made up my mind for sure, but I've been thinking it over for a long time. It's very wily of the family if it prophesied [this].

We've known each other for more than a year. We met at a dance where Mrs Forbes-Robertson took me. She is a Pole and introduced me to a great many of her compatriots and we've been great pals and comrades ever since. When first I knew I was fond of him, it all seemed so strange and such a jump into the unknown that I didn't a bit know if I could do it and be happy and I didn't want to be engaged and perhaps break it off at the last moment.

So I waited and waited 'til I quite knew my own heart and mind and 'til I knew his and now I am sure of us both and confident that our love for each other and our mutual love for our work will help us over the rough places and trials of matrimony and the bother of not being blessed with too much money. He has about £160 a year that's all, but will have more as the property is not divided among the younger children till the youngest comes of age in about four years' time. I don't want him to settle any money on me. It's not necessary as I have my own.

He is a widower and has a child which is with his mother. He married very young and was most unhappy. His wife deceived him and there was a great scandal, her lover tried to kill her. They tell me he behaved wonderfully and was awfully good to her when she was deserted, ill and broken-hearted. He took her back and looked after her. She died of consumption a year ago.

Being a Pole, he has to have papers of identity and passport. I have seen them but of course they are in Russian and I don't understand them. I've met a cousin of his but he has no relations here now. He was educated to be a barrister but gave it up for painting and has already a gold medal. I am telling you anything about him I can think of. You must ask what you want for it's hard for me to know exactly what to say.

If possible, we should like to be married the end of May as we both want to have the summer free to stay quietly in some place in the country and paint big pictures. I am very anxious to do a thing and try and exhibit it [*sic*], and one wants three months clear. We both feel that the less time wasted over getting married the better. Ceremonials are a great bother and quite prevent hard work and if we are married later it cuts the summer up so. Also we want to work together.

I have paid Julian up to April 29th and of course I don't want to lose any of that if possible. I don't the least know about settlements. I imagine that if one had come into one's property that they were unnecessary since the 'married women's property act' was passed, perhaps as I am marrying a foreigner, my money had better be settled on me. Of course I will make a will and leave him what I can, but during my life I shall certainly keep control of what little I already have! Which only amounts – as far as I can gather – to the right to spend the interest as I wish. I don't quite see how a settlement can be drawn up 'til the question of Mabel's money is definitely settled by her marrying or not within the given time and I certainly don't want to wait for her.

I've taken a long time to decide to leap a great obstacle and having once made up my mind, I shan't be out of a fuss and quiet 'til I have got through the awful ceremonial which I thoroughly dread; a wedding has always presented itself to me as the acme of disagreeables for the bride. The letters, presents, appalling parade in church, breakfast etc, are so barbarous and public. For me, the less the better.

I should like to be married in London also, it's a little less of a show and a lot less important. I only got your letter after coming home after school too late for the evening post. It's a mere chance here whether they arrive at eight in the morning, midday or evening.

I have just this morning Sunday received another letter from Mama. She seems to think it will take some time to get married. Couldn't we both come and stay at Lissadell later on after Julian's is finished and paint there? Then there would be no hurry to get married. The thing is we don't want to waste the summer, we want to paint together and of course, we can't do it unless we marry or go home.

Casi has just come in so I can tell you more from him. First his name is Casimir Joseph Dunin de Markievicz, his title is 'potomsturemyj dvoranin' [*sic*] which means son of a count whose family has been on a certain property for seven generations. He says that if you wish to make enquiries as to his family status you can do it through the British ambassador at St Petersburg, who will have to make enquiries at the heraldry department. Or else he can get his papers officially translated here into English.

As to his money, he comes into it in four years, 'til then he receives about £160 a year through trustees. Also he has the right to be maintained with some servants, horses; everything. After his mother's death he will inherit about the same thing as he has. His cousin whom I met Wierchelowsky [*sic*] is the son of a man who is in a very high position in the government; he is *Conseiller-secrétaire d'État* – comes after the chancellor. He has one other uncle of the same name – Markievicz – who is a general. I think if you want to know it would be much the simplest and quite enough to get his papers officially translated. Another way of finding out if he is genuine would be to write to the War Office as he served in the Imperial Guard, which is only for the noblesse but it would cost a lot and they would only be able to certify his family and position.

Also possibly they might not answer as they are not bound to. Another thing they can just get some official statement as to my family and to send it to his mother. They are very proud and don't care a bit about money but would like to be sure I am 'noblesse'. He says they will take his word for it; but myself, I would like them to have no doubts.

Now good bye.

Best love,
Yrs,
Con

To Josslyn Gore-Booth   *[Undated].*

My dear Joss,
I enclose his two addresses. His home in Russia is only occupied by an elderly relative who keeps cats! And who I always compare in my mind to Augusta [Gore-Booth]. And here, he is in for the moment a friend's studio, as he sub-let his, which was large and expensive, directly his big pictures were finished. He made a good bargain and got nearly double for it. I tell you this in case you wanted to make enquiries. We will see about his papers being translated.

I don't think you need have any doubts about him. I have met so many of his friends and compatriots coming and going who all seem to respect and admire him. Also, Mrs Forbes-Robertson who is a Pole has known him for years. Of course, I may be prejudiced but as far as I can see there is nothing that is not perfectly open and simple about him and among the colony of Pole and Russian artists and students here, he seems to hold a much higher position than the other men of his age. He has introduced me as his *fiancée* to a great many.

One thing I have not thought to say or you to ask and which is perhaps the most important of all is his relations with Russia. Thank goodness he hates politics and has never meddled in any plots or belonged to any political societies. He is on the best of terms with the Russians, belongs to the club of Russian painters and is exhibiting as a Russian. This is all of grave importance, as if a man is known to be political and patriotic, he is liable to be seized and sent to Siberia on the merest suspicion.

He wrote to Mama; didn't she get a letter enclosed in mine? I can't agree to going home for a month without him, I have no intention and see no need to leave here 'til he comes with me. We would only be wretched and not work. If you read my letter again, you will see that what I said was, if we waited, we must wait together and work. He is not in a good studio and is only doing a couple of small things, and when they are finished, wants to start something serious and get married at once so as not to waste time.

I am quite pleased and willing to wait a bit and make everything as pleasant as I can and have no objection to anybody making any enquiries they like. But I wish you to understand that I have quite made up my mind to marry him and nothing could stop me – humanely speaking. It is difficult to explain politely, but the plain English is this, that I don't recognise that you or anyone else has any more *right* to make enquiries and ask questions than I should if you were in a similar position. Don't think I don't appreciate your affection and interest and fully realise the bother of it for you. I am extremely grateful – and for my part, as I know he's all right and have nothing to fear. I should be very glad for you all to be satisfied.

I take it you like things to be put plainly and won't be offended. I am very glad you think I have acted with sense and I hope you will continue to think so.

Of course, I am a very poor marriage for him, but his mother was quite nice and kind and was only anxious for his happiness. However, his brother and sister may not be so pleasant. He has not heard from them yet. However, it won't much matter if they do object though of course we would prefer that they were pleased.

Now goodbye and I hope things will square up all right. I really see 'the Lord's' hand in it all.

Yrs,
Con

Ireland, 1901–1916

After many letters concerning the exact nature of Markievicz's social standing, financial arrangements and the possibility of a Roman Catholic wedding ceremony to satisfy Casi's mother, the pair married on 20 September 1900. On 13 November 1901, their daughter Maeve (later written as Medhbh by Constance) was born at Lissadell.

George 'Æ' Russell helped persuade them to return from Paris to live in Ireland, and in 1903, after a trip to Poland, they moved into a house called St Mary's in the Dublin suburb of Rathgar. With them was Staskou, Casimir's son from his first marriage, then about eight years old. They quickly immersed themselves in the cultural life of Dublin, holding their first art exhibition in October 1903, and becoming involved in the thriving theatrical scene and in Hugh Lane's campaign to open a municipal gallery for modern art in Dublin. In 1907, they were among the founding members of the United Arts Club.

Around 1908, Constance joined Sinn Féin and Inghinidhe na hÉireann and began renting Slate Cottage in the foothills of the Dublin Mountains at Sandyford. In April 1908, she campaigned with her sister Eva in the Manchester North by-election, helping to defeat Winston Churchill. At home, the theatre and gardening remained major interests.

To Josslyn Gore-Booth   *17 October 1908.*

My dear Joss,
Many thanks for your letter and cheque for £2-3-1.
    We are very hard at work rehearsing Casi's new play. It's going to be very funny. We have got the funniest North of Ireland girl

acting that you ever saw [Nora Fitzpatrick]. I have just been lent a new typing machine and it's rather old and stiff and won't work properly. Everything seems to slip about, but I think, on the whole, it's more legible than my fist.

I am getting the pots ready for the bulbs; I think the scented one was *Barrii Cons* [*sic*], but indeed I'm not a bit sure. My *Primula Capitata* are so lovely still and are so very large and fine and I've got quite a lot of roses out still.

This garden is much more satisfactory than St Mary's. There is more sun and less wind. The slugs though seem to prosper quite as well as the flowers.

Now good bye, love to you both.

Yrs affect,
Constance de Markievicz

Although Constance was a republican and labour activist first, she was a staunch supporter of the women's suffrage campaign. Hanna Sheehy Skeffington, a founder of the Irish Women's Franchise League, became an ally and close friend.

In March 1909, Constance gave a lecture to the National Literary Society on 'Women, Ideals and the Nation'. Later that year, she founded Na Fianna Éireann. With money always tight, she had rented out St Mary's and began a brief flirtation with communal living at Belcamp Park, a seven-acre estate five miles north of Dublin's city centre. Despite Casimir's protests, she would stay there until April 1911, moving into Surrey House, in Rathmines, later that year. In July 1911, she was involved in protests at the visit of the newly crowned King George V to Dublin.

In early 1912, a resolution demanding inclusion of women's suffrage in the Home Rule Bill sent to all Irish MPs by the Irish Women's Franchise League, and supported by Constance, was ignored. British suffragettes, the name given by the British press to women's suffrage activists who believed in taking direct and militant action for the cause, were jailed after throwing a hatchet at British prime minister H. H. Asquith on a visit to Dublin in July 1912. They went on hunger strike.

To Josslyn Gore-Booth

Belcamp Park,
Raheny,
Co. Dublin.
1 December 1909 (received).

My dear Joss,
I don't know how to thank you. Your letter came as a complete surprise, for I really did not think you cared a bit for me, or what became of me. I am awfully thankful. It is a great relief, I really did not know what was going to happen, and Eva would not let me get my own money. I could see no way out for I had counted on that.

It is a wonderful load off my mind. Everything seemed so black this morning. This is a big house, but we've got it very cheap and the garden is in good order and ought to pay.

I hope you are all right again. The weather here has been so awful. Casi, I am glad to say, seems to get fitter every day; he must have been even worse than you were. This is a very healthy place, you ought to come for a few days next time you are up. You could give me suggestions for the garden.

I wish I could thank you properly; but I feel quite bewildered, it came as such a wonderful surprise and shock.

Yrs,
Con

To Josslyn Gore-Booth

No address.
10 August 1911 (received).

My dear Joss,
Until I got a letter from you, it never struck me that anyone would believe the charge against me, so I'm writing to tell you what really happened.

Miss M. [Molony] was very seedy and got muddled in her speech and gave the impression that she was going to abuse the King. The police rushed to the lorry, I was sitting and got up and stepped over in front of her so that in case they were violent I would be able to save her for a bit, she is so delicate. A policeman tried to seize me by the ankles. I stepped back and reached forward and pushed him back. I did not kick or throw sand. Another policeman caught me from behind and I was dragged away. I did nothing to warrant any arrest.

On advice, I am taking a counter-charge against the police. Unless they are able to get a great number to perjure themselves, or unless some fool – wishing to make a heroine of me – lies about what I did, I must win.

The Nationalists are very keen that the question of freedom of speech and of the police interrupting meetings without the authority to do so should be fought. They say that the whole thing was illegal from the police point of view, but of course, it's hard to fight the police, as they are such liars. The men who employ them do not know what truth and honour is. We are engaging council. Everyone has been awfully kind and sympathetic, but it's a great bore and worry.

With love to mother,

Yrs,
Con

To Josslyn Gore-Booth   *c. August 1911.*
                                                        [Fragment].

Everything here has subsided again, and Dublin is its usual peaceful self and we are all praying that King George will not come again for many a long day.

Even if I were not a nationalist I should object to Kings' visits for they but bring out the worst qualities in people: all sorts of snobbery is developed in people, which leads to such trickery, such meanness, such lies and misrepresentation. Everyone using every means to get himself noticed; no trick is too low for a man if he sees a title the other side ...

The Third Home Rule Bill was passed in 1913, despite the vociferous opposition of Ulster unionists and their allies in the British Conservative

Party. The workers' lockout of August 1913 began when Dublin United Tramway Company drivers and conductors went on strike.

On 31 August, the arrest of James Larkin after a rally in O'Connell Street saw police baton-charging the crowd, with Constance among the victims. Over 400 were treated in hospital. Casimir wrote a letter to The Freeman's Journal *voicing his horror at what he called 'Bloody Sunday' – the first use of a term that would recur in Irish history.*

In October, a soup kitchen for striking workers and their families, supervised by Delia Larkin and Constance, opened in Liberty Hall and remained open until the following February. That same month, the Markieviczs were forced out of the Dublin Repertory Company by their business partner Evelyn Ashley because of Constance's political profile. Casimir could no longer earn a living in Dublin and left Dublin in December to work as a war correspondent in Albania. The World War intervened, and he would never live in Ireland again.

In November, the Irish Citizen Army was founded by James Connolly and Captain Jack White to protect workers and trade unionists; a week later, the Irish Volunteers began recruiting. Cumann na mBan, working in conjunction with the Irish Volunteers, would follow in April 1914. The Howth gun-running took place on 26 July; a week later, Britain declared war on Germany and in September, the Government of Ireland Act 1914 was passed but it was suspended for the duration of the war. John Redmond controversially encouraged Irish men to join the British army, so splitting the Irish Volunteers. While 140,000 remained with Redmond in what became known as the National Volunteers, about 12,000 hard-line republicans, led by the movement's founder Eoin MacNeill, declared Redmond's policy at variance with the aims and objectives of the Volunteers. They broke away, still calling themselves the Irish Volunteers. James Larkin left for the USA and would not return until 1923.

Constance heard from Casimir in April 1915; he had been severely wounded while fighting for an Imperial Hussar regiment in the Carpathians. She was left to deal with his debts. Staskou set off to join his father in the Ukraine, his fare paid for by Josslyn Gore-Booth. In August, O'Donovan Rossa's funeral in Dublin became a set piece for republicans. Plans for a rising were already well advanced.

To Josslyn Gore-Booth   *Surrey House,*
Leinster Road,
Dublin.
1 June 1915 (received).

My dear Joss,
I owe about £100 – grocer's alone is £51. The others are butcher, coal, rent, St Mary's etc – it's all house things.

Unluckily I let Casi raise money (£100) on the lease of St Mary's; he paid it back but never gave me back the document, or there would have been no bother. Casi will send me money when he arrives and I can easily pay back bit by bit now. I am alone for the moment. I'm in an awful hole. I reckon though that now I can run this on about 30/- per week.

I should have been all right if I had not Staskou. I was economising hard when he turned up and I was paying off back numbers. He minded so dreadfully about having clothes and odds and ends of things and Russian lessons that I gave him what he wanted as well as keeping him and let the bills rip.

I owe a few pounds for chemist and dentist (Staskou) specs, and vet for dog. I could not tell to a pound or two, as I would not ask for accounts unless I had the means to pay them.

Yrs,
CdeM

To Josslyn Gore-Booth   *Surrey House,*
Leinster Road.
11 June 1915.

My dear Joss,
I want you to do me a favour and lend me a few pounds for Staskou. Casi sent what should have been £30 and that is the very least he ought to have in his pocket for the journey, but the exchange is so bad that he only got £24-12! That would be very tight even in times of peace and just now one does not know where one may be held up.

I am very sorry to bother you, but I am weighed down with debt myself – having him here made it impossible to economise and make up for what I spent of my own in that last starvation month of the strike. Then I can't get my income tax rebate money because Casi is away, and prices in Dublin are so awful. So everything is rather unfortunate for me. One needs something in hand to face [higher] prices – everyone seems to be helped except the people with the small incomes!

A most tiresome thing has happened to the 'Builders' Co-op'. We are building a stable for the co-op bakery. Their architect measured out the premises for us and now the 'Petrol Oil Co' claim that we have encroached on their foundations. Of course, this is absurd, as you can leave gaps of 6 inches between every house in a street, but they think that by objecting they can make the bakery pay up! So we are being delayed and held up, which is most inconvenient. We don't want to sack good workmen, and we can't afford to keep them idle while the solicitors talk and send in files ...

[rest of letter missing]

To Josslyn Gore-Booth   *Surrey House,*
                                                                 Leinster Road.
                                                                 18 June 1915.

My dear Joss,
Thanks for yours. I do hope you are really better. I had no idea that you were so ill. Staskou has had a horrid cold and it's so impossible to make a boy take care in fine summer weather. Molly's [Joss's wife] cheque sent him off with enough money for any immediate necessity. If he gets caught or interned in Germany, he may want more but he has enough to keep him 'til he can get more.

I can live very cheaply now that he has gone. While he was here it was nothing but money, money, money, as well as having to give him far better food than I require.

I have a lovely hedge of eating peas, also beans in my garden. It grew inches during the showers we had the last few days so I shall have great vegetables in about a month; carrots and turnips too and salad and tomatoes.

I am raising some money to pay off what I owe so that I can pay by the week as I used to before the strike. It's the only way to keep out of debt for unbusinesslike people with small incomes. It's so hard to realise how things mount up – getting rid of S. is a great relief. I did not like the responsibility at all of an idle youth in town; also the expense.

I am awfully grateful to Molly for the cheque and so is he. He got a very nice warm coat and went off very pleased with himself.

Now goodbye,

Yrs,
CdeM

To Hanna Sheehy Skeffington   *June 1915.*

My dear Mrs Skeffington,
Many thanks for yours. Hope the pamphlet will be out this week. Printers very tiresome!

I hope Mr S. is better – the weather is rather awful. There is a rumour going around from the Castle that his heart was affected and that was why they let him out. I daresay it's not true, but I thought I'd better tell you, as if that is so, he ought to rest *absolutely*. But of course your doctor would know.

Miss O'D. Rossa says he is going to America too early and that people won't go to lectures during the desperately hot weather and thoroughly advises him to wait a month.

Have you a lot of introductions?

Yrs affect,
Constance de Markievicz

Easter Rising, 1916

In advance of the 1916 Rising, Markievicz was made a lieutenant in the Irish Citizen Army. Although her original responsibility was to liaise between the various rebel outposts, using a car belonging to Dr Kathleen Lynn, Michael Mallin asked her to stay with his group when she arrived at St Stephen's Green, a large public park on the south side of Dublin's city centre, overlooked by the Royal College of Surgeons in Ireland on its west side. After one day of fighting, the rebels retreated to the RCSI, where they would remain until they surrendered on Sunday 30 April 1916.

28 April 1916.
[Unsigned – in Markievicz's handwriting].

TIME 11.15 am
PLACE Turkish Baths
TO C/O of Commissariat
PLACE College of Surgeons
Please arrange for meals for 23 men here today at 3pm.

For her role in the 1916 Rising Markievicz was court-martialled and sentenced to death. That sentence was commuted to life imprisonment purely on grounds of her sex. Initially she was held in damp, dismal conditions at Kilmainham Jail, enduring the agony of hearing her close friends and comrades shot dead by firing squads. After her court martial, she was moved to Mountjoy Prison, an imposing Victorian prison on the fringes of Dublin's city centre. The authorities then decided to move the republican prisoners to British jails, where they would be less accessible. The series of almost 100 letters to her sister Eva Gore-Booth begins in Mountjoy. Eva had been allowed to visit her sister in jail, and she later described the heavy uniformity of such places, with their imposing outer walls and grim interiors punctuated by barred windows and heavy iron doors, all designed to keep 'undesirables' at a safe distance from respectable society.

To Eva
Mountjoy Prison,
Dublin.
16 May 1916.

Dearest Old Darling,

It was such a heaven-sent joy, seeing you. It was a new life, a resurrection, though I knew all the time that you'd try and see me, even though I'd been fighting and you hate it all so and think killing so wrong. It was so dear of Esther [Roper] to come all that long way too. Susan [Mitchell] too, for I expect lots of people will think it very awful of her! Anyhow, you are three dears and you brought sunshine to me, and I long to hug you all!

Now to business. Hayes and Hayes, 41–42 Nassau Street, are agents for Surrey House. They wrote to me re giving up tenancy, and very decently secured the house, which had been left open. There is no lease. I had one for three years and since it finished, I part paid each quarter. The house was in very bad condition when I bought it. The house is very untidy, as I had no time to put it straight after the police raid. If you could get Bessie Lynch she would be a great help. There is a charwoman called Mrs Boylan too, whom Bessie would know and who is very honest.

My valuables are all with a friend (silver and jewellery). I don't know how much it will cost to store furniture. I don't know whether it would be cheaper to pack it into a tiny house and put in Bernie to care [for] it. There is a lot – I don't want anything thrown away. I am rather unhappy about the pictures. Egan, Lr Ormond Quay, might store those hanging on the walls and my illuminated address from the Transport Union. He has some pictures of ours already.

Don't store furniture with Myers; he was a brute to his men in the strike. You'll want to insist on their bringing proper boxes for the books, as they are awfully careless. The china too wants care. Then there are the acting things. You'll probably want to buy a tin trunk or two, and get them packed with naphtha balls.

There are wigs in the bottom of the kitchen press and in the cupboard half-way up the stairs. They want to be put by with care. The linen too, such as it is, wants to have the starch washed out before it is put by. If you could only catch Bessie Lynch, she knows the house so well and is such a good worker. There are a lot of crewel wools in the big press on the stairs: they want to be put with naphtha balls too. If someone could house the wigs and them I'd be thankful.

On the right of the fireplace in drawing-room is a sort of a desk. The same key fits it and the big brown press upstairs. One of my friends has the key. If you have not got it, pull out top drawer and push down and push lock back where it pokes through. Small centre drawer is locked: there is nothing in it. But my bank book may be there and in a small drawer to the right, there are papers for recovery of income tax. Some more of them are in the pocket of my coat that is here. I haven't recovered income tax for two or three years, Casi has to sign and it's an awful nuisance, so I always let it run on until there was something worth recovering. There should be now.

Could Susan get my clothes that are here and look after them for me? There is a little brown case with drawing things that Susan might keep for me. I told you that Cochrane and Co. were trying to let St Mary's. It should be put down at Norths, Dockrells and a couple of agencies. I think my name should be suppressed and it should be let in yours.

Of course, my household bills are not paid. John Clarke of Richmond Street is my grocer; Ferguson, Rathmines, my baker; Kehoe, butcher, and Hendrick, oilman, are both Rathmines. I owe two coal bills: one to Clerkin, Tara Street, and the other to a man I forget in Charlemont Street, on the right-hand side as you face the bridge, but close to the chemist at the corner where the trams cross. I owe also a trifle to Gleeson of O'Connell Street for a skirt, and to the Art Decorating Company, Belfast. But there is no hurry about any of these. Don't pay anything unless you know the bill is really mine, as people have played queer tricks, getting things on credit in my name before now.

You poor old darling. It's such a bore for you. I feel rather as if I were superintending my own funeral from the grave! There is a very old book of music in the drawing-room. It might be valuable. If you have time, bring it to a Mr Braid at Pigotts, and ask his advice about selling it. I promised to let him have a look at it, as he says it is unique. I had no time to leave it with him.

I left a green canvas suit-case, a small red dressing-case and a brown handbag with Peter Ennis, the caretaker of Liberty Hall. I've had them there some time. I dare say Peter's arrested, but he wasn't mixed up in anything, so he may be out. I left my bike knocking round the Hall too.

I miss poor Poppet [dog] very much and wonder if he has forgotten me. Poor Mrs [Lillie] Connolly – I wonder where she is, and if you got him from her. I do feel so sorry for her. Her Belfast address was 1, Glenalina Terrace, Falls Road, Belfast. She was so devoted to her husband. Also she has four children at home and only the two older girls working. With regard to Bessie Lynch: what I had in mind for her was to start her washing in a small way in some work after the War. She is a beautiful laundress. Of course she would want another girl with her to do accounts, etc., but you could let her know that I haven't forgotten her, and the ten shillings a week is only to keep her safe and happy until something can be arranged. It's much better for people to earn their own living if they can.

Poor Bridie Goff [Gough] ought to get a month's wages, at least. She was arrested with me. Bessie would know where she lives: somewhere in Henrietta St. If you can't find Bessie, advertise for her in the evening paper. I hope you found Mrs [Agnes] Mallin. I wish I knew, for it worries me so to think of her.

I nearly forgot the little Hall in Camden Street. Mr Cummins, pawnbroker of Richmond Street, is the landlord. If things quiet down, I'd like to go on paying the rent for them as hitherto. A little boy called Smith, living in the Piles building, could find out. The landlord, of course, might know. He was quite nice.

I feel as if I were giving you such a lot of worries and bothers, and I feel, too, that I haven't remembered half. Anyhow, it's very economical living here! And I half feel glad that I am not treated as a political prisoner, as I would then be tempted to eat, smoke and dress at my own expense! In the mean time, all my debts will be paid, I live free, and after a time I suppose I will be allowed to write again and see a visitor. I don't know the rules. But do try to get in touch with Mrs Connolly, Mrs Mallin and Bessie Lynch for me. I would be sorry for any of them to be hungry, and I would be sorry too if they thought I had forgotten them, for they were friends.

By the way, the garden seat and tools might be of use to Susan. There are a few decent plants too, which she could take if she likes, and a couple of decent rose-trees.

Now, darling, don't worry about me, for I'm not too bad at all, and it's only a mean spirit that grudges paying the price. Everybody is quite kind, and though this is not exactly a bed of roses, still many rebels have had much worse to bear. The life is colourless, the beds are hard, the food peculiar, but you might say that of many a life, and when I think of what the Fenians suffered, and of what the Poles suffered in the 'sixties, I realise that I am extremely lucky. So don't worry your sweet old head. I don't know if you are still here, so I am sending this to Susan to forward. I hope that I shall live to see you again some day and I shall live in hopes.

With very much love to you three darlings. I can see your faces when I shut my eyes.

Yours,
Con

To Josslyn Gore-Booth   *Mountjoy Prison.*
                                   [Undated; c. June 1916].

My dear Joss,
I've just been handed two letters from you, one dated May 15, the other June, which I see you posted together.

I can't conceive why Eva who is my trustee and therefore the most natural person to look after one's things should be passed over. I suppose it is because she is a woman!

She and I are always in such sympathy that I believe she would know what I wanted before asking me. Hayes (the solicitor who let me Surrey House) wrote me that he had secured it as the police told him it was open and that they were afraid of it being looted.

About packing the things – would you ask Miss M. F. Mullen [Madeline ffrench-Mullen] if she could superintend it (George Russell will know her address). If she can't, Nellie Gifford, 8 Temple Villa, Palmerston Road.

Both these people would do anything for me and neither are people who have to work. Susan Mitchell would if they both could not, but she has so much to do with the paper and her house. I want them to be careful to collect all bits of paper with notes of poetry on them. Bessie Lynch would pack, she is very capable and honest. My little servant Bridie Goff would help too. She should get a couple of pounds.

One thing I forgot – I left my false teeth in a cup in the pantry (they were broken). Could they be repaired and sent [to] me? I'd have to get a new bottom now – Gaga knows the name of the dentist. I expect they would make no difference here as I can only eat slops.

I instructed Mr Cochrane, solicitor, Harcourt Street, to try and let St Mary's for me. The lease should be in the Bank of Ireland. Casi was hard up and I let him borrow on it. I think it's all paid back. I had at first a 3-year lease of Surrey House, it ran out and I just paid what was due. The house was in a bad state when I took it.

I'd like the cottage to be kept. The people next door, Mrs Mulligan, care for it. I owe her £1 – I usually gave her 10/- per year to care[take] it and let her use it when I don't want it. This year I promised her £1 for various reasons. Her husband died and prices are so high. Daniel O'Connell Fitz-Simons, Moreen, Dundrum is the landlord. He and his wife are great friends. Dan never asked me for rent except [when] he was hard up.

I believe one gets out on a ticket of leave in about 15 years. By then the cottage would be a perfect place to retire to end my days and I like the luxury of feeling that one root still remains and is not torn up. Sentimental perhaps but it won't cost much.

One thing that might bring in a little money – just before the fight I drew 3 Xmas cards to be printed. I gave them to Percy Reynolds, a clever boy. He was arrested – I would like him to get half the profits if any. Susan M. could write the verse. They must be done in Ireland or not at all. I shall have heaps of money rolling in and it will have to be invested in Ireland. Some I'd like to use to help bolster up things which might not pay, but would help the country. But they must be Irish, that's all I care about. I am most grateful indeed to you. One grows very philosophic and one feels that one's possessions and treasures matter so little.

You might write to Casi too. I don't suppose any account of rebellion was allowed into Russia and he and Stas won't know what has happened to me. He might get it into his head that I have eloped or something. You better shell him with a few picture P.C.s [postcards] and just put on it that I'm all right but unable to write.

I really might be much worse off.

Yours ever,
Con

From Lady Gore-Booth to Josslyn   *Ardeevin,*
Sligo.
17 June 1916.

My dearest Joss,
I don't know that I am right in sending Eva's letter, but it all seems such a stupid muddle that you better see her views. Of course you won't refer to having seen the letter to her.

I can't help agreeing with a great deal she says that somebody ought to do something, and not leave Con's wretched things over the floor – *why* do you keep the key and not allow Miss Mitchell to go in as Con wishes? If you have power to do this, surely you have power to act about letting the houses etc.?

Eva distinctly says in every letter that she has nothing to do with the business things and only wishes to carry out a few private wishes of Con's, which naturally she will not send you unless Con wishes her to do so. I don't see how they can affect the business part you have to do – Eva tells me Con wishes Miss Mitchell to have the key and look over her things and no doubt told her what to do with them – I can't imagine why you won't let her have the key of the house.

What use would it be to you to know Con's private wishes [as] she has told Eva, except how much money to send weekly to the people she wants to help. Would it save time, expense and worry if you went to Dublin and settled it up? Send back Eva's when read.

Love Mother.

To Eva   *[On unofficial paper].*
                               No date; c. July 1916.

I am, alas! going into exile. Make a point to try and get in to see me. I believe you could by influence. Do you know [J. A.] Seddon and is he an M.P.? He and I were great allies in the Strike, and he might be willing to help. I know he liked me personally. He might get the Labour people to put 'questions' anyhow.

Remember, I don't mind being in jail, and if it's better for the cause, I'm prepared to remain here. My only desire is to be of use to those outside in the long, tedious struggle with England. Nothing else matters really to me.

I believe that by rules, I am entitled to receive and write one letter on moving, so that if you get no letter in a few weeks, write and say that previously, at your visit, I arranged to always write to you. Quote this rule and ask why you have not heard. They would do a good deal to avoid any fuss and to combat the idea that we are being ill-treated.

This is *d'être* [unofficial] paper and written under huge difficulties!

Remember it is only by pushing and sort of discreet threats and making yourself disagreeable that you will be able to do anything for us.

I am going to Aylesbury – [I] shall be quite amiable, and am not going to hunger-strike, as am advised by comrades not to. It would suit the Government very well to let me die quietly! I won't do work for the army, that's all. I look forward to seeing you the whole time. Put on your prettiest hat when you come! Give Esther my best love. I shall never forget her coming.

What does enemy [England] think of it all? My family must be quite amusing about my latest crimes! I wonder so many things and am getting quite clever about noticing trifles and details. I told you to write to Casi and get the news through. It would have to be very diplomatically done to evade censor. You might try. Now I must stop.

Very, very best love. Am going to Aylesbury. Let friends know.

To Eva   *[On unofficial paper;*
no date, no address].

You see, the gap has been thrown and I have found a real friend, and it just makes the whole difference: both mentally and bodily. She is taking awful risks for me and both body and soul are ministered to. Tit-bits of news and 'tuck'.

I want you to give her a copy of our book, with your autograph. Try to find some person connected with nothing that has not too grand an address, who could then just send her a picture postcard with her name and address and to whom she could then write and let her know if she was going into town and call for news. Also give her tit-bits of rebel news, that must not be sent through the post.

Trust her absolutely and let not your right hand know what your left hand doeth (Esther of course excepted). None of the crew or the family must even guess, for people will talk.

You had probably better not try and see her again, as you are both probably under watchful and protective eyes.

At present, anyhow, I see my friend a lot. I am sending you also some things to do for me. No hurry about them. Love and kisses.

To Eva   *[Scribbled on unofficial paper;*
                                              no date, no address].

Darling,
Got yours – ever so much love. If it's better for the cause to leave
me in quod [prison], leave me. Being sent to Aylesbury. You can
probably get a backdoor influence – Duchess of Bedford is a 'visitor'
there. I want to get my teeth done, two ought to be stopped. I am
so glad M [Medhbh] was amused and not shocked! Best love and
many kisses and hoping we may some day meet again.

Mountjoy and Aylesbury Prisons, August 1916–July 1917

On 7 August 1916, Markievicz was escorted across the Irish Sea to Aylesbury Prison, where she was classified as a common criminal prisoner; other Irish rebels arrested after Easter week were classified as internees and treated differently. Aylesbury was a forbidding Victoria pile in Buckinghamshire, first opened in 1847 as a county jail and later converted into a women's prison. The entrance was through double doors, with the first door banged shut and locked before the second one opened. Constance, jailed as a common criminal, joined a mix of petty thieves, prostitutes, swindlers and murderers, many of them with mental health problems. Initially, she was placed in solitary confinement; her small cell was enclosed by an iron door with an 'eye' in the middle of it. In the early days, she would pace her cell, trying to avoid the all-seeing 'eye'.

The day began at 6 am when prisoners washed and dressed and ate a breakfast of six ounces of bread and one pint of tea, usually cold, in their cells. Work followed; hard or soft, depending on the sentence. Those, like Constance, sentenced to 'hard labour' got two ounces of cheese and a small piece of bread at 10 o'clock to keep them going. Lunch at noon typically consisted of two ounces of meat (fish on Fridays), two ounces of cabbage, one potato, thick gravy and six ounces of bread. Supper at 4.40pm was a pint of cocoa or tea and six ounces of bread; the prisoners were perpetually hungry and always on the look-out for an extra onion or turnip. At 5.30pm, the prisoners were locked up for the night. During her sentence, Constance's weight went from a healthy eleven stone to a gaunt seven and a half stone.

Her first job was in the sewing room, where she made prisoners' nightgowns and articles of underwear from coarse calico. She was allowed one book a week and, after a few weeks, was permitted to write one letter a week. It was a dull routine for a woman of Constance's prodigious energy and she asked to be moved. Her next job was cleaning the prison kitchen and she became an expert at scrubbing floors.

Once free, Constance would paint a graphic picture of the dirt and filth endured by all prisoners, who lived in fear of picking up 'loathsome diseases'. She also described the disturbed mental state of many prisoners; one tried to kill herself by cutting her throat, while another set fire to her cell and almost died of burns. Others tried to hang themselves or swallowed buttons and huge needles. Talk was forbidden in the prison and the lack of companionship proved the greatest of hardships for Constance.

Little of this came out in her letters; she was determined to be the model prisoner and not to worry her family.

To Eva   Aylesbury Prison.
                                                    8 August 1916.

Dearest Old Darling,
The one thing I have gained by my exile is the privilege of writing a letter, but there is very little to say, as I do not suppose 'an essay on prison life' would pass the censor, however interesting and amusing it might be!

What you have called 'my misplaced sense of humour' still remains to me, and I am quite well and cheerful.

I saw myself, for the first time for over three months, the other day, and it is quite amusing to meet yourself as a stranger. We bowed and grinned, and I thought my teeth very dirty and very much wanting a dentist, and I'd got very thin and very sunburnt. In six months I shall not recognise myself at all, my memory for faces being so bad! I remember a fairy tale of a princess, who banished mirrors when she began to grow old. I think it showed a great lack of interest in life. The less I see my face, the more curious I grow about it, and I don't resent it getting old.

It's queer and lonely here, there was so much life in Mountjoy. There were sea-gulls and pigeons, which I had quite tame, there were 'Stop press' cries, and little boys splashing in the canal and singing Irish songs, shrill and discordant, but with such vigour. There was a black spaniel, too, with long, silky ears, and a most attractive convict-baby with a squint, and soft Irish voices everywhere. There were the trains, 'Broadstone and North Wall' trams, and even an old melodeon, and a man trying to play an Irish tune on a bugle over the wall. Here it is so still and I find it so hard to understand what anyone says to me, and they seem to find the same trouble with me. 'English as she is spoke' can be very puzzling. One thing nice here is the hollyhocks in the garden. They seem to understand gardening here. There is a great crop of carrots, too, that we pass every day, going to 'exercise' round and round in a ring – like so many old hunters in a summer.

I had such a lovely journey over here. My escort never had been on the sea before and kept thinking she was going to be ill. I lay down and enjoyed a sunny porthole and a fresh breeze. There was a big airship (like the picture of a Zeppelin) cruising about when we arrived. I was awfully pleased, as I had never seen one. I long so to fly! Also I'd love to dive in a submarine.

I dreamed of you the other night. You had on a soft-looking dark blue small hat, and it was crooked. You had bought tickets and three donkeys, and you were going to take Esther and me to Egypt, of all places! When I woke up I had to laugh, but it was wonderfully vivid. Look it up in a dream-book. I dream a good deal ever since I was in jail and I never hardly did so before.

I'd love to show you all the doggerel I wrote in Mountjoy, though I know you'd only jeer – in a kindly way. I love writing it so, and I've not lost it. It's in my head all right!

When's your next book coming out, and the one with my pictures, if it ever does? They were very bad. I can do much better now. I was just beginning to get some feeling into my black and white when I left Ireland. I made quills out of rooks' feathers that I found in the garden. They are much nicer than most pens: you can get such a fine, soft line.

My darling, I repeat – don't worry about me. I am quite cheerful and content, and I really would have felt very small and useless if I had been ignored. I am quite patient and I believe that everything will happen for the best. One thing I should enjoy getting out for, and that would be to see the faces of respectable people when I met them!

I don't like to send anyone my love, for fear that that most valuable offering would be spurned. I expect, though, that Molly [sister-in-law] has a soft spot for me somewhere. Very best love to Esther and to Susan and all the 'rebelly crew', if ever you come across them. Do go to the Transport Union headquarters if ever you go to Dublin. They'd all think you were me, and they would love to see you and you could tell them about me. Now best love old darling and send me a budget of news and gossip, when you can write, about all my pals and my family, and anything amusing at all. I laugh when I think of Mordaunt and Mabel.

Yours,
Con(vict 12).

To Eva   *Aylesbury Prison.*
                                                21 September 1916.

Dearest Old Darling,
I wonder if you expect this. I was always a rotten correspondent and hated writing and now it is such a joy. I could go on babbling for ever, though there is nothing to write about. I did love seeing you and Esther so by the way and I hope she got her hat all right. Yours was very nice. You don't know what a picture the two of you made, all soft, dreamy colours. (Moral: always visit criminals in your best clothes, blue and grey for choice, if it's me!)

I am now going to see if 'anything arises out of the minutes' – i.e. your last letter. First, tell Ottoline Morrell not to get into my boat, unless she has the health of an ostrich. I often think how lucky it's me not you that is here. Give her my love. I would have liked to see her very much, and have since found out that I may have three visitors! But I must give their names.

Puzzle – how [to] find out for next time, so as to give their names? You may answer this, but it's very hard to tell now who will be able to come here in January!

Is James Webb Lady Cecilia's husband? I know several of the name. He was a dear and awfully nice to me when I was young.

I've been dreaming again. A school of village boys, perched on high, high stools at enormous desks. You the schoolmarm, in blue. Boy turns round, in a blue holland pinny with shorts, bare legs and socks and E.'s head and a beard! It seemed quite natural! He had been writing X's on a paper divided into squares, two on the top line and three on the bottom thus:

X X

XXX

Thank Susan [Mitchell] and Violet [Russell] a thousand times for settling the house. It must have been an awful job. I'd love to write to Susan. Tell her how I am and that I often think of her the right side of the bars in Dublin.

I wish that for your next visit you would try and get a statement of accounts from Joss. I want to know what bills are paid. Some might easily get left out otherwise, as people would not know where to send bills. Find out if he did anything about Christmas cards. I wrote him about some drawings I had done. I hope Mrs M[Mallin] is getting her pound a week all right and that she can do without my 10/-. Give all the crew my love. Tell Andy Dunn to go on singing. [Marie] Perolz will know where to find him. I often think of the 'click' [clique] and the refugees and our kitchen teas. Tell Andy too that later on we'll try to get someone to teach him, and ask him to give my love to Mr Nugent, if he will accept such a gift from a felon! By the way, convicts can have photos, so send me yours, I always forget to tell you this – and Medhbh's.

Talking of dreams – five minutes in the day and think of me, I will think of you at the same time and we'll do it as often as we can. Tell me what hour when you write. Don't hurry to answer this, as news may come of Casi.

I send my love to all my friends in the Transport Union and the Co-op. Tell them that I am often with them in spirit, and that I have nothing but happy, pleasant, busy memories of them. Mr [Thomas] Foran is a friend there, of course he may be in jail! So many of my friends I know nothing about. Mr Billy O'Brien too, I'd like to be remembered to, and oh! So many more! – and I don't even know if they're alive!

Where is Bessie stopping? Give her my love. I think she would be very wise to go to America. Give her a letter to 'John Brennan' [Sidney Gifford Czira] if she goes. 'John' would remember her, and would, I am sure, like to see her, and she would be something from home for Bessie. Do you know what the other Gifford girls are doing? Tell Perolz to give them my love and to Medhbh Cavanagh. She and Perolz are great pals.

By the way, did you remember about the blue serge dress? P. [Perolz] has the trunk. The key, a small one, was in a red leather bag left in L[Liberty] Hall. The second key was left in a house that was burnt. My lace, with a lot of household goods, are in the trunk. The dress is at the bottom.

I wonder if 'Mr P.' [Poppet] has forgotten me? I often think of his nice brown eyes. Do you remember how Reginald [Roper] played with him at Manchester? I am not sure which Mr Power you mean. Is he 'Mark' and very good-looking and a friend of Violet's?

I am now going to lapse into verse! I want you to criticise. Tell me something about metre and what to aim at. I am quite humble and I know I'm not a poet, but I do love trying.

RAIN

High walls hang round on every side
A cage of cruel red,

The sickly grass is bleached and dried,
As brick the flower bed.

The fierce rays of the sun down beat,
The burning flagstones scorch our feet,

As in the noonday's blighting heat
We walk with weary tread.

Upon our cheeks a blessed breeze,
And in our weary ears
The rustling talk of happy trees
Glad that refreshment nears,

A softly soothing, gentle drip,
Wee drops for grass and flowers to sip,
God's chalice for the moth's grey lip
Or angels' happy tears.

Of course, I know it's only jingle! I loved the metre of the dedication you read me out. Trying to do a thing oneself makes one appreciate anything good much more. Write me a verse or two in your next letter and tell me how to get to work! Don't tell me to wait 'til I am blessed by the 'gift'!

Don't worry about me. I am quite happy. It is in nobody's power to make me unhappy. I am not afraid, either of the future or of myself. You know well how little comforts and luxuries ever.

You remember 'They shall be remembered for ever' [From the play *Kathleen ní Houlihan* by W. B. Yeats and Lady Gregory]. What we stood for, and even poor me will not be forgotten, and 'the people shall hear them for ever?' That play of WB's was a sort of gospel to me. 'If any man would help me, he must give me himself, give me all.'

I love hearing about all the people you write about. I remember Clare Annesley's mother so well. She was very beautiful and I used to love looking at her. I hope some day to meet C. A. and Ottoline M[Morrell]. I remember her so well, though I never got to know her. I'm longing to see her.

Tell Miss [Sarah] Reddish I often think of her and of Mrs [Sarah] Dickenson and all the others, and of the great election we fought and won. Tell Mabel that her sick soldier never came to Dublin. I wrote to him to (I think) Tipperary. I remember Mr McNeil [unknown friend] now quite well; he is awfully nice. Fancy Gaga doing the Grand Tour again! Please give Medhbh £1 of my money for birthday with my love and ditto for Christmas.

I am so glad about the book. I hope that it will go well and it's a great joy to me to think I may help to sell it, and that my little gift of drawings may be worth something to my old darling.

There are the most beautiful cloud effects here. East and south over big old elms. They are really wonderful. Did not know that England produced anything so heavenly! Oh! for the Dublin Mountains and the soft twilights and the harvest moon on cornfields! I must write a poem about cornfields.

Best love and many a hug to you and Esther. Love to Miss F. M. [ffrench-Mullen] if ever you see her and all rebels and felons, comrades and friends!

Always thinking of you.

Yrs,
C de M

To Josslyn Gore-Booth   *Aylesbury Prison.*
                                                             17 October 1916.

My dear Joss,
Many thanks for yours. Please pay Casi's bills and please send him the receipts. Register or insure them.

Re St Mary's – £50 is very little for St Mary's. But of course, I can't judge here – for four years it would be all right, but eight years would mean over £100 loss to me. But you can judge better than me and have probably done so by now. Anyway, I am quite content to leave it to you and in any crisis ask Eva, who is like my second self.

It is hard to remember if I owe anything more. Casi owed a bill of about 15/- to 'Ceppi', a frame-maker and cast maker on the quays. It might be paid.

I am afraid I am writing very badly but I am beginning to forget how, and my hand won't work properly from want of practise!

Lyons is the only bill to question. It ought to be an Xmas gift either for Casi or me. Eva will tell you. This is all like living to see yourself dead and your business all being wound up and 'amens' being said.

Income tax refund – I had the papers for two years' refund. The full papers for both (Mr Cooper's and the dividend ones). If they were not in the drawer of the desk, they may be in the box I left at Miss Perolz's when I heard that the house was going to be occupied. Eva thinks the police opened the box and took papers. Try and get them back if so – there was not a scrap of writing that had anything to say to a rebellion on it or even political; some of Casi's letters, the unfinished text of a society play and some poems. Nothing except personal things; some photos, lace and scarves and blouses – just a few things I valued. I believe all my clothes were looted! However they would not be much use to me here.

I am very sorry you are having so much bother and selfishly thankful that I have not got to do it for myself. I always wished Casi had been a financial expert who would have run the house and given me so much a week pocket money. Anyhow here I have no expenses.

Eva gave me messages from Mr and Mrs Cooper [possibly the politician Bryan Cooper, who was from Co. Sligo]. Please tell them how glad I was to get them and give her my love – Eva had so much that she will never remember all!

Let me again repeat that with regard to St Mary's, I can't possibly judge shut away here and I know you will do the best you can and that it is really a gamble and I am really grateful and know that you will act for the best and will be quite content whatever you decide.

I should just like to know about my 'business affairs' now and then but shall always be pleased and grateful.

Yrs,
Constance de Markievicz

PS: I have signed enclosed document but am afraid it will be of very little interest to you to see my court martial. They went into no particulars – I have nothing I wish to conceal and anybody may see it (I mean the record of proceedings). I gave Eva a full account of all that occurred at C. M. Don't bother about rumours. My enemies will make a monster of me, my friends a heroine and both will be equally wide of the truth. I really did very little, for we were not in the thick of it at all.

Yrs,
CdM

Lady Gore-Booth to Josslyn

Ardeevin,
Sligo.
19 November 1916.

Dearest Joss,
I am so glad you have had a satisfactory letter from Con and look forward much to seeing her handwriting again – it is so much better for you to get into direct communication with her, it is never very satisfactory to go through two or three people. Everything gets wrong and misunderstood. Of course, Con has much more common sense than Eva, who is all sentiment – her whole heart is with Con and she will do anything to help her but seems to go about it in a foolish way.

The old man will be very interesting at having his dreams come true – it's rather odd.

Lovingly,
Mother

To Eva

Aylesbury Prison.
[Unofficial paper; no date, no address].

Darling,
This will go tomorrow, with my love. For God's sake be discreet. I am all right and not a bit unhappy. I love the book, it's a real joy. They have put the rose in the triangle on its side, didn't I put it upright?

Ask me all the questions you can think of. The doctor here (Fox), a woman, is a devil. She is going to be governor, but rules are so strict that she can't hurt me in any way. It makes all the difference having a friend here. Don't count on my getting out for ever so long, unless a real fuss is made (home and America). I don't see why they should let me go.

You should get 'questions' asked on anything you can think of; the company one is in, starvation, etc., and try to make them publish the trials. You've probably done all this! I am so in the dark. They don't want a continuous fuss.

Let me know trades union conditions for workrooms *temperature*. The trades unions should have a visitor or inspector here. They should start jail reform. The people are all poor people, and they should see to them.

Best love and kisses to you both, I love being in poetry and feel so important!

Yrs for ever,
Con.

To Eva   *[Unofficial paper].*

These questions should be asked [of] me and all political prisoners at a visit:

What do you weigh? What was your normal weight?
What do you get to eat? Can you eat it?
How much exercise do you get per day?
How often do you get clean underclothes?
Are you constipated? Can you get medicine?
What temperature is the room you work in?
What is your task? ie, how much do you do in a week?

If they won't let me or any of the others answer, push to get answers by every possible means. The women I am with are the gutter rats of England, quite different from Mountjoy. Prostitutes and widows [jailed] for baby murder; others for abortion. Make capital of this in Ireland and America. One nice Irishwoman I want you to help when she comes out – Murphy is her name. She has been so nice to me, but be cautious. If others find you out, I will always give you some tokens or password, but some may try and blackmail you.

On 6 December, Liberal leader David Lloyd George replaced Herbert H. Asquith as Britain's prime minister and formed a coalition government with the support of Edward Carson of the Ulster Unionist Party, and the Conservative Party leader, Andrew Bonar Law, who had Ulster roots. Later in the month, Irish prisoners were released from British jails under a general amnesty. Constance remained in Aylesbury, despite the best efforts of her sister to have her released.

To Eva   *Aylesbury Prison.*
                                                     29 December 1916.

Dearest Old Darling,
I was waiting and wondering who ought to write first, and now I've got 'St Ursula' from you and can contain myself no longer.
   Mr G. [Gavan] Duffy interviewed me yesterday and we talked my trial up and down. Of course, I forgot to ask him about Casi and Staskou's things that were lifted by the police! But no matter. He seemed very capable and careful, and he took copious notes.
   Do the following lines fit onto the poem I sent you before? And do they improve it?

   We're folded in a sheet of rain,
   Clasped to the heart of things
   My spirit slips the yoke of pain
   And one with nature sings.

   I am the cloud that floats so free
   The boundless space, the deep blue sea.
   Of Heaven and Peace I hold the key
   And poise on golden wings.

I am not quite sure if it's sense. Words are such odd things – they suddenly become alive and mean all sorts of things on their own and not what you meant at all. And they simply run away with me and I can't manage them at all.

I have begun another poem, but one is so hustled here that somehow one can't do much. But I love trying and trying to put things into verse. It seems to show one so much of the beauty and the secret and symbolic side of life that one never dreamt of before.

All that has happened to me seems to have opened such wonderful new doors. I seem to pass through it all now as a dream. Day by day slips by and I am not unhappy. I just live in a sort of expectant peace and feel so very close to you.

Christmas day has come, and more and more beautiful cards. They seem to me to be symbols of the wonderful love and friendship that is waiting for me and fighting for me outside. I am blessed with such an extraordinary number of warm-hearted, true friends. If I had not got to gaol, perhaps I would not have found it out. You see, there is compensation in everything.

Your beloved letter has just come, such a joy. But still no card of your own design. 'Brownie' is a darling and a real friend. Give her my love and tell her I'm afraid her key was lost. Doesn't that sound mysterious? She is not one of the 'crew' but just a dear friend of Casi's and mine, gay and warm-hearted.

Talking of keys, do write and ask Ella Young for mine. I lent her nearly all my keys and she never gave them back. She wanted to open something. On second thoughts, don't. I'd sooner lose the keys than fuss her, and in any case, they are probably lost, and I certainly don't want them!

My head is quite turned with the reviews you sent me! Those poor rough scribbles! If ever I get out I'll do a lot more. I've learnt such a lot since. This is a real jail pen, vile, and I couldn't make it do what I wanted in the drawing at all.

Don't make yourself miserable, darling, about me. I am often afraid that you are much more unhappy than I am. I feel a quiet, peaceful, a *nunc dimitis* [now let us depart] sort of feeling. All my life, in a funny way, seems to have led up to the last year, and it's all been such a hurry-scurry of a life. Now I feel that I have done what

I was born to do. The great wave has crashed up against the rock, and now all the bubbles and ripples and little me slip back into a quiet pool of the sea. I am getting even more sentimental than you – in spite of the censor's cold and unpoetic eye! – but that's how I feel, quite peaceful and calm.

Tell me about W. if you think of it and Maud Gonne. Give my love to the doctor [Lynn], Madeleine [ffrench-Mullen] and all of them. I love Susan's verse on my card. Wish her a very happy Christmas, with my love. I got three copies of that one, but none of the others.

I had a really lovely dream the other night: try and interpret. A wonderful crimson sun rose in the corner of my cell, slowly passed up and along and stood over my head. It was followed by a gold one and that by a blue one, and they all gave such wonderful lights, and when they passed over my head they left a luminous opalescent glow of colours that mix and yet keep their own peculiar qualities. It is difficult to explain but it was wonderfully beautiful.

Still more cards came to-day. Such a joy. I inquired about yours, and it came, but I cannot have it until the Home Office has been consulted and approved! My curiosity is most vivid! What can you have put on it?

I am so glad that the Aonach [Aonach na Nollag, the annual Sinn Féin Christmas fair] went off so well, and love all the news about the Hall. Madeleine and the dear doctor are splendid. Good luck to them and to M. – and the paper. My soul feels flattered and I'm longing to see you again. It will be quite soon now. I hope it will be all right about Clare A.

Some of my 'army' sent me cards. I never had so many in all my life before. Mrs Murray Robertson [widow of Scottish architect John] sent me such a lovely one. Try and meet her. She paints lovely fans (New English Art Club) [founded 1885 as an alternative to the Royal Academy] and knows Mrs Dryhurst. She is awfully nice.

Now, darling, the limit is approaching and I must be bidding you good-bye. Give my love to Ireland and all her children, my comrades, and to my 'Poppet' and to his foster-mother. I loved the card they sent. Just room enough to tell you how beautiful I think 'dew-pearled cobwebs'. Your words are like colours and lines – so restrained, vivid and pure. I love the end of 'Maeve' so. The peace she found was, I think, rather like mine. But I've gone a step further, I don't need hazel boughs and mystic streams. I've found it in jail. Don't say 'How conceited!'.

> The wandering winds of Christmas time,
> The twinkling of the stars
> Are messengers of hope and love,
> Defying prison bars.

> The birds that fly about my cage
> Are vagrant thoughts that fly
> To greet you all at Christmas time –
> They wing the wintry sky.

This is supposed to be a Christmas card! For you and all friends. I have already got 46 and love them, such beauties. But I have not got the one you said you were drawing yourself. You, Esther, Reginald and Beatrice Collins sent me a picture gallery. But who sent Monna Liza [*sic*]? Thank Gaga for her two and Medhbh. They were so pretty and such nice poems. Tell M[Medhbh] I wish I were on the boat (picture) with her!

However, I am quite cheerful, for Christmas has brought the world of art and life and hope into my cell. I have all the cards arranged upon the bed and they are the greatest joy. Thank Evelyn and Molly. Evelyn [Mordaunt's wife] sent me a 'family group' and Molly [Josslyn's wife] a most attractive poem written out. I wonder if she drew the dear little design at the top. I wish Evelyn herself had been in the group, but there's Medhbh, Beg [*sic*], Gaga, and the two little boys.

Love and thanks and best wishes to all.

My blessing and love to you,
CdeM
PS: I was so sorry about Ernest [Kavanagh]. He was a bit of a genius. Will write something. Tell Maeve [Cavanagh MacDowell – his sister] to collect his drawings, original and reproductions. Will bring them out some day.

To Eva

Aylesbury Prison.
27 January 1917.

Beloved Old Darling,
For goodness sake do take care of your dear old self and don't run
any risks. This English climate is so awful that I wonder how you
get along at all. Every day for months it seems to freeze. I long for
our more considerate and gentle climate, that always gives you a
peep at the blessed sun and a soft warm drizzle. I see the sunrise
every morning, and it is most beautiful and quite worth the trouble
of walking out to see it, though I need hardly tell you that it is not
my will-power that guides my weary legs!

As I knew you were not coming, I was not disappointed at not
seeing you. Esther and Clare were like a bottle of champagne to
me, they brightened me up so. I thought Clare lovely and rather like
her grandmother, whom I knew quite well. It's such a joy to look at
pretty things. I thought my 'Poppet' looked so fat and well; I longed
to hug it!

I am so inquisitive about the baby in your letter. You say 'I hear
a lovely little baby has taken the place of <u>Seon Hard</u> Constance
Georgina Dunin after you.' [*sic*] I cannot read underlined bits and
am much puzzled.

I loved your card. As you say, the idea at the back of yours and
mine was somewhat the same, but yours was far superior. I loved
the group of children round Roseen. You had a wonderful feeling
in it all – movement, proportion and design were all excellent. The
tone was very nice too. I feel so proud of it being done for me, and
of being in three poems! My head is getting very swelled indeed.
Didn't you tell me that Miss [Viola; a writer and poet] Meynell
[Alice Meynell's daughter] had me in a poem too? I'd love to hear it
some time. I like your new poem very much, especially verse three.
Your poems have a magic effect on me. They transport me away to
beautiful lands of dim sunshine and pearly waves, where beautiful,
stately people drift gracefully about. They are all like you and have
wild aureoles of golden hair and long white fingers!

I'm awfully interested in astrology; do try to read Medhbh's fate
in the stars. Nobody ever remembers my birth hour exactly so you

will have some trouble there! Couldn't you work back from some other date in my life, such as my wedding day? I was late and was only just in time to get married that day. Or twelve o'clock, Monday of Easter Week? – which *I think* was the moment we started on our 'divine adventure'.

Please give the old Miss Trevekes [*sic*] my love. How sweet of the poor old dear to want to see me. And Emer [Helena Molony].

I don't understand from your letter whether the shop is still going in Liberty Hall. Which room do they mean by 'the old band room'? The band changed rooms so often! Give my love to Emer and tell her I got her card and think of her often, and Miss [Winifrid] Carney, who is interned with her. I got very funny and instructive cards from both! I really did love my cards. I never loved any Christmas presents half so much. I did enjoy seeing the photos of M. and the children that Esther brought. Please give her my love and thank her for thinking of it, it was a great pleasure to me.

I want you to write and thank little Ronan Kent for a card he sent, also old Mrs [Margaret] Pearse. The boy is probably at St Enda's School. It was awfully nice of them to think of me.

I am getting off this letter as quick as I can as they have taken to reckoning your next from the date it goes, not from the date you get your sheet of paper, which, if you delay writing, allows them to rob you of a certain number of letters in a year. I delayed a fortnight over the last, and that fortnight is lost to me in letters.

[12 lines deleted by the censor]

I'm afraid that my writing has got rather bad. Send me some Sligo news about you, family etc. I am still reading your [*The Triumph of*] '*Maeve*'. I think Connaught should be spelt 'Connacht'. Someone else has probably told you this long ago but you asked me. I do love Maeve's last speech, but it would be very difficult to make a stage success of. I long to give you a lecture on writing a verse play. It could be done and a success made of it.

I wish we could collaborate. Aren't I getting conceited? But I feel I understand audiences and stagecraft and play-producing – by this, I mean the whole process – from author to the meanest usher. I include all these as material that goes to produce a dramatic performance, and they must all pull together. You can't play organ music on a Jew's harp, and you give your penny whistles organ music to play. You also have too many variations of the beautiful theme taken up by unsuitable instruments and so you produce a beautiful poem in dialogue but not a good play. Some day I may get a chance of trying to explain. I can feel it so well, but can't do it myself.

I am longing to know how you are, but am not anxious about you; I *was* for two days some time ago, but then got into my head that you were better, and now I feel confident that you are getting on all right though it may be slow. Don't hurry to get up.

I've been writing ...

[12 lines deleted by the censor]

With best love to all my darlings and many hugs and kisses to you. 'Beyond earth's barred gates' every morning at 9 o'clock, I seek you there.

Yrs,
Con

To Eva   *Aylesbury Prison.*
                                                   27 February 1917.

Dearest Old Darling,

The sun is shining, the sky is so blue and the horrid red walls make it look bluer still, and I seem to see it shining through your golden halo and touching up your blues and greys, and then I think perhaps she is in a murky English fog and I grudge it being able to touch you and envelop you in its embrace. And then I think: perhaps the same fog will blow over here, and will have us both in the same grip – and so I wander on, quite drivelling.

I loved your last poem and letter. If you can think of it, do bring Miss Meynell's poem next visit. I am burning with curiosity; I think I told you, but can't be sure.

Please tell 'Crew' [*sic*] not to publish any unpublished poems of mine without asking me (through you). Anything once published they can do what they like with, but there are one or two I don't want published. I was so glad to hear of K. [Kingston; cousin] the old darling. I'm sure he's a rebel in his heart. He's one of the people I should really love to see. He and I were so very sympathetic always. Tell him I was so glad to get a message from him and give him my love. He always feels like part of the family.

The greedy starlings are making such a row on the window-ledge, fighting most rudely over the remains of my dinner. This morning a wedge-shaped flight of wild geese flew over us as we were exercising, making their weird cackling cry, and they brought me home at once. Do you remember the wonderful monster, supposed to be a cow, that Joss concocted, to stalk them from behind or within, and how they fled shrieking for miles at the sight, and how unapproachable they were for weeks owing to the fright they got? The Trojan horse was nothing to that beast.

I have just been reading your letter again and can't help wishing that I were Percy's cow or pig! Who is the D ... at Barrington St.? I can't read the name, and where is Street? Give Father Albert [Bibby] my love and tell him I often think of him.

Lord MacDonnell was an old friend, also his wife and nice daughter. He always impressed me as a very straight man, although he was a politician! I liked him very much.

Give E[Esther] my love and tell her I would have sent her a gilt-edged invitation card, but the censor won't allow me! I'd love to see her, don't let her not come if she says she is coming. Once she gets a pass she must come!

I was glad to hear of Mrs Mallin, and so interested to hear that the boy is learning to draw. Perhaps I shall be able to help him, some day. Who knows?

What a lot of letters I am letting you in for, you poor old darling. It would probably upset Mrs Mallin very much, seeing me. It would bring it all back to her. They were such a devoted pair. The last things he said to me were about her. If you are writing to any of the [Liberty] Hall crowd, tell them I got their cards. The Co-op. girls sent a joint one, and the Norgroves sent me one each. Tell them to remember me to Mrs Norgrove and ask for news of her husband.

Now I'm going to write out a poem, about another jail-bird – a thrush. It's true!

He sang the song of the waking Spring,
The song of the budding tree,
Of the chrysalis cradling the butterfly's wing
And the waking to life of each earth-bound thing
That the sun comes out to free.

He sang of himself and of five blue eggs
Black-spotted and warm and alive,
Of baby-birds hopping on uncouth legs,
Of worms lying cool by the sheltered hedge.
Oh how he would live and thrive!

He sang of the sunrise, all azure and gold,
He laughed at the prison wall.
The joy of his song made him happy and bold,
He forgot that life could be cruel and cold
That each shadowy nook could a foe enfold.
His wings could defy them all.

In the air was the rapture of dawn and Spring
But the glittering sun was cold.
The wind from the west, with its sweet salt sting,
Was quenched from the north with his haste to bring
Clouds discoloured and lowering
Which down on the day he rolled.

White on the world the snow-flakes fall
And cold and death have their sway.
They beat on his wings in a smothering pall,
And close at the foot of the prison wall
Which loomed above him so endless and tall
Frozen to death he lay.

Away into space the storm-clouds float
And the earth is again awake.
Cold from his heart the snow-flakes float,
The reviving sun kissed his soft-dappled throat,

But it never will throb to another note
Nor thrill with a sparkling shake.

He will never build the nest of his song
Nor sing to his brooding mate.
Was he right to rejoice or was he all wrong?
Do hope and faith but to fools belong?
Is courage all a mistake?

No effort is lost though all may go wrong
And death come to shadow and change.
He gave his best, and simple and strong
Broke the darkness which lasted the winter long
With Spring-time's triumphant melodious song,
A melody wild and strange.

And the air had thrilled to his morning song,
The ripples of life and glee
That floated, all rainbow-tinted, along.
Striking a note that rang true and strong
On the strings of Eternity.

It's very long, isn't it? And they say that 'good things are done up in small parcels'. I love your birthday poem so much. You've missed your vocation. You should be a poet laureate. I will make you mine!

I'm sure no one had so much poetry written about them spontaneously before, while they were alive. Ordinary kings and queens have to pay for it, so they get rubbish. Pegasus, being thoroughbred, will not stand a spur – even a golden one.

I wanted so to talk about [William] Blake and about horoscopes the other day, but of course forgot about both! I wish I'd known Blake. I would love to argue about light and shade with him. He was all wrong – and strange for such a great man, he took the superficial view that shadow is to soften and conceal. It never seemed to dawn on him that bad draughtsmen may use shadows for this: but a Master, such as Rembrandt, has as true an outline as [John] Flaxman [British artist], and each shadow is a definite thing with a shape, as much, so as an arm or a leg. But I must not write lectures on Art or Blake! I have no room and you no time to read.

Take care of yourself, you blessed old dear. I am very well, and luckily for me escaped my usual bad cold, which generally gets hold of me in January. The frosty weather always agrees with me.

Last night I dreamt I was walking on the top of the cliff beyond John's Port, [St John's Port, Sligo] a ripe cornfield with poppies on my right, when a great khaki-coloured snake rushed out of the corn and slithered down the cliff! You didn't tell me if you found any meanings in the colours of the winds.

Molly Byrne is a great girl. I wish I could write her some songs. She sings with such go and has such a nice voice. Give her my love and tell her I long to hear her sing again and I often think of the times we had together.

Give Susan my love. It's awfully good of her to help Bessie. By the way, if Bessie marries, I promised her £10 to set up. If she married, it might help things, so ask Susan to let her know I have not forgotten. I don't even know if she wants to marry! And remember, in setting her up, I don't mind a few pounds more or less, but her mother must not live with her. She's a devil.

Please ask Joss to give Medhbh £1 to buy an Easter egg.

You are so encouraging about my poetry, and a little bird tells me all the time that it's twaddle, and I laugh at myself and go on and inflict it on you.

Now I am arriving at the 'wall' and so must pull up. Love to Esther and Reginald and all friends and rebels. Bless your sweet old heart.

Yrs,
Con

PS: I hope you like being a 'respectable friend' (see preface [a list of rules appended by the prison authorities to each letter] to this letter).

[Scrawled around edges of the pages]: Tell Gaga she might have sent me some Sligo news. It's always amusing. Love to all. You have not quite got my point about plays but no room. Bless you.

Thank God February is a short month. I shall see you again quite soon. Much love and take care of yourself.

Give my love to Mrs Barrett at [Liberty] Hall. She was Shawn Connolly's sister and a great friend. I've heard nothing of her. I often have a funny fancy, almost real, that I am sitting between you and Esther holding a hand of each. So sentimental!

On 19 April 1917, the USA entered the war. Irish–American pressure on the British to settle the 'Irish question' increased.

To Eva   *Aylesbury Prison.*
                                                              5 May 1917.

Dearest Old Darling,

When I came up to my cell after seeing you I found this old blue sheet, the bird's own colours! So I begin at once.

I loved your drawings. They are quite wonderful. You have a wonderful gift for line and a great imagination. All you need is the knack of wagging a pen and that is practice. You want to go on and on and on. Your figures have such grace and life. Do bring more next time.

Did I ever thank Reginald for his Easter card with its tricolour messages? I loved it, and those cards of good pictures are such a help to look at.

I want you to send the following messages to Father Albert: he was such a wonderful friend.

[11 lines deleted by the censor]

I neglected this epistle to the 'Birds' Nest' all Sunday, for I suddenly got a craze to work out Clare's book-plate and it came out much nicer. I've started Esther's too; I've got some more ideas for it and it is coming out better than I expected. I am going to do your birthday card all over again. I was really rather seedy and that is really why I went off into that wild smudging that you saw. I cannot wag a pen monotonously unless I am very fit, and I am feeling fine to-day.

I have some of Gertrude's primroses, some roses and carnations in my cell and I talk nonsense to them and they are great company.

Suddenly I heard you shouting to me this morning. I wondered so what you were trying to tell me, for I couldn't hear. One's imagination plays one such odd tricks.

Last night I dreamt too, such a strange beautiful dream. I was in an artist's house. He was a sculptor – German or Norwegian I think – and everything was very, very old, simple and massive. The windows were long, low slits with tiny panes, like some palaces in the time of the Huns and Goths, and the only picture there was of a girl, all in blue, with a mushroom hat of iridescent blue feathers, yellow-gold hair and a pale face. While I was looking at it, the figure suddenly looked down at a paper lying in its lap, and I realised that it was you! There were such lovely lilies growing in carved stone jars in that house and through the windows the sun shone on trees and a river.

I am still reading Blake diligently and I like the two you quoted immensely and I too was struck by the prophecy. Do you know 'The Song of Liberty'? It ends with 'Empire is no more and now the lion and the wolf shall cease.' I wonder if that is a prophecy too? I don't understand anything else in it from beginning to end! Tiriel, Har and Heva etc. also puzzle me much. I suppose they are really only fancy names for quite commonplace articles.

I have just been given Fr Albert's gifts, so please say 'Thank you a thousand times' and tell him I love the beads in my own rebel colours!

No one who has not been in jail can realise what a joy it is to get a coloured picture post-card! The *Life of St Francis* too looks awfully interesting. By the way I got a card from Squidge; give her my best love and thanks. I got a letter too from Father A. He is a real dear. I am already looking forward to your next visit in the flesh. They are like flashes of sunlight. I forgot – did I ever tell you the first cell I had here was haunted – it was haunted by a man. I often wondered if he was Irish, but he never spoke, 'tho he often kept me company. Your letter still smells delicious. I have it here under my nose.

I wonder so who is acting 'tail' and who 'dog' in Dublin now? The younger generation of rebels will have a great chance now of building up and doing things for the country. I have great faith in the young.

These last few days the trees have simply flung out their green leaves. They did it at night, so that I should not learn their secret! The one thing I am learning here is to watch everything closely, whether it is trees or black beetles, birds or women. The sparrows are delightful – like men at their best. Someone once said 'the more I know men, the more I love my dog', and I think I rather agree. Dogs don't lie; I don't suppose birds do!

What's Gaga doing over here? And what's happening to Coz Con [Muncaster]? It's tragic, the way things break up and change. He spent his whole time for such years building up that place, and now I suppose the next man will either alter everything or let the whole place drop to pieces. I should like to have seen it again. It must be rather awful for Gaga.

Dusk is coming on and the blue bird will have finished pecking at her evening meal by now and is probably preening her feathers and wondering what I am doing. Again, another day! I don't know why I have delayed so long over this. Laziness and dullness, I suppose, but really, if you come to think of it, I have nothing to talk about, only vague nonsense. The Chapel was a treat this morning, with the smell of the lilies. How I love the smell of them! I think they are your flower.

(Saturday) I have just seen the Governor. Miss Emily Norgrove wants to visit me. Of course, I'd love to see her, but I don't want her visit to interfere with you. (I wish people would go to you about visiting me and let you arrange. I'm so afraid of someone getting your pass – by accident.) It's so impossible for me to arrange and I only want what and who is convenient to you and naturally I am delighted to see any friends.

There is only a week now 'til I see you. You probably won't get this 'til afterwards. I have written one more verse to the B.B. It ends in the middle of a sentence. Here it is. Next verse not done enough to send:

Then my soul strikes the magical key-note
And the circle of wonder is born
When all beautiful thoughts that are free float
In a vortex out to the dawn,
While the air grows heavy around me
As the Presence encloses my soul
And I know that my Blue Bird has found me,
That together we rule and control.
(I am sorry for the censor!)

I dream by day all sorts of vague ideas and theories about sounds, all sounds being musical notes. Echo will only call back to you when you pitch your voice on certain notes. Certain notes are re-echoed by dogs, who howl if you play to them on the violin or piano or sing to them. There is a certain pitch that carries best in every different hall. I think that there is a lot of natural magic in sounds.

Now darling I am forced by the limit of a sheet of paper to stop. That's an awfully nice photo of you drawing. I wish Esther were in the room too. Give her my love. Have you heard anything of Susan lately? She sent me such a nice card. The 'brown wind of Connaught' is blowing. He will kiss you for me and ruffle your curls at sundown. He passes here on his way from Ireland.

Best love,

Yrs,
CdM

[Around edges]: This will reach you just in time to give you birthday greetings.

There is a small sycamore tree here in the garden. It's not very 'paintable'. I am having an egg for breakfast! Alice Milligan's card was prophetic, only it's not a duck! They say there was another air raid. I hope you were not alarmed or deafened.

Bye bye again old darling. This is such a foolish dawdling old letter.

To Eva   *Aylesbury Prison.*
                                                    9 June 1917.

Beloved Old Darling,
How short your visit always seems and how much must always
remain unsaid, unless the powers that be provide me with a brand-
new and absolutely clean and unwritten tablet for my poor old
memory.

I meant to have asked you where the meeting was that you could
not go to, and where Dr L. [Kathleen Lynn] spoke. I also wanted to
tell you to ask Susan for a motto to illustrate for the book-plate she
probably has, but I'd love to do her a motto.

Now don't work and worry yourself to death about me, you old
blessing. I am wonderfully content and I know that all is going well
with Kathleen [Ireland] and that there is nothing I can do in my
own country that others can't do as well. The hours slip by, like
rosary beads of dragons' teeth, with your visit a big glowing opal
bead to mark the rhythm. Don't I drivel?

It is really very curious that you should write a poem on and give
a lecture on St Francis, for I have been thinking of him a great deal
and thinking out pictures of him. I could find out very little about
him here, then F. A. [Fr Albert] sent me his 'Life' [of St Francis] –
'out of the blue' as they say – and then your letter came.

I have your poem copied and decorated it already. It's very
beautiful (the poem) [to Dora Sigerson Shorter]. Did I ever tell you
that Squidge sent me a card? I want you to give my love and thanks
to her.

I am so interested in little Doyle's horoscope. You must make
it out for Janey, his mother, for me to give her if ever I get out!
Perhaps you may drift across them, but I am sure she would be
most interested in it and would love to have it signed by you and
dated, to put by until he grows up. You have hit one nail on the
head in it in a wonderful way.

What you poetically term my 'ascetic way of living' certainly
has great compensations. I think that something I might call
the 'subconscious self' develops only at the expense of your
body – of course with the consent and desire of your will. To

develop it, it is necessary to cut yourself off from a great deal of human intercourse, to work hard and eat little, and as your subconscious self emerges, it comes more and more in time with the subconscious soul of the world, in which lie all the beauties and subtleties you speak of.

I think, too, that any friendships worth having have their roots on this plane: and, too, that this is the secret of the monastic orders and of the hermits and philosophers from the beginning of the world, especially of the Eastern mystics.

It used to puzzle me so when I read of girls – like Maud's sisters – becoming Carmelite nuns, and I could never see either the sense or the use of it. Since I have been here I understand it absolutely, and I know that for people with a vocation the compensation far outweighs the things you give up.

You ask me if the flowers last. They are wonderful. One lily – I threw it away on Monday – lasted one month and two days. I think it knew that I loved it. I am always going to keep a flower or leaf in water from one visit to another.

I am glad that I am president of so many things! I should always advise societies to choose their presidents from among jail-birds, as presidents are always such a bore and so in the way on committees! I always rather liked taking the chair, for the fun of bursting through all the red tape and when remonstrated with, I could always corner them by saying, 'ridiculous English conventions! Surely an Irish committee is not going to be bound by them?' Now they'll be able, on all the committees in Ireland, to waste all their precious time tying up their minds and other people's in red tape. Notices of motion about rubbish taking the place of the divine inspiration of the moment, and then all that twaddle about amendments and addenda and procedure of every kind!

I wonder whether you would get dignified and shocked? It is such years since we served on committees together; not since we went out to force a Suffrage Bill through Parliament. I have no ambition to have a vote for an English Parliament, and don't suppose I would use it. I don't think that Parliaments are much use anyhow. All authority in a country always seems to get into the hands of a clique and permanent officials.

I think I am beginning to believe in anarchy. Laws work out as injustice, legalised by red tape. You have such a lot of real good news and interesting gossip in your letter. You always manage to tell me about the things I most want to hear about.

The Fianna news was very cheering, and isn't the Doctor [Lynn] splendid? When one considers that her paying patients must almost all be in the enemy's camp! I call it awfully plucky and fine of her to come out in public the way she does. It's wonderful too the amount she does for the poor. I feel so proud of having introduced her to the real Ireland. One has such wonderful luck sometimes. If another doctor hadn't suddenly lost her mother, I should never have met ours.

I think my handwriting is getting awful. I think the sort of work I do is bad for writing. Do you ever hear of Mrs [Lillie] Connolly and her daughter Ina, they were great friends of mine? Ask for news of them, next time you write to the doctor or any of them. Ina was a splendid girl. Ask too if the Feis has come off yet.

Do you remember the verse labelled 'Introduction' at the head of Blake's 'Gates of Paradise'? Judges ought to take it to heart.

I am already beginning to get excited over your next visit and to wonder whom you are going to bring. I wonder if any of my visitors will ever get into jail themselves? Take my advice, and don't you, for you are not strong enough. Some people it would be very good for. I am sure that six months of it would do Percy a lot of good!

I saw a lovely moon the other night, and in my mind's eye began to play billiards with it. I rolled my mind into a great ball and cannoned off the moon into the B.B.'s window. If you think of it, the moon is the apex of so many triangles. I would have loved to hear your lecture on the 'Peace of St Francis'. You can tell me something about it, if you've room, in your next letter.

It's so funny to me to realise that I never wrote letters until I got into jail! And it's really quite an amusing game! You're so awfully good. I sometimes find it on my conscience that I give you so much to do. I must be an awful nuisance. Don't wear yourself out, that's all.

Did you ever visit the catacombs in Rome? The old paintings must be so interesting. I have just been reading about them. I have always longed to go to Rome. That and the Pyramids, also perhaps the Parthenon, which you would almost have to pass; I always feel I know these places quite well.

This morning, when the flutter of wings came at nine o'clock, I was peeling swedes. They, you may not know, are a kind of turnip largely eaten by sheep! We have been eating so many lately that I feel I shall soon begin to 'baa-baa'. But they are very good indeed. You should try them, though perhaps as a Veg[etarian], you already know them.

Now, darling, the limit is reached and there is no space for love which would require a very big one and remembrances to all friends. I hope Esther will be coming again soon. I long to show her the book. I know she would understand.

Best love and bless you old darlings.

Yrs,
CdeM

Free Again, July 1917–June 1918

Markievicz was released from Aylesbury Prison on 17 July 1917 and returned to an ecstatic welcome in Dublin. She rented a house with the Ginnells and resumed her life of organising and public speaking for Sinn Féin. As she had long threatened to do, she converted to Catholicism.

In mid-September, thirty-eight prisoners held in Mountjoy Prison began a hunger strike. They were force-fed: strapped to a chair, their mouths were forced open and a tube inserted through either the mouth or the nose. The process killed Thomas Ashe.

At a meeting of the Sinn Féin executive in December, Constance was appointed to head a Department of Labour along with Cathal O'Shannon. She was one of four women elected to the executive, all with links to the 1916 Rising.

To Josslyn Gore-Booth   *Frongoth [sic].*
10 September 1917 (received).

My dear Joss,
How stupid of Strachan [a Dublin removals man?]. Please wire him as I want my things moved in on Monday.

Mrs Ginnell and I are sharing a house. It will be handier if I get arrested again. As to money, I quite understood what you sent me – but I used to have £336 a year. Say I had £300 and the rest filled up the £100 you found, then there is about £80 due for the other three months. It's a year and three months since I was locked up – roughly I concluded that I should have something to live on and a little to spare and I don't understand.

I didn't like to bother Eva, as she is ill, and you know as long as I can get on somehow, I don't worry or fuss. You told me money would be due to me in August; I have not received any. The National Aid sent me a cheque to 'take a holiday' and I get expenses when I go to speak at meetings and I can get a dinner for 3 pence at Liberty Hall. Pea soup, bread and tea, a much better dinner than you get in jail. So I have rubbed along until now, but now I am starting a house again, I want a little cash.

Yrs,
C deM

To Eva   *143 Leinster Road.*
                                                   26 September 1917.

Dearest Old Darling,
We have just heard of Thomas Ashe's heroic death in the Mater Hospital last night. Dr K. [Kathleen] L. [Lynn] went up and actually was admitted. He was just drifting off into unconsciousness, and she waited 'til he died. Isn't it all wonderful and terrible? I don't know how they find the courage to do it. I feel afraid myself. I don't a bit feel sure that I could do it. It's different from fighting somehow, it is so awfully cold-blooded. Dr. K. L. thinks that it was the forcible feeding that did it, that they forced some into his lungs, because at the Mater they say he died of pneumonia.

Drs D. and C. of M. [Mountjoy] jail sent for a Dublin doctor to help feed our men. Eight refused, to their everlasting credit. A Dr Low, English from Amiens Street, did it for them. Isn't it wonderful to think of these boys in Mountjoy? Some are just rough country lads, all going in smiling and confident and facing up to things like this.

I had a talk with Liddy and with Brown [IRA men] during the hour they had to wait under arrest at Limerick Station. Both said they knew what they had to do. I said: 'Think it over before you hunger strike, for they will let you die, and it would be fatal for the cause if you gave in to save your life.' I told them that there was no need for them to strike, and that it was terrible suffering, and in fact tried to persuade them not to, but the one idea that is in every one of their minds is, 'We are soldiers pledged to Ireland, and we can fight in jail as well as out, and die in jail as well as out, and it is up to us to do it.' I think the English are trying to goad us into another rising, to wipe us all out.

General L. [Lowe] is reported to have said that M. [Maxwell] shot sixteen, but he will not stop 'til he has sixteen hundred if he gets the chance. They have machine-guns and armoured cars parading the streets here and in every corner of Ireland, and masses of soldiers in every district. When I gave a lecture in Cork they mobilised a regiment, with four machine-guns in the neighbouring streets.

The charges against our men are really so absurd too; no one speaks more strongly than I, and I am left alone. J. M. Donagh never spoke very strongly. No one is preaching rebellion. We are all talking of organising the country into a strong constitutional movement, with the Volunteer Force behind, whose immediate duty is to keep order ...

[Last page lost]

To Josslyn Gore-Booth   *143 Leinster Road.*
                                                    28 December 1917 (received).

My dear Joss,
A happy Xmas to you. Sorry I've been so long about writing but I've such a lot to do and think over that somehow my own things don't get much attention.

Xmas time being a time of peace, I want to put the burden of unanswered letters off my mind and to propitiate you for I know how annoying it must have been not to get an answer. I always meant to write, but when one's hardly ever at home, it's very hard to sit down to do anything that isn't of desperately immediate need.

Many thanks for all you've done. I didn't pay Strachan yet because he was so tiresome. He delivered all my books wet and a lot were mouldy and very much damaged and, too, nobody ever pays a big bill on the day it's due and I don't see why I should. I suppose he's afraid I may lose my money.

I see that I can only get paid according to your letter from 1915 (end of) as a 'femme sole' that I believe was a new law passed. I wonder if being paid would invalidate a joint claim paid from Casi and I [*sic*] for two preceding years. I am going down to [an] office about it presently and I have a friend and fellow rebel who has an office for 'refunds' so I expect I will be all right.

Now goodbye – wishing you and yours a Happy Xmas and heaps of good luck in the new year.

Yrs,
Con de M

PS: Casi's letter very cheerful, he's painting and running theatres with great success. Not much news in it. He says he wrote a work about Ireland when he heard I was released and that it made a 'great row'. All the nobility's privileges have been taken from them (thine too!).

To Eva   *[Fragment; no address].*
                                                    [Early 1918].

... fear of air raids and no revolution looming. We are all organising for a strong constitutional movement now. I believe that by International Law, we have, by Easter Week, earned the right to be in at the Peace Conference at the end of the War, and that's what we are now aiming at.

I know that you will be glad that we do not contemplate another 'scrap' at present, and we are making our men do police duty at meetings and keep order, and they are doing it very well. We are trying to prevent all low electioneering tricks and our men are a wonderfully decent, sober, and orderly crowd. The other side is supplying drink to the separation-allowance women [families of soldiers fighting in the war got a 'separation allowance'] and trying to organise riots, so far unsuccessfully.

Do you know, I sometimes almost regret jail – I loved your visits so? And now you are so far away and life is such a rush. I think the greater the gloom, the brighter the spots of sunlight. That's one of the things that makes even the horror of jail bearable.

Holloway Prison,
June 1918–March 1919

*With the World War in its fourth year, and the attempted
imposition of conscription causing outrage in Ireland, the British
used the pretext of a 'German plot' to arrest over seventy Sinn Féin
activists. Markievicz was one of them. In early June 1918, she found
herself interned in Holloway Prison, London, since 1902 a women's
only prison, where she was joined by Maud Gonne MacBride and
Kathleen Clarke.*

*Conditions in Holloway were a big improvement on Aylesbury, with
the three women classed as internees rather than common criminals.
In each cell was a camp bed with a mattress that seemed made of
hay, and coarse sheets and blankets. As internees, the women were
allowed to have food, clothes, books and approved newspapers sent
in. In the early days, they were locked up for twenty-three hours a
day, getting one hour's exercise out of doors. The prison diet consisted
of cocoa, margarine and 'a thing called skilly', which Clarke found
so repulsive she could not eat it. When Clarke and Gonne became
alarmingly thin, they were put on a 'hospital' diet that included milk,
rice pudding, tea and, later, an egg. Markievicz persuaded the doctor
to give them two hours of fresh air a day and soon they were allowed
to spend as long as they liked out of doors. In the end all three were
moved to more comfortable conditions in the hospital wing. At this
point they were allowed regular visitors.*

*Their main enemy was boredom. All three read a lot. They
decorated their cells, grew plants, did needlework and, in the case
of Markievicz, painted. After Maud Gonne was released in early
November, the remaining two were given a gas ring and took to*

cooking their own stews and other 'messes'. As is clear from the letters she wrote, Markievicz kept a close eye on the news and often commented on the bigger stories of the day. Irish republicans were attempting to have their case for independence heard at the Peace Conference in Versailles, which would follow the ending of the World War. This would be chaired by the American president Woodrow Wilson, who hoped to establish a League of Nations to prevent any future world wars. Since he was depending on British support for this, the Irish had little chance of a hearing in Versailles.

To Eva   *[Holloway] c/o Chief Postal Censor,*
Strand House,
Portugal Street, London.
[Undated fragment. Possibly June 1918].

Dearest old darling,
Re enclosed – £10 is your B. present, £5 just for things for me. Am quite rich. I earned your present and was dying to send it to you. Thank Clare for dressing gown with my love. I've worn it a lot, do you think I might keep it and get her another? I'd like to keep the dress too, it's so handy and cool and get one instead for whoever it belongs to, if I may.

Asparagus was a great joy. You might send me a bottle of mixed pickles some time. Tinned apricots were lovely. Do try to make some arrangements about books for us. Library here very bad and books so dreadfully dirty and *so old*. M.G and I are very fit and well, but poor Mrs Clarke is very feeble. Are there no depths ... [letter cut off].

... 'plot' being made public! The petty teasing too of not allowing even the usual internment conditions. No visits and shutting us up soon after 4 (devil's time), really 3 o'clock by God's time.

And this awful letter paper too. I'm so thankful you are not living in London, as if so, air raids would be a horror.

I sometimes think they arrested us to try and provoke another rebellion in Ireland, do you think that is so? To get a chance to shoot down 'the Irish' again. Bye bye darling, my heart is divided ...

To Eva   *Address to 'Holloway', c/o The Chief Postal Censor,*
Strand House,
Portugal St.,
WC2.
[Undated; soon after arrest].

Dearest Old Darling,

At last our extraordinary captors have given us leave to write – three letters a week. It sounded generous, until I got the paper supplied! A very English generosity I call it. Let me tell you and our common enemy the censor that there is no German plot! Very likely you won't be let know this, for I believe myself that it is all a political game, and that the English Government wanted a German Plot. Further than this, the whole affair is a mystery to me, why I was kidnapped, etc.

Our policy was very open and simple: to try and get the Powers to bring up Ireland's case at the Peace Conference (as Lord Salisbury brought in Greece) and, with all this talk about Freedom of the Seas, we have a great chance.

By the way, I wish you'd worry the Irish Government for my attaché case: it has some oddments in it that I prize and some notes about Ireland's claim to Sovereign Statehood that will no doubt interest the English, but they will be disappointed if they expect plots! There were some manuscript poems, too, that I had no time to read. I was always disappointed myself when I saw the headings of 'PLOTS' and found it related to cabbages and potatoes!

Talking of newspapers, they won't give us Irish ones: nothing but foreign ones, with no interest but the war news. What is the point of it all?

I love all the local gossip so. You are such a clever old darling, and all the things you sent have been such a comfort. We share everything. The 'sparrow grass' [asparagus] was delicious. I think my cheque-book is in my attaché case. When I can get at my money I will send you some. Do you mind (I know you don't) my keeping your cool things for the moment? It is so hot here.

Poor Mrs Clarke will never stand this. She frets for her boys and she has never got over the shock of her husband's and brother's murders. She nearly died and has been very feeble since.

Now this wretched paper will hold no more. Please thank Esther, Reginald, Clare and Patricia Lynch for all they sent us. Poor Poppet! Fancy arresting him! Bella [Dulcibella Barton] of course will take him.

Now bye bye and don't worry about me as I really wanted a rest. I had the German measles just before I was seized!

Yrs,
Con

To Eva   *Holloway Prison.*
                                                     8 June 1918.

Dearest Old Darling,
How I long to see you. I am getting more and more bored and inquisitive here! What is the meaning of it all? We wonder more and more. Is it political or military? Anyhow, it is not to their credit and will certainly rebound on our oppressors. Myself, I think it is about the best thing that could have happened for Ireland, as there was so little to be done there, only propaganda, and our arrests carry so much further than speeches. Sending you to jail is like pulling out all the loud stops on all the speeches you ever made or words you ever wrote!

I've been reading the Billing [libel] trial, a show-up for England! What a judge, what a jury and what a crowd! I wonder what a 'competent authority' would think of the merits of that and of our 'German Conspiracy'? It's really comic opera.

We are only allowed foreign papers here, which is one of the mean and petty ways of a great Empire to tease its imprisoned rebels, as there could be no practical reason for not allowing us the Irish papers. We are not allowed Labour papers either, even English ones!

Mrs Clarke only got news of her children today. She is in a fair way to break down, as she has been fretting so about them and neither ate nor slept. She simply lived for them and is one of your ideal mothers.

Now I want you to write to the Dublin Military Authority. They have sent my attaché case, having removed all letters and papers and my cheque-book. Now they did not steal Mrs Clarke's letters nor M. Gonne's letters, so why mine? Manuscript poetry, letters and notes of my own (typed and in copybook) for lectures and speeches. The notes are on Ireland's Geographical Status and her claim to Sovereign Statehood and on various industries and history. This is a very dull note. I can't say anything nice because of the censor's prying eyes.

Much love to you and much dislike to him.

I gCuis na hEireann,
Constance de Markievicz I.R.A.

To Eva   *Holloway Prison,*
[Undated; soon after her arrival in Holloway].

Dearest Old Darling,
I do love your letters so, they are such a cheer. The cards are a glory. That head of Christ by Leonardo [da Vinci] is one of the wonders of the world. Those copies of *Colour* [art magazine] that Esther left are an inspiration. I've hardly let them out of my hands. They are such a painting lesson, when one can't get much nature. Canned fruit is A1. It and Dulcibella's vegetables keep me alive. Bless you all, you kind and charitable people. Tell Gertrude I would love cigarettes! I feel that I forget to thank you half enough.

Mrs C. loves the fruit and she finds it so hard to eat enough. M.G. has a splendid appetite, luckily. I do a little cooking, too, and make 'savoury messes' with rice etc over a gas ring!

Fancy you meeting 'Miss Holland'– old beast; how we hated each other, and do still; but I guess Ludwig would have loved even me, if she could have seen into the future! I wonder if she is alive, and if she has made her former pupil out? Good luck to her and hers.

By the way, how often does Joss pay money into the bank for you and me and when?

Kitty [Ireland] seems to be flourishing. I'd love to see her. So sorry that I can't see you at present. You'll understand my attitude, I know, and be patient. It's very slow here and everything seems to be going at a great pace outside. Empires and Governments seem to be rather like the Gadarene pigs just now [about to plunge into the abyss].

Many thanks for Litvinoff's book. Poor Russia. I often think about my Polish relations. Poor Casi hated wars, revolutions and politics: and there he is – or was – in Kiev, or in the Ukraine.

Now Auf Wiedersehn darling,

Yrs i gCuis na hEireann,
Constance Markievicz

With the tide turning in favour of the allies in the World War, the attempt to enforce conscription on Ireland was dropped on 20 June 1918. Markievicz was thrilled at the news.

To Eva   *Holloway Prison.*
22 June 1918.

Dearest Old Darling,
I am radiantly happy! Don't be alarmed. 'Stone walls do not a prison make', etc. I've just got the result. Such a victory! Our arrests did it! For we were not at all certain; in fact, most doubtful of results. Ireland is always true to those who are true to her. Putting us away cleared the issues for us, so much better than our own speeches ever could.

Send me your stories to read when they come out, I am longing to read them. I don't think I have any talent that way myself. Could you send me the *Herald*, *The Dreadnought* and the *Socialist* (through the censor)?

Thank Reginald for his book. I had procured the Programme History for him and had begun a letter to him, when I was 'took'.

I am quite well off, for a wonder, and you can buy me any book you think, and also some stockings with thick soles. I passed yours on to Mrs C. who came with nothing but what she stood up in. Water-colours too, and etching materials. I wish I knew how long they meant to keep me, so as to know what to get in. The whole thing is really laughable. My companions I think of as 'Niobe' [heroic mother of Greek myth] and 'Rachel' [heroic mother of Christian myth], as they are the two most complete and perfect – though now, alas mournful – mothers that I ever met! It's really very bad luck on the kids to lose parents.

I loved 'Mrs Fits, the rubbish woman'.

Have just got a bundle of Irish papers with all the back news, through the censor! Do you think he read them? So funny. Just at present I wish I could challenge King George to mortal combat, box the censor's ears, ask many questions of Ll George in the English Parliament, publish a newspaper in America and kiss you! etc., etc.

Best love,
Constance de Markievicz, I.R.A.

To J. P. Dunne   *Holloway Jail.*
                                                      Business Letter
                                                      5 July 1918.

A Chara,

I entirely agree with you when you state that the child belongs not only to the parents but to the community and I believe all thinking Irish people to be of the same mind. It was owing to the subjugation of our nation that the terrible workhouse system that you also condemn was ever introduced; it is up to us to get rid of it.

The whole economic situation of Ireland has reduced our workers to such a terrible state of poverty and uncertainty that one bows in admiration to the splendid mothers of the lovely children that they have given to Ireland with such unthinkable suffering and self-sacrifice. Your efforts have my warmest sympathies.

If ever I am free to come back to Ireland, I will see you and consult with labour as to what I can best do to help Ireland do justice to their mothers in their great work.

I gCuis na hEireann,
Constance de Markievicz, I.R.A.

To Eva   *Holloway Prison.*
                                                19 July 1918.

Dearest Old Darling,

I haven't heard from you yet this week. I wonder if yours has been stopped by that wretched censor? There seems to be no method in his madness at all.

I am so glad that you are out of town. London is such a horrid place. Sight, ears, smell, morals and sense of beauty are offended at every moment in this most odious town. (Is this politics?)

You once asked me about Kingston [distant cousin]. Give him my love if you see him again and tell him to get to see me if he can. I dare him. Of course I'd love to see him again. I'm very interested in Greece, and you will be surprised that I like your play very much and I would like to act in it.

Please write to Miss [Madge] Daly, 15 Farrington Street, Limerick, and tell her that her sister [Kathleen Clarke] is better. She is a great friend of mine and has been very kind to me and I would like you to know her.

Dulcibella is such an angel, she never forgets us. She sent us raw onions this week. I ate one as big as an egg, and quite believed, for one awful moment, that I was in Aylesbury again and had stolen it!

How long are they going to keep up the pose that they are afraid of our seeing even infants? I wonder so what will happen to Wilhelm [Kaiser], also to George [V] and his cousins. The present popular howl must be very disagreeable to the ears of many alien cousins, who have given their whole lives and energies to the country of their adoption. W.'s alien father [Frederick III] was such an old dear, too, and his native mamma [Victoria, Princess Royal, daughter of Queen Victoria] a real crawling old snob. Perhaps you have forgotten W. I often laugh when I think of him.

There is no point in my seeing a solicitor. What can he do but spend my money? There is no German plot, and it is more satisfactory to sit tight than to appeal to law or the want of law that put one here.

Bushels of love,

Mise i gCuis na hEireann,
Constance de Markievicz I.R.A.

To Eva   *Holloway Prison.*
                                                    31 July 1918.

Beloved O. D.,

Got your letter dated 27th last night. Censor is mending his manners and apparently doing a day's work for a day's pay!

I wish I had your book. I would illustrate it, just for fun. Send me a couple of those reproductions (coloured) of Florentine pictures, Christmas cards on brown paper mounts, to copy costumes from and I'll do you a picture for your play.

Today's *Irish Times* twice alludes to Ireland as a 'Domestic Question'. Liars!

Greek history is very blood-thirsty; everything I ever read pales before it. So excited about your new poetry book. My head is so swelled! I shall soon have to wear a new hat.

After all, darling, you may call yourself a pacifist, but I never inspired you to immortal verse until I had fought in a Rebellion! Do you read the *Irish Independent*? If not, do so, for this last fight of the children to play innocent games is too funny for words.

So glad you wrote to Madge [Daly]. I am giving myself the pleasure of augmenting your birthday present, as my bank-book has just come and I am quite wealthy! Spend it on a spree or take a holiday or otherwise amuse yourself.

So glad you agree about solicitors; same applies to party, always excepting Alfie who is a friend.

I'd very much like to see Kingston – we used to be great pals. Mrs G. has been very tiresome and odd. I don't wonder at Bella. I think she must be annoyed and jealous at not being arrested! It is so tiresome trying to write telegraphically!

Am sending cheque to Susan. Love to Kitty [Ireland] and the children; I'd do anything to help them. Old Mrs Murphy makes me unhappy. Does she want a few shillings? D--- [Damn], the end of the page!

Love to you both,

Yrs i gCuis na hEireann,
Constance de Markievicz

From Hanna Sheehy Skeffington   *3 Belgrave Park,*
Rathmines,
Dublin.
8 August 1918.

Dear Madame,

I expect you already heard I'm back in Dublin [after 18 months in USA]. I got your news from Mrs [Wyse] Power. I wish I could have seen you. I first thought we would meet, but now that seems unlikely. I was so sorry to hear you had measles, but trust you have now recovered and that you keep your health and spirits – the latter I'm fairly sure of always.

I met many friends and admirers of yours out west. Kitty's [Ireland] divorce will I think be granted. On those matters westerners have wider ideas than the old world.

I am well and so is the boy [son Owen]. My trip did me good in many ways and I was very glad of the experience, tho' of course I'm now glad to be at home once more. Send my regards to your companions – we follow your career with great interest. I trust your sister is well and that you get news and papers. I would like to hear from you and Madame Gonne but I know you all have many correspondents and limited opportunities for writing.

I hope we'll all meet again in happier times.

Yours affectionately,
Hanna S. Skeffington
Is there anything I can send you or do for you? Please command.
HSS

Hanna Sheehy Skeffington met Constance sooner than she expected. Two days after writing this letter, Skeffington was arrested in Dublin after returning via Liverpool from her long sojourn in the USA with her son Owen. She was deported to England and spent one day in Holloway, but was quickly released when she began a hunger strike. She received permission to return to Ireland on 17 August and, with Helena Molony and Madeleine ffrench-Mullen, immediately organised a meeting at Foster Place in central Dublin to protest against the treatment of female Sinn Féin prisoners in British jails.

To Eva   *Holloway Prison.*
                                                Undated.

Dearest Old Darling,

Many thanks for things. Poor Staskou. I'd hate him to be killed or wounded. He did love life so. He was attached to the Russian Volunteer Fleet at Archangel and was interpreting. When you get back, try and find out through any and all Russian agents. Russia must be an awful place to be in.

Do tell me about Joss and the C.s [neighbours?]. It seems such a shame to sack him. I felt it was coming and two years ago, it had begun. I remember telling C. that nothing counted with Joss and that he need not count on friendship if he ever dared disagree or got on J.'s nerves. But what brought the crisis?

The censor has no method. The letter you wrote on receipt of the cheque was delayed until after I had got the next you wrote! We are now only to write on 'domestic and business subjects'! I would like to remind the sweet rulers of this Empire that they have constantly affirmed that 'Ireland is a domestic question'!

Poor old Gaga, how frightened she must be crossing! [the Irish Sea for her Grand Tour] I don't think the peas were from her after all. So glad that you will be seeing Hanna. Give her my love.

I was so interested to read some of [Stephen] Hobhouse's experiences [jailed as a conscientious objector in 1916], and thought of the time I kissed you at Aylesbury, and the row, and of how the Realm trembled! But I did it!

I'd love to read your pacifist novel. How do you manage love-scenes? Have you a collaborator? I feel that I could help! You old darling! What an epidemic of plots there seems to be! They don't seem to have put anyone in jail over this last. I get more and more puzzled. Why this secret imprisonment?

Best love – Auf Wiedersehn.

Yrs i gCuis an hEireann,

Constance de Markievicz

P.S.: Please get me a 6″ pot prepared with leaf mould to re-pot sweet geraniums.

To Eva   *Holloway Prison.*
                                               22 August 1918.

Beloved old darling,
It was a real joy to see your lovely old face grinning behind its
specs again. I wonder is the realm tottering ever since? Lots of
paints, etc., come, and the brushes are a dream. One tube of oils
by mistake. When you return it, you can get it changed for 'Saturn
red'.

Your poems are the pick of the basket (anthology). I simply hate
poems in slang. The Cockney accent makes me stop my ears. War
certainly does not inspire great literature. You always get away
from the obvious, from local colour, the exact date, time and place
and take root in eternal truths. So one can always, if one is in touch
with the eternal, and the roots of things. One can always pick you
out and appreciate you. But those fools who depend on lost 'h's'
and a battle in Flanders are too dull for words.

I wish you had brought me some drawings to look at. The worst
of prison is that it is such an ugly place. Please agitate to get the
papers that were stolen from me out of that attaché case.

Fancy Gaga still doing the Grand Tour! I was so soon fed up with
the intense respectability.

Did Clare [Annesley] get my letter? How I wish I were painting
a cornfield with a white cottage. Now bye bye dear and bless your
poor old heart. Love to you both.

Mise i gCuis na hEireann,
Constance de Markievicz

To Eva   *Holloway Prison.*
                                               3 September 1918.

Beloved old darling,
Your last letters have come in quite decent time and are such a joy.
Do take care of yourself, stay in bed and don't worry about me. I
put up 1 lb. last week, and I'm painting a lot and using this jail as

a rest-cure! As far as I am concerned you can be quite happy, for I really wanted a rest.

The bottled jellies were lovely and the grapes charming. I have hung three bundles up on the bars of our cage, where the sun shines through them.

That cheque I sent is for you, with my love. I will send another for the fur coat. Let me know about how much. No hurry. It's Miss Daly who is trying for a visit, not Mrs. [Daly]. We are so glad that you can put her up and look after her.

Two lovely little Florentine picture-books arrived from Clare. A great joy. And papers, etc., from Patricia [Lynch]. People are so kind. Mrs C. is much more comfortable the last few days. I had been getting a bit anxious, she is so frail. She has a wonderful spirit, and we joke away. We yelled over your last letter with the big 'D' (omitted). Don't go to jail as a proxy: it would kill you, and one Irishwoman is better than a dozen Englishmen, even conscientious ones!

There are wasps here. One walked up my leg yesterday, but we parted amicably. They never sting me and I never kill them. We are affinities. Perhaps I was one in my last incarnation!

Goodbye,

Yrs,
Constance de Markievicz I.R.A

To Eva   *Holloway Prison.*
                                           11 September 1918.

Dearest Old Darling,
You don't say anything about your health in the letter just received and I feel anxious. Esther does not look too well in the photo either. It's awful for you two dear old crocks that somebody else's detestable war keeps you out of Italy; why don't you go to Ireland for a bit? Anyhow you'd get food there. You'd have great fun, too, as everyone would mistake you for me, as before. And then you'd get everything you'd ask for and much more. Dulcibella's home is so lovely. I always wanted to take you to Glendalough.

Maud Gonne has been very ill with a rash, but she is on the mend and up again. We were most anxious for some days. She is very nervous about her health and always afraid that that old lung of hers will come against her.

We were frightfully excited about the Peelers' strike [strike by police in the UK]. Why don't the jailers do ditto! And by way of sabotage, destroy the jails? Did Clare get my letter? By the way, you might send me an old picture postcard if you find a pretty one as they don't count as letters, and would be a help to painting. I'm working quite hard and doing quite big things and improving a lot. Jail is so hideous, which is a bore. I've done Deirdre and Medhbh and more horses. I love the two wee books of pictures – they are a great help. I look forward to your book so much. Write my name in it before you send it to me.

Best love to you and all rebels.

Yrs i gCuis na hEireann,
Constance de Markievicz

To Eva   *Holloway Prison.*
                                                18 September 1918.

Beloved Old Darling,
I do hope you are better. It's awful to think of you ill, and me so chirpy myself. Thank God you are not here. Your last letter was lovely and I could see that you were really better.

With regard to this new visiting scheme of the Eng. Govt., I didn't like to worry you until I knew that you were better, so I didn't tell you definitely; but I would not like anyone to submit themselves to such an indignity just for me. No, no, no! Either sign, or see me with a wardress present (according to jail rules); but once we Irish rebels pledge our word we are to be trusted, and to be watched and spied on after one's word is given is more than I would put up with. It is a nuisance but unavoidable, and one is not looking for a bed of roses! One does not expect honourable treatment. People always 'judge others by themselves'.

We are all right. M. G. is better. K. C. is not so well; she suffers so, but has such a wonderful spirit. She never complains but makes the best of everything. I want you, when you are well, to arrange for someone to bring flowers for the Church, at my expense, enough for two posies for the two vases on the altar. You would probably find a Catholic girl in some Irish society who would undertake the job. Flowers to be left at the gate 'for R. C. Priest'.

I have got my vote registered all right, in spite of Unionist objectors, censor's delays, etc. This was part of a batch of good news from the 'western front'.

Much love to you darling, Esther and all good rebels.

Yrs, i gCuis na hEireann,
Constance de Markievicz I.R.A.

To Eva   *Holloway Prison.*
                                                     8 October 1918.

Beloved old darling,
Letter just came. Give my love to Janey [Coffey] and tell her she must come to see me if ever I get out, and that I thought of her at the time of the St Patrick's pilgrimage. I was in here at the time.

The coats came on appro. Bad value. Green one nice, but *must* have the fur below the knees, and it's a little too short too. Weather is warm, so there is no hurry. I don't think [illegible] is a very good place. But perhaps it is, on consideration. I have not shopped there for such years. Don't like 'Coney Seal' anywhere at all.

My 'baby' wrote to me, but put no address; poor little fellow has been very ill.

I am making a border for your 'Dora Shorter' poem, it's very nice. Your P.C.s [postcards] are such a joy. Don't let Squidge or anyone else see me under the present absurd regulations. As you say, it's my funeral, and I'm dancing at it! A little patience, and won't we talk! I feel quite capable of talking not only the hind but all four legs oft that belted ass, the British Empire.

Do you remember [Arthur] O'Shaughnessy's poem, 'And three with a new song's measure'?

Mrs C. is better again, thanks to a filthy bottle, a painted chest and being rolled in cotton wool for a week. One of the few times I've known a doctor to be of any use.

M. G. is awfully nervous about herself and will end by fretting herself into a consumption, but I don't think she's physically ill, but awfully unhappy, can settle to nothing, just frets and fidgets; we are awfully sorry for her but are helpless. She just cheers up when her family leave things or write.

We are awfully sorry for her, but I don't think much use.

How's your health? I hope electric treatment is right. Watch it carefully yourself as English doctors are often fools and never intuitive.

Best love old darling.

I gCuis na hEireann,
Constance de Markievicz I.R.A.

To Eva   *Holloway Prison.*
Yours posted 10th just arrived
Yours posted 15th arrived yesterday!
18 October 1918.

Beloved old darling,

We *must* take what you call an 'absolutist' stand here, and giving an undertaking cuts the ground from under our feet. Living up to your principles is always d..nable [damnable], but it's particularly necessary just now. Madge [Daly] could explain at length, if you wrote her. We are going on all right.

Mrs C. is really a little better at last. For the first time since we have been here, she seems really to be on the mend. My weight goes steadily up and I'm getting quite 'round and rosy'. M. G. is all nerves and fancies but physically I don't think there is anything the matter with her.

We got some lovely marmalade left at the gate. I think it must have been Patricia [Lynch]. If you come across a pot of raspberry jam do send me one. Mrs C. and I make puddings out of spare bread and put marmalade in and are thinking that a change would be nice. Aren't I the greedy pig? Gaga wrote me another amazing letter, certainly there's no fool like an old fool.

Just re-read your letter and will try and be exact about visits. We are asked, above and beyond the jail rules of having a wardress present at visits, 'to give undertakings in writing not to talk politics and our visitors not to carry messages or make reports'. Under these conditions we refuse visits. Is that clear?

I do love your letters so. We roar over them. How's your health? I'd love to be looking and talking you almost off your head, but I'm painting away here and have a lot of things to show you. I'm sorry to be tiresome about coats but I *must* have one long enough.

Best love – and oh, the cards are a *real* joy.

Yrs i gCuis na hEireann,
Constance de Markievicz I.R.A.

To Eva   *Holloway Prison.*
                                              21 October 1918.

Dearest Old Darling,
So glad to hear you are a bit better. How I wish I was there to fuss over you. I wonder where you are? My imagination visualises you and E. in resplendent raiment and on verandahs and in wind-swept pine woods and in comfortable, civilised beds.

When you come back, if it's not too much bother, I want you to send anything you send here to *me*. It's so exciting getting things. If it means a lot of arranging, of course don't bother, but do if you can. You are such an old darling.

Cloaks no good, *must* have one long enough. The authorities have supplied me with shoes, stockings, costume, etc, so for a jailbird I'm not so badly off! Health splendid.

Such an interesting packet of newspapers came from P. L. [Patricia Lynch] on Saturday. She's really an angel and I'm most grateful. Mrs C. much better. She really has a hero's soul and makes the best of everything, she is an ideal jail-bird. Your P.C.s are such a joy. I have finished copying out your Dora S. poem, with border and caps. I'm longing for you to see it.

The world seems to be more topsy-turvy than ever. What hypocrites people are! Do read P. S. O'Hegarty's *Unconquerable Nation*. I wish I could get it for you, but the Realm might totter if I tried.

I'm glad you think there is a chance of our being let out. I suppose it will suddenly strike them that we are less powerful out than in, and then out we shall go! In the meantime, we are quite cheerful and resigned (that is, Kathleen C. and I) and don't worry.

Best love to you and Esther and all good rebels.

Is mise i gCuis na hEireann – take care of yourself you O. D.!
Constance de Markievicz I.R.A.

To Eva   *Holloway Prison.*
                                [Undated; probably October 1918].

Dearest old darling,
Many thanks for your two, which came through quite quickly for a change. I am glad you got mine about the better distribution of food so quickly.

How mad the world seems to have grown! What *do* they all want? Do you think they will go on fighting and lying and talking hypocrisy until a great plague comes to sweep all their armies away? Poor democracy, so much is being done in its name.

I do hope you are taking every precaution. We are safer here from infection than anywhere else, so don't worry about us. We are warmed with hot pipes and well ventilated, and there is nothing in our conditions to affect our health.

Please send me toothpaste, a box of sweet soap, a sponge, and hair mixture – Jaborandi. If you consider that I cannot get a fur coat for the money I sent, I will send you another cheque. Isn't it absurd to lock up doctors for nothing just now?

Just had such a gorgeous box of sweets from Ireland! Blackball, chocolates and all sorts of luxuries. Please thank whoever sent me fags. I'm afraid I don't see much chance of our liberation. I don't know why they put us here, so it's very hard to make a guess what the tyrants will do with us.

By the way, has anyone had the imagination, patience and perseverance enough to make a map of the land where the Czecho-Slovaks and the Jugo-Slavs are born and bred? They interest me enormously. They are rather like something Alice found in Wonderland!

M. G. is much more nerves than anything else. She worry, worry, worries and 'knows she is going to die'. She is thin but has a very good appetite. She'll get all right if she gets out.

Best love.

Mise i gCuis na hEireann,
Constance de Markievicz I.R.A.

On 29 October 1918, Maud Gonne MacBride was released from Holloway on medical advice.

After the armistice with Germany that ended the First World War on 11 November, a general election was called for Sunday 14 December 1918. For the first time, women aged over 30 could not only vote but also stand for election. Markievicz agreed to stand in the Dublin St Patrick's constituency as a Sinn Féin candidate.

To Eva   *Holloway Prison.*
                   [Undated; after Gonne released on 29 October].

Dearest Old Darling,
I will buy the thing I made Mrs M. but don't let her know that it's *me* buying it. Just say that you can sell it for £1 and don't say to whom. Don't send her more money than that: it would be like dropping water through a sieve! But I'd like just to give her that.

I'm afraid she is too old to work, as she never had to, and you must learn young. She has a sister, who, she says, is comfortably off in Manchester or Liverpool.

Don't take Mrs G. seriously: she is rather touched – 'nobody loves me' – and she is always seeking someone (female) to hold her hand, take her shopping and do all her errands for her. She can never find even a friend, because she is so absorbed in 'No. 1'!

I'm painting away and quite content. It's great fun trying to do water-colours. We have been moved into a more comfortable lodgement: the realm will be endangered if I say more!

So sorry you are in the grip of the 'flu. It's almost as bad as being in the grip of the English! I've heaps of books still and some of them will take a long time to read. Do take care of yourself and don't overdo it.

By the way, according to 'information received', the men are allowed larger sheets of paper for letters and two sheets! Trust the English to always make a point of worse treatment for women.

By the way, shall you 'stand' for Parliament? I wouldn't mind doing it as a 'Shinner' as an election sport, and one does not have to go to Parliament if one wins, but oh! to have to sit there and listen to all that blather!

Much love from yours i gCuis na hEireann,
Constance de Markievicz I.R.A.

To Eva   *Holloway Prison.*
                                  [Undated; after Gonne released].

Beloved Old Darling,
Just seen alarmist reports from M. G. [on 'flu pandemic]. Do try and calm her! We are far safer here than outside from 'flu, as we are all to ourselves on a landing and exercise alone. I believe there are a few cases among the seven or eight hundred persons shut up in here.

Please write a reassuring note to Madge D. [Daly]. People get so excited when they read these exaggerated pars [paragraphs], in the shrieking dailies. Please thank Reginald for things, and I do so love the cards – his little book of etchings was a joy.

I've *heaps* of pickles and anchovy – enough for a couple of months. I'm getting fat; gone up a stone. So sorry to hear about your pains; hope Esther is not bad. I often long to see you. Isn't the whole thing a miserable bit of petty tyranny and spite? So English! Send me in a common scribbling block and an exercise book, when you've time. No hurry, as I've still got paper. The red chrysanthemums look so lovely in my cell.

Aren't the small nations of the world having a fine old 'beano'? It does make me laugh. We can't be kept out of our own for ever, if only the wave rolls on! Do you remember Blake's prophecy? Do write it on a card for me some time. Did Shawn [MacBride] ever show you some doggerel of mine I think he had? My letters seem to grow very dull, but these sheets are not inspiring.

I sent cheque for [the] boy to go for change of air straight to Dublin.

Best love and keep your heart up.

Yrs i gCuis na hEireann,
Constance de Markievicz I.R.A.

To Eva   *Holloway Prison.*
                                                4 December 1918.

Dearest old darling,
I do love your post-cards! So glad that you are better. I wonder if you are doing any election work? Don't overdo it.

I see that [John] Maclean is out and am so glad. He is a hero. If the whole situation were not so tragic it would be laughable. The English election is like *Alice in Wonderland* or a Gilbert and Sullivan Opera. The *D. News* and the *Chronicle* are a treat.

Thank God we are not a materialistic nation! Anyhow, it keeps you out of a lot of trouble. It seems to me that the Germans – in the far end of things – will have really won the war, as they have gained a victory over themselves or, rather, materialism.

Did you see some absurd yarn in *D. News* about a cypher letter and Sinn Féin? I wouldn't be a bit surprised if they don't start a new 'plot' to keep us in. It is so easy to get a poor fool to carry a letter for a few shillings.

You sent me such a lovely picture of a rock garden, I longed to be there. Please tell Molly O'Neill, 6 Gloucester Gardens, Bishop's Road that I wrote to her to Hove about two months ago. Thank her for the things she left for me. I enjoyed them very much. It's such a bore not knowing how long they intend to keep you. There is nothing to help us calculate! I suppose that we are just a card in their hand and will be played when they think it suits them. It's hard on Mrs Clarke. I'm thankful to say she is better again, but I don't think she'll be really well until she has an operation. My weight is nine and a half stone and am very well.

So M. G. went home! Had she leave? I wonder whether she'll be sent back. It's very mysterious why they ever took her, but they are, luckily, sometimes very stupid.

Best love darling.

Mise i gCuis na hEireann,
Constance de Markievicz I.R.A.

To Eva   *Holloway Prison.*
                                             12 December 1918.

Darling,
I haven't heard from you for an age. I think the censor is an evil person. One of my letters re election was stopped and he just pinched it. Evidence, I suppose, of a new 'plot'! I was actually allowed a big bit of paper to write an Election Address on! I wrote one in such a hurry that it's probably not sense. *The Freeman's Journal* is putting all sorts of rubbish into our mouths! It's not fair to shut us up and not let us answer! Luckily the Irish people never believe the daily papers, especially *The Freeman*, which is reported to be run by English gold – I mean – Treasury Notes!

By the way, buy me Cole's new book. Brailsford and Hobson have been such a delight. I am studying them over and over again. Please thank Miss Moorhead for lovely dressing-gown. I was just going to write out for one.

Who is 'Whimsical Winnie'? I love her.

Did you see that one of us died at Usk [Richard Coleman from Swords, Co. Dublin]? It's not in the English papers. Do you get the *Independent*? I told them to send it to you. We are so lucky here. Usk is evidently very hard. However, it is quite good for the cause to die in Jail, and I'm sure he did not grudge the sacrifice.

I was wishing that you were not a pacifist the other day. It would have been so funny to have impersonated me in Dublin, but they'd have thought that they had gone mad when you (or I!) began to speak, and rainbow-tinted words on the beauties of Peace began to fall from your (or my!) ruby lips! I drivel.

Such beautiful white lilac came. By the way, what has happened about flowers for church?

With love and take care of yourselves.

I gCuis na hEireann,
Constance de Markievicz, I.R.A.

To Hanna Sheehy Skeffington   *Holloway Jail.*
                                                    12 December 1918.

My dear Mrs Skeffington,
Many thanks for your card received some days ago. I have received so few letters since the election campaign; before that I began to think that the censor was holding them up! I don't even know if my election address was let go. One letter I had written previously was not allowed to go. I don't know why and they keep the letters they fancy for three days.

One cannot help but laugh at the delightfully fair way this election is being managed, our opponents are making full use of the opportunities that are being lavished on them to misrepresent us in the press and we are gagged and cannot answer them. Luckily our people have no delusions with regard to the truthfulness and honour of the subsidised daily press. With this long delay between the voting and counting, any villainy may be tried. Also the 'absent' voters seem to me to give unlimited scope for trickery. It would look very funny if Sinn Féiners only won when unopposed! The death of poor Coleman in Usk; how terrible for them. We are so lucky here. There has been so little influenza and we are so well out of any infection, but I forget; you saw for yourself. We wonder so how long they will keep us and what is at the back of it all? Do you think they have a Pigott [author of the fake Parnell letters] up their sleeve?

I never feel it matters much what happens to us and I have such a sure conviction that things are going all right for Ireland; we are only pawns in the game. It has been so good for the country having no 'leaders', they have all had a chance and learned how to think and act. Leaders can be such a curse!

I see that you and yours have been doing splendid work for me. One reason I'd love to win is that we could make St Pat's a rallying ground for women and a splendid centre for constructive work by women. I am full of schemes and ideas.

And now good bye and good luck. Love to yourself and remember me to my friends in your league.

Mise i gCuis na hEireann,
Constance de Markievicz I.R.A.

On Saturday 28 December, the election results were announced with a landslide victory for Sinn Féin. A day later, Markievicz was told of her election victory. She was the first woman to be elected to the House of Commons. Always happy for an excuse to goad the censor, she began signing her letters 'M.P.' and 'T.D.', before coming up with an Irish version of the same, and finally TD after the first sitting of Dáil Éireann in January 1919.

To Eva   *Holloway Prison.*
                                                  6 January 1919.

Beloved old darling,
We are still revelling in your gifts. Do you know J. A. Hobson? I once
met him and liked him so much. Since reading his last book, I want
to meet him again. Do try to get in touch with him. It's all true what
he says and I want to ask him a score of questions.

Wilson [American President] seems to me a very dark horse.
I hope they won't get him assassinated. The elections were
very cleverly rigged. English people seem to be both foolish and
unprincipled. I don't think our people would ever rise to cries of
'Revenge!' We conquered by telling them that each one of them
must learn to carry the cross for Ireland and that without pain and
self-sacrifice, our country would be lost. Do you remember Yeats'
'Kathleen ni Houlihan' – 'If you would help me, you must give me
yourself, give me all'? That's what the elections mean for Ireland,
and something great for Ireland must come out of it.

Your letter was very good, but I was sorry that you omitted
Rachel, who is the most suited to the job of the lot. Don't push
M. any more. She has quite lost grip from long absence. Do you
know St Malachy's prophecy? I've just illuminated it and it's fine.
I ring the changes between broad and soppy brushwork and fine,
light illuminating. Wait 'til you see all I've done. I've begun to write
several things too, but don't get on, as I simply can't tear myself
away from my painting.

It's such a puzzle to me why they keep us. English spite I suppose.
Perhaps they are going to wait until they have made the world
safe for Democracy! It's certainly not safe in Ireland just now. We
pray that Wilson does not lose his head and his soul, wallowing in
drawing-rooms and getting his eyes progged out with the spikes of
crowns!

Bless you and all yours,
Constance de Markievicz, I.R.A., M.P.

To Eva   *Holloway Prison.*
                                            17 January 1919.

Dearest old darling,
Fur coat is beautiful, so snug and warm. Many thanks for the thread
I got from Limerick at last. Do write to M. She sent me things and I
can't spare letter.

Bella need not worry. I'm not thinking of taking her back
[Poppet?]. But she has good points and knew every detective in
Dublin by sight. Thank women candidates for Telewag [telegram].

How soon is civilisation going to be fed up with the fat
Englishman? I see that they have great new schemes for the
betterment of mankind, and that helpless coloured people are
praying to be under their beneficent rule. Anyhow, they are
incubating baby Frankensteins [Dr Frankenstein's monsters] all
over the globe and scattering dragons' teeth, even among their own
democracy.

I see no more reason for our release than there was for our
jailing, so don't delude yourself with hopes. Some day someone will
have an Idea, and we shall be free. The only pity is that Englishmen
have so few ideas. They can do sums and say long prayers and
buy their way through life, and that's all. They certainly don't like
idealists or people who are ready to support the principles they
teach.

If you have a friend who does not mind shopping, get them to
see if you can still get big model engines, signals, rails, etc., like Bug
[unknown acquaintance] had, driven by methylated spirit. Any boy
would understand.

Who told you about Mrs C.? I can't read it. She is so fretted at
being away from her boys. I can't make out why they keep her. She
is not sleeping now and is so feeble. It's very puzzling, why they
keep some and let others loose. In some ways it is a blessing that
they are so stupid. I often laugh when I read the papers.

Is mise I gCuis na hEireann,
Constance de Markievicz I.R.A., M.P.

To Eva   *Holloway Prison.*
                                    [Undated; after January 1919].

Dearest old darling,
We cannot accept the new scheme they have offered us for visits, as
I don't see how one could possibly keep the promise one is asked
to give.

They want us to promise not to talk 'politics'. Today life is
'politics'. Finance, economics, education, even the ever-popular
(in England) subject of divorce is all mixed up with politics today. I can't invest my money, without politics; buy clothes without
politics. Art is all political, music is battle tunes or hymns of hate
or self-glorification, and so I simply do not know what they mean
when they say we must not talk politics.

What the censor let through is no criterion. He did not like
some of the Christmas cards sent me, I find! So I refuse to keep this
promise that I don't understand. I never deliberately said I'd do a
thing without believing I was capable of doing it yet.

'An Exile's Dream of Ireland' I would like for the picture. I don't
like making capital for myself out of being in jail! I see an awful
account of Kathleen in today's paper. It was cruel, cruel putting her
in here.

I do love the purple chiffon Clare sent me. It's a joy on a dull
day. I'm quite fat and well and working quite hard at painting;
Colour [monthly art magazine published 1914-32] is such a help.
I think I am safer here from 'flu than anywhere else. Do take care
of yourself.

Clare looks so lovely on the postcard. Could you not get someone
to write to M. O'N.? [Molly O'Neill] Date it from a hotel en route for
Ireland and then she won't call and sit! I fear I am an awful plague.
Are you taking care of yourself? I feel so bad when I hear of you up
here on bad days and at unholy hours. I wish I could give you some
of my strength.

When I read of Dev, I thought of O'Shaughnessy's poem; ['Ode'];
the lines beginning 'One man with a dream'. Mercifully, there were
three, not one. [One man with a dream, at pleasure,/Shall go forth

and conquer a crown;/And three with a new song's measure/Can trample an empire down.]

Mise i gCuis na hEireann
Constance de Markievicz I.C.A., F. d P. [possibly Feisire de Pharlaiminte – direct translation of Member of Parliament into Irish].

To Eva   *Holloway Prison.*
                                                       22 January 1919.

Beloved old darling,
Thank you for the things. You sent fixative but no blower. Thank Esther for hers. I know J.A. Hobson slightly and want to meet him again. You might buy me his new book. I want to read up imperialism and earlier peace conferences and anything about Empire building and theories about internal construction of a state. I would buy any good books that might be useful to pass on. I want to get together a little library of Economics and Welt-Politik [literally world politics; originally describing Germany's imperialist foreign policy from 1890 onwards]. Is there any hope of there being a white rook among the birds of prey engaged in tearing up carcases?

Did you read Miss Brodrick's letter in the *Daily News*? It's quite good. The English must be so bored that the only result of having put us in here has been to put them in a false position before every honourable person and to give the young people at home the chance to develop themselves and to learn to do without 'leaders'. I don't believe in leaders myself; I had just time to fix up my end before I was 'took' and it has had great results with regard to the women.

Could you order the *Dreadnought* and *Herald* regularly for me? They sometimes come and sometimes miss. How is Sylvia [Pankhurst] about Ireland? She had one very stupid par. [paragraph].

Do you ever see our Labour paper? Tell me if you don't and I will get it sent you. Why do you put your letters in two envelopes? Is it to support trade?

This awful weather does not agree with Mrs C. It is not too warm here at all. She is so fragile. Can you tell why she was arrested at all? I never knew such brutality. She led the life of a semi-invalid. The lily you sent was such a joy to us and the altar flowers were lovely.

Now goodbye darling, love to you both.

Mise i gCuis na hEireann,
Constance de Markievicz, I.C.A, F. de P.

To Eva   *Holloway Prison.*
                                                    30 January 1919.

Dearest of Darlings,
I do hope you are minding yourself this awful weather. Mercifully for us the police strike did not come off, so there is still a stoker who stokes, and we are not too bad.

K. C. in bed with a bad cold. Hanna S. could have been an M.P. if *she* had *wanted*. A seat was offered her. She is not altogether an S.F. I think, and I *know* prefers to work from the women's platform. I quite agree with your estimate of her.

Do try and worry out why that December letter of mine was held up for so long. I certainly had nothing in it that I thought would be delayed. I've sent several test letters; only two were stopped. One thing I am quite grateful to that diabolic lazy man the censor for: he has taught me a lot of useful things – caution, for one. If one had more paper and a less odious censor, one might have been tempted to be indiscreet. Not about policies, I shall always stand against 'Secret Diplomacy', not in pompous speeches and newspaper articles, but by speaking out myself.

Saying things that might get others into trouble is all that I fear. It's awful to think that even Art is conquered by militarism. Fancy anyone wanting to paint awful war scenes when they could paint reapers or the sea.

[James] Connolly was such a prophet. He said war was going to be between the fat man and his Black flag and the Workers and their Red flag and now it has come! He also saw victory for the Red. I am growing pessimistic and wonder how they will abuse power when they have got it.

Did you see the latest Hun atrocity in Ireland? St Enda's school! I am filled with wonder at the patience and discipline of the people. So few retaliations, for which I am thankful.

Best love to all,

Yrs i gCuis na hEireann,
Constance de Markievicz I.C.A., M.P.
PS: Please send Hobson's *Life of Cobden*. Miss C. J. Cole (Sylvia's friend) seems to be a person of ideas.

To Eva   *Holloway Prison.*
                                                  6 February 1919.

Dearest Old Darling,
Yours and E.'s [birthday] presents are such a joy. I have hung the garment where I can look at it when I am painting, it's such a gorgeous colour.

Write Carlisle [George Howard, 11th Earl of Carlisle; son of Markievicz's cousin Rhoda L'Estrange]. Tell him where I am and that I can't write and that if he can get me out I'll lunch with him at the Carlton! Or anywhere else.

I get such funny letters from the ends of the world, and I begin to understand why M.P.s employ secretaries. My election was a foregone conclusion. I must know most of those who voted for me. The Transport Union is strong, ditto S.F. Everyone had to concentrate on the 'doubtfuls'.

Isn't Dev great? [de Valera escaped from Lincoln Jail on 4 February 1919]. That's not his portrait in the *Daily Mail*. I'm afraid they'll hold the rest of us all the longer now, out of spite.

Don't come up here [Eva's home at 33 Fitzroy Square was due south of Holloway Prison.] this awful weather. I shudder to think of you out in it. I don't go out much. It's not the sort of weather for a jail! Yes, get Hobson's book, and what about B.[Bertrand] Russell's? Ask for my watch here next call, it's losing [time].

I'd love a run to John's Port or up Ben Bulben. Do you remember when we went up years ago, on my birthday, in the snow and mist, and how grand and mysterious it was?

I heard from Kitty the other day. Very good news. Uncle and the other relations turning up trumps. I've got the menu of the Historical Banquet for you, with a lot of signatures on it. Mrs W. P. [Wyse Power] sent it. My cards are so nice in the album. If I ever get out, I shall have such a queer lot of parcels.

What hypocrites the Allies are, and us in jail for doing what they boastfully pretend to have done! Anyhow, I think the old tin kettle must burst soon. Democracy must learn something out of all this, and then?

We are really so sane in Ireland and it really would be 'safe for democracy' if the Armed Forces were withdrawn. Aren't we a patient and long-suffering people?

With best love to you both,

Mise i gCuis na hEireann,
Constance de Markievicz I.R.A., M.P.

On 18 February, Kathleen Clarke was released from Holloway and went to stay with Eva Gore-Booth at Fitzroy Square before returning to Ireland escorted by her sister Madge and Michael Staines. During her trip home, she fell ill with 'flu and ended up spending seven weeks in a Dublin nursing home. Constance was released three weeks later and visited her.

To Eva   *Holloway Prison.*
                                                19 February 1919.

Beloved old darling,
Here I am, all alone in this Englishwoman's home! Luckily, I always find myself good company. Of course, I miss K. very much, though for the first time in my life I was thankful to see the back of a dear friend. Give her a good 'scholding' and a hug from me and tell her the tea-pot's broken, not by me this time! I've no one to bully now, and she requires it. I hope she is being good and staying in bed or resting up. Weren't you shocked when you saw her? And they dare to talk about German atrocities – the hypocrites! But it will all react in the end.

I'm almost sure it was St Hubert; think it must be a misprint [clearly referring to something written to her by Eva; St Hubert is the patron saint of humane hunting]. I'm now doing 'Heroic Death'. It's rather nice and illuminating is great fun, for a change. You can get such nice colour. I wish I'd ever looked at any in my life.

Have you heard where Dev is? What a gossip you are having! Do you know a girl called Evans on the Vote? She wrote me such a nice letter, and is publishing, or has published, one from me.

So glad you saw Mrs S. [Sheehy Skeffington]. It's not much good holding meetings about Russia, nobody minds talk nowadays. It wasn't talk blocked conscription: it was the astounding fact that the whole male population left at home and most of the women and kids would have died sooner than fight for England, and they simply did not dare exterminate a nation.

Our contempt of money and our taking jails and death as all in the day's work must puzzle the British more than a little.

You criticise our election organisation! The Enemy says it was efficient, perfect, etc. It was practically nil! So everyone butted in, women and children taking a very prominent part. I believe it brought out a lot of women speakers.

Now good night, love to you all,

Yrs i gCuis na hEireann,
Constance de Markievicz I.R.A., M.P.

To Eva   *Holloway Prison.*
                                    24 February 1919.

Dearest Old Darling,

I was informed this morning that my last letter to you was kidnapped en route. I am puzzling my head as to why. It was such unimportant blather that I had not made a note of its contents. I always do so if I sail near the wind or when I occasionally write 'acid tests'. Kathleen too, having just had free intercourse with you makes it all the funnier. They are all like a comic opera.

I suppose it was spite and that they want to break our spirit. The only thing that I remember in it was that I asked you to write to Molly O'Neill and explain that I simply could not write to my friends and not to mind not hearing. Maybe they are afraid of my sending messages to her!

Isn't K. C. a dear? So patient and so unselfish. Her only thought was not to give me trouble, as if any little thing I could do for her was trouble! I do hope she'll lie up. She is really very bad and will only kill herself if she runs round. I quite forget that she is not here and I start talking with her occasionally.

It's so funny being alone and never seeing anyone with whom one has common interests of any kind. At Aylesbury we had a certain community of hatred that gave one mutual interests, and the mutual sport of combining to pinch onions, dripping [melted fat from roasted meat] or rags! Doesn't it sound funny and mad? But it kept one going.

I can't be bothered about exhibiting. I'd have to go through so many forms and would probably not be allowed to do so, even if I asked humbly for leave to do so. If you have anything of mine fit, I don't mind your sending, but don't sell.

Best love,

Mise i gCuis na hEireann,
Constance de Markievicz I.C.A., F. d P.

To Eva   *Holloway Prison.*
                                                26 February 1919.

Dearest old darling,

Did K. give you a cheque? I got such a nice letter from another sister, saying how kind you were. I was so glad that you were able to repay them a little for all their goodness to me. Their house was a home to me, when I was 'running' round that part of Ireland. They fed me up and looked after me, and I just came and went as I liked.

Will you send someone (not a duchess!) or go to see Annie Lancaster, Ward C, Mental Hospital, New Southgate? She's an old Aylesbury comrade and used to be called Dyer. Give her some money to buy little extras, with my love, and tell her why I can't write and where I am. It's near here, I believe. Write if you can't go. Mrs W. P. [Wyse Power] who attends to my correspondence in Dublin tells me she wrote twice to me.

Colour [magazine] is such a joy, so are the gaudy ribbons you sent. They help me with my painting. Colour is like everything else. It depends on the relationship of the many to each other, the air, life, etc., for their beauty. Alone, a colour is meaningless: merged in the waves of life and light and combined with other colours, it equals the one composed of the many, assumes emotions, which it can convey to you: it acts, has qualities and personalities. This sounds odd but it's true, and it is only as people grasp this that they are of any use in the world. Do you think Nellie has? Joss has not. Charlie has, in his own line.

Poor Sidney, what on earth has he been up to, he has an awful heritage on both sides to fight. I always felt tolerant of wild acts but I hate a sneak. I hope it's not drink, he's so young.

Thank Clare for things yesterday, and oh! do thank Mrs McKenna. It was misery not knowing the time. What's happened to Cooper? I wonder if the censor will object to this? He certainly is an awful fool. I'd love to tell him so, but find some relief in writing it!

Love to all,

Mise i gCuis na hEireann,
Constance de Markievicz I.R.A., F. d P.

To Eva   *Holloway Prison.*
                                [Undated; after Kathleen Clarke's release].

Beloved darling,
The censor stopped my last to you. Said it was political. I did not
consider it so. I discussed the morals of politicians and my own
future!

I am drawing a lot. When you have time, send me some small
rough boards for water colour or a rough block, very rough; neutral
tint, cobalt, brown, and pink in tubes, and some very fine pens –
crow quill – or nibs; some blue darning silk for stockings, sweet
soap and a hand looking-glass, round if possible, with a handle
which folds over, so that I can stand it up for my face and hold it to
look at my drawings. Also some nice cold cream. Please send my
bank book to Coutts, get it made up and return it.

Ivy was not contraband, and I loved it and the home news. I
hope Kathleen's health will not suffer from her return to town.
Poor old Gaga! I think some vegetables must have come from her.
Very grateful. Poor Kitty! Judging from the papers, the War enables
people to get divorced quite easily. I wish her luck. I wonder what
cousin Sam [USA] thinks of it all.

Pickles are excellent, but smaller bottles would be more suitable.
So sorry you did not see Janey [Coffey]. Give her my love and do
try to see her. I'd hate to think she went back to the old game. Do
send me English Labour papers occasionally and an odd picture
one. The books are a great joy. I loved the pictures in Savoy and will
take great care of them all for you.

I am reading Henry Brailsford. He seems to be a man after my
own heart. I wonder if I would be after his!

A dear little photo of you and E. in the flat is with me. Best love
to you and all my friends.

Mise i gCuis na hEireann,
Constance de Markievicz I.R.A.

'On the Run',
March–June 1919

Markievicz was released from Holloway on 10 March 1919 under a general amnesty. She returned to Ireland and took up her place as a TD (Teachta Dála) in the first Dáil Éireann, which had been established in January 1919. Since this was soon outlawed and the War of Independence against the British was raging, she and her fellow TDs were 'on the run', moving from one safe house to another and using numerous ploys to evade capture by the British troops and the Royal Irish Constabulary. With policemen abandoning the force in large numbers, the RIC was supplemented by the fearsome 'Black and Tans' – demobbed and shell-shocked soldiers sent to Ireland from the trenches of northern France, mainly to keep them off the streets of Britain. They wore an improvised uniform of British army khaki and RIC bottle green – hence the name.

To Eva   *10 Richmond Avenue, Fairview, Dublin.*
[After March 1919; release from Holloway].

Darling,

I had a wonderful journey. Mme Nancy O'Rahilly [widow of The O'Rahilly, who died in 1916] and Mrs [Nell] Humphreys [sister of The O'Rahilly] met me at Holyhead, and they had secured sunny seats on the boat. The sun on the rippling sea was divine, and the sea-gulls gave the finishing touch to the reality of freedom.

I was met by deputations of everybody! M. S. [Michael Staines] and Joe McG. [McGrath] (both on the run), and C. M. B. [Cumann na mBan] at Kingstown with bouquet. Howling crowds everywhere. They took me to a hotel and fed me. I was extremely hungry. It was all very official. Just deputations from all the organisations, run mostly by the women. S. McG. [Seán McGarry] was there, very pleased with himself. We motored into Dublin to Liberty Hall. Last time was nothing to it. The crowd had no beginning or end. I made a speech, and we then formed up in a torchlight procession and went to St Patrick's.

M. had dropped from the sky into our midst. We held one meeting for me and one for J. McG. (escaped Usk). The constituency certainly appeared unanimous, and it was unparalleled in Irish history, they say. Every window had a flag or candles or both. You never saw such excitement. K. C. [Kathleen Clarke] is better and was glad to see me. Maeve [Maud Gonne] also was looking much better.

I'm already very busy. We celebrated the Commune on the eighteenth, and Mrs Humphreys is giving me a party to meet fellow MPs on Saturday. Liberty Hall is capturing Ireland and growing on every side. The Women Workers have a palace and everything is booming here.

Talking of Sligo, the Town Hall was captured by S.F. [Sinn Féin; in the borough election of 1919.] There was a wild meeting of trustees to fight it and Joss actually refused to attend. He also refused to lend motors or give petrol to [the] parliamentary party, saying that all his employees belong to the advanced party and he was not going to oppose them. It is curious that it is to his family alone that he does not allow freedom of thought. Of course, they all say he is secretly S.F.

Mise i gCuis na hEireann,
Constance de Markievicz I.R.A.

To Josslyn Gore-Booth   *Liberty Hall.*
Undated; c. March 1919.

My Dear Joss,
Many thanks for yours. I am so glad that you have heard from Casi [on 20 January from Teatr Polski, Warsaw]; please send me his address, as

I was not able to answer his last. I got it just before I was arrested and it must have been destroyed as I could not find it when I came back.

Yrs,
Constance de Markievicz

After spending five weeks in a Dublin nursing home recovering from the 'flu, Kathleen Clarke travelled to her native Limerick where she was reunited with her three sons, who were staying with her sisters. Constance remained as a lodger at her Dublin house on Richmond Avenue.

To Kathleen Clarke   *Undated; mid-1919.*

Dearest Kathleen,
I was so thankful to hear that you were not flattened out with the journey – though I am not yet convinced that Limerick in a state of siege is the best place in the world for you; excitement always seemed to play the very Dickens with you in jail.

I am all alone now in charge! The bird is my great responsibility; it's very fit and well but does not sing. The cat is going to have kittens any moment, so the O'Hegartys left it 'til after that event, as they are afraid of the journey for it. It's an extraordinary animal, it always woke up and sent for baby Shawn when he howled and seems awfully lonely without him.

I haven't heard of a house yet, Noyk [solicitor] is also looking out for me. I quite envy you in the very joys of Asuger [*sic*]. I wonder how long you will stay there; such a bore for you not to be able to get out to the country at all. Thank Madge [Daly] for her letter, give her and all my friends in Barrington Street my love. You must feel very proud of the people, it's such a wonderful stand they have taken [Limerick soviet, 15–27 April 1919], and it will have a worldwide effect and influence.

I am full up with work as usual – even more so – so have no time to be lonesome. Some of my pictures are already mounted and look lovely. I have no fixed date of exhibition yet. Any chance of your being fit to attend in the next few months, as I would put it off for the pleasure of having you.

Love from,
Con
PS: Have begun a moonlight sketch in garden.
[In margin] Tell Madge I dispatched Eva's things.
One photo for you and one for Madge in garden by Miss Smith.

To Éamon de Valera [after he offered her the job of Minister for Labour in the first Dáil].

31 Richmond Avenue.
30 May 1919.

A Chara Dil,
I can give you all my time for Ireland's work.

Mise i gCuis na hEireann,
Constance de Markievicz

To Eva   *[Undated fragment].*

How I wish you had been here! But it would have killed you. You were very wise to refrain.

You will be pleased to hear that people in command are not in favour of a fight just now and do not want to shed useless blood. I haven't seen Dev yet. O'Reilly is doing awfully well, they say. I wish I was there. I wonder if I left much behind with you? Poor you! I hope it did not fuss you too much. I was greatly impressed by Cole. I am sending you a letter for Ll. George, etc. I'm almost run off my legs already.

Cork Jail,
June–October 1919

On 15 June 1919, Constance was arrested and sentenced to four months in Cork Jail for making a seditious speech. By then de Valera had left Ireland for the USA; he would not return for eighteen months and, in his absence, Michael Collins became de facto *leader of the Irish republicans. While in prison, where conditions were not too onerous, Constance got news of her stepson Staskou for the first time in many years.*

To Eva

Cork Jail.
14 June 1919.

Dearest Old Darling,
Clare has just written that you are ill and I am so sorry that I just got arrested, for I know how that will worry you. But you needn't bother, for I am in excellent health and spirits. I am here for advising girls not to walk out with the police and a few other remarks of that sort. The whole thing would make a very funny story for a magazine!

I'm afraid the green brooch was not very nice, but it was the nearest thing I could get to what I remembered of the old, but it strikes me as having too much silver and too little pattern. Some day we'll find a better one.

I have been so busy since I was back in Ireland and had a lovely time. Spent two days among the mountains with Bella and saw and hugged 'Mr. P.' [Poppet the dog]. He was like a stunned person when he saw me, I thought he was going to faint. Certainly animals are more human than some people, especially English politicians.

This is the most comfortable jail I have been in yet. There's a nice garden, full of pinks, and you can hear the birds sing. I have heaps of friends here, who send me in lots of very good food – in fact, all my meals. Our people are such darlings. In Dublin, my meals were sent in, and at Mallow, when they made sure of the police being able to identify me and changed and improved the warrant, a girl gave me a teapot of lovely tea and some cakes to keep me going.

I wonder if Gaga realised she was talking sedition when she used to abuse Maggie Campbell for walking with a policeman, years and years ago. It was a terrible crime in her eyes, and she sacked Medhbh's first nurse for doing ditto! I wonder what her present point of view is! Someone ought to warn her of the risks she runs

I can't help laughing all the time. Anyhow, I'm alright, so don't you worry. I got in at the psychological moment, if I mistake not!, and I'm glad.

I'll write again soon, so take care of your dear old self. Do write me a line if you can. I know I'm a selfish devil to ask you.

Love to Esther and all the love of my heart to yourself.

Mise i gCuis na hEireann,
Constance de Markievicz

To Kathleen Clarke   *Cork Jail.*
                                                                   15 June 1919.

Dearest Kathleen,
Here I am in yet another jail, adding to my experience! I was in the midst of an article on 'Prison Reform' for *New Ireland* – this week's – when they took me. I wonder whether they'll ever let me out to finish it. The charge is an absurdity and boils down to advising people to avoid the police; girls not to walk with them, boys not to drink with them. Swift's immortal phrase 'Burn everything English except their coal' is also damning evidence against me. I don't know what the Peeler's [policeman] thoughts were, who or what he believed I was urging people to burn. I laugh every time I think of the funny scene I

went through! You'd have thought the Peelers would be grateful to us, urging our crowd to avoid them, especially in a district like Knocklong! [Two local policemen were shot dead during the successful rescue of Republican prisoner Sean Hogan by his IRA colleagues from the Cork train after it stopped in Knocklong in May 1919.] When you think of it, mine is so much the safest policy for them.

Molly will have told you that she saw me in the Bridewell and brought me an excellent dinner. You never saw such a display of military and police as there was at King's Bridge [Heuston train station, Dublin] and who came down to Mallow with me! I felt very important and had to laugh at Mallow. I thought they were trying me but it was only a dress rehearsal for the police, to be quite sure that they could identify me and to get their story down pat. After going through the performance, I was put back on the motor lorry and away back to the train and on here. Some kind girls at Mallow pushed a pot full of tea and some cakes into my hands, a boy gave me fags. In Cork, I was recognised by friends, who sent me in supplies.

Mrs Mina O'Hegarty and Nora Wallace visited me on Saturday; they brought me strawberries and other nice things. I do hope you are none the worse for the excitement and worry. I felt quite guilty for bringing trouble on the house, though I know you wouldn't wish it otherwise, you great soul.

My love to the boys. It's a great education for them. This is the most comfy jail I was in yet! [With] my love and may God bless you.

Mise i gCuis na hEireann,
Constance de Markievicz I.C.A.
P.S.: [at top of letter] If I get a big sentence, I shall put all my energy to learning Gaelic!

To Eva   *Cork Jail.*
                                                            21 June 1919.

Dearest Old Darling,
Just got yours and so sorry to hear that you are ill. I'm fit and flourishing. I have lots of friends here and saw Miss McSweeney

[Mary MacSwiney] today, who is writing to you and will keep you posted. She is a dear.

The joke about my identity is this: the two policemen who recognised me and swore to it being me who made the speech had never really seen me. I spoke at 11.40 pm. There were a few rough torches and a huge crowd. In the background cringed the police. After the meeting, I transferred my hat, coat, and a long blue Liberty scarf you gave me years ago, to a girl. These police, who swore they knew me, followed her around Newmarket, while I looked on and laughed. So you see what liars they are!

We showed Sylvia [Pankhurst] a lot of life while she was over. I like her. She's a sport, and brave as brave. I told her about Molly O'N. So glad that the latter has been released. I wonder if your Donnelly is anything to do with the publisher who married Nellie Gifford. I got a card from her today from America.

Kitty [Ireland] seems to be having a great look-in just now. Everyone seems to want her. I think she'll get her divorce all right in the end. No one can say she is not entitled to it. Our precious cousin 'Bender OR' [*sic*] I see has not defended himself and is free. I wonder the King's Proctor did not intervene. She was worse than he. It was a wicked marriage. I remember it so well, she was years older than him and he was just hooked by that disreputable mother of hers – one of the last good works I did before getting lifted was to help organise a scheme for raising money for the starving Hun babies. I am wondering how many more will get arrested over it! We ought to get a good deal of money over it anyway, for people over here, being poor, are very generous.

I got lovely roses too yesterday, and such heaps of strawberries and cream too. Friends are so good to me. If you want to be really appreciated in Ireland, go to jail!

By the way, have you done any more horoscopes lately? And can you tell me how often I get to jail? And shall I be hung in the end?

I feel quite cheerful and happy. My arrest came just at the right moment. Also I wanted a little rest and change of air! The climate here is lovely and the situation perfect, on a hill, facing to the south.

When they motored me to Mallow to be tried, they headed the procession with an armoured car, and several tons of soldiers and police, armed to the teeth, came in other lorries. It was Gilbertian [like a comic opera written by Gilbert and Sullivan]. Mallow was in a state of siege. The only thing they hadn't got was an aeroplane.

Now goodbye, darling, and good luck to you. Take care of your precious self and don't hurry back to London. Was the evening dress a success?

Best of love to you and Esther.

Is mise i gCuis na hEireann,
Constance de Markievicz

To Nora Connolly   *Cork Jail.*
                                                          26 June 1919.

My dear Nora,

Would you kindly ask some of them to send me on *Dreadnought* from the Hall? Any of you may of course open it and read it first. Also I left a photo in drawer for Inchicore Hall. I wrote the man's name on it, who will call.

Did you see Mr P. on my 'case'? I call it wicked. He has taken the opportunity of my being locked up to try and create an impression that I am advocating a general pogrom of the police. If he succeeds in creating this impression, he will also create a situation of grave danger for every policeman in Ireland. I shall not be responsible for this – much as I dislike those spies and informers, I would never advocate a pogrom. I hope the police will realise what Mr P. has done! All I wish is that people – by socially ostracising them – should render them harmless and prevent them getting information, also make them ashamed of themselves.

My whole proceedings have been 'Gilbertian' from my arrest and capture, my journey by special train, with about 30 police and 30 enemy soldiers armed to the teeth; [and] the Preliminary Exam when the Peelers got a look at me as to identify me and rehearsed their version of my speech.

The Sergeant swore to hearing me tell the people to treat the police like 'leepers'. For a moment I could not think what he meant; at the court house he had learnt to say 'lepers'.

I was charged with urging traders to boycott the police and with holding a proclaimed meeting; but no further mention was made at my trial of either of these charges. The first was a lie and of course there is no evidence for the second. So the Peelers contended themselves by swearing that I had told people to ill-treat their children at school; a lie which I contradicted in my statement, for I would not be represented as making war on children, that is the police's game – not ours.

But it was really quite pleasant hearing first a Sergeant and then a Constable telling a delighted crowd of Sinn Féiners how they ought to be treated; everyone enjoyed it I am sure, except themselves.

I told you about how I slipped out of the market? And how they couldn't recognise me a short time after the meeting? Fancy their daring to swear to me after that. I wonder so who concocted the speech they made – as mine – for them. I think it was built on a little leaflet I saw going around. It was too dark at the meeting to take notes and both repeated the same yarn. I had notes to speak from, but could not read them.

I think I got a card from Kerry, something effaced on it, signed 'Mairghead' – was it from the soldier girl? Give her my love. It's pinned up by my bed. Tell Cathal how sorry I was not to see him. Hope he'll be around this way again. Miss McSweeney and Miss Wallace will arrange about visits, so if anyone is going down here, let them send a car ahead so that there will be a visit to spare. What trouble 'the two D.s' seem to have made. Thomas Foran's idea of arbitration by the Dáil is very good. I saw that in the *Daily H*. The papers bring such good news that one could be happy anywhere. I was so anxious 'til I knew that Dev had got through safely.

I think we are close to the time when, no matter what happens, it will be all right for Ireland. Her oppressors are gradually getting their due, the distrust and opprobrium of the world, and they are tottering towards their end. So I'm quite cheerful and content to serve patiently here for a while for 'the Glory and the Honour of Ireland'. Special love to your mother. I was sorry not to have got to see her.

My greetings to all good rebels.

Mise i gCuis na hEireann,
Constance de Markievicz I.C.A.

To Kathleen Clarke   *Cork Jail.*
                                                          2 July 1919.

Dearest Kathleen,
Many thanks for yours. How heavenly the garden must be; so
interested to hear about the grapes; I hope it will be a good crop.
I am having a surfeit of strawberries and cream, and fresh eggs.
Everyone here is so kind and thoughtful, they feed me like a fighting
cock. For the present I am taking your advice and enjoying it. As
you say, food makes a lot of difference to me – they send me such
lovely milk too – they all know my fads! Porridge, milk, raw eggs
and puddings, so I'm all right.

Molly O'N. has just got 11 days I see for a speech in a park in
London! It read very funny and rather mad; she tried to take a
stand but didn't know how so she began by pleading 'not guilty'
and acknowledging the court by defending herself and ended in a
burst of defiance and refusing to pay the fine. I think it was quite
creditable and that she did her best and is in jail.

P. S. [O'Hegarty] told me you were looking better; I was so glad
to hear it. I'm so interested to hear of the [wall]paper, do send me
a pattern – then I'll be able to see the room in my dreams. I hope
Mr B. O'Connor will mend the eaves, or it will come off directly the
weather changes. Did Miss C. ask you to send me my bank book? It
should have come by now; it's a large square envelope with 'Coutts'
printed on it.

You didn't tell me what you thought of Maeve's house; what a
joke the 'Baby Bolshie' must be in glasses! I wonder how you like
giving lessons; teaching to me is a fascinating job, if your pupils
want to learn. What are you teaching them?

Our poor reception! I suppose they put it off, when I was 'pulled'
and you rather a crock. I was looking forward to it so as I love an
outdoor fête and I wanted another peep at all E. O'C.'s lovely prints
too.

There were three leather straps fixed together on the floor of the room I was in, they are Tommy [Tomasina] McGarry's. Would you ask one of the boys to bring them to her with thanks. Give her my love; and Seán [McGarry; Tommy's husband]. I am writing hard and getting on with my education. Jail is a splendid place to study in; you aren't interrupted. You never tell me how your health [is]. P. S. was the only one who gave me news.

The weather is dry and warm; when it gets wet I'll ask you to send me my old shoes with the American laces and woollen stockings, but not yet. Later, too, I'll ask you to send paints, but I'll send you a list of what I want. At present I'm spending all my energy on studying. Many thanks for the things you sent. I never paid Molly [a maid in the Clarke household] anything, so you'll have to do it for me! It was Good Friday, I think, I took her over.

I often picture you all; Daly inventing things, Tom climbing up ropes, Emmet dancing around and you calmly scratching about and the way the boys used to be longing to turn the hose on me! How merciful they were – at their age I would have done it.

Best love to you all.

Mise i gCuis na hEireann,
Constance de Markievicz I.C.A.

To Eva *Cork Jail.*
5 July 1919.

Dearest Old Darling,
Just delighted with your letter. I did not get the tale about King Billy out of C. K. [Charles Kingsley], I got it in a novel and ran it to earth in Haverty's *History of Ireland*. Another rather sweet and almost prophetic yarn is about Henry II. Before he finally appropriated Ireland (mentally at least) he sent a messenger to the Pope to ask permission to crown his son John as King. The Pope permitted this atrocity, but sent Henry a crown of peacock's feathers, tied with gold wire, to perform the ceremony with! You could write a poem about that.

You are right to a certain extent about [John] Mitchel: he was certainly not a Bolshie, but that made it all the more wonderful that he took such risks and went in so whole-heartedly for the Revolution. You cannot imagine Gaga with a gun in her hand! He was a queer mixture. The oddest thing about him was that he was against the freeing of the black slaves in America. Of course his reason was that the English were on the other side, and the reason why the English Government were so keen on Emancipation was that slave labour, being unpaid, enabled the Americans to undersell the English tea-planters (Jamaica, etc.). The English originally established slavery in America.

He had wonderful instincts about politics. He prophesied the War with Germany, and his ideas for Ireland were far better than those adopted. He was one of the divine ancestors of Easter Week. I think they all failed because they had no policy. They were all writers and theorists, but could neither organise nor frame a policy. Fintan Lalor had ideas, so had Thomas Davis, but they never seemed able to evolve a policy or an organisation to work their ideas. Perhaps the country was not ripe. I agree with Lenin that 'if the conditions are not there, no sort of propaganda will hasten or impede it'.

Pearse was rather like the '48 men in that, but thanks to Tom Clarke and Seán McDermott, the organisation was there, and Connolly had the brain, so that when the moment came they were able to grasp it. Pearse wrote beautifully and spoke beautifully, and they say he wrote his speeches and got them off by heart. He was the only orator I ever listened to; he had a fine delivery, a beautiful voice and a poetic and sincere way of putting things, and what he said was always interesting and made you think. Connolly was quite different. He was no orator and had a bad delivery, but he never made an uninteresting speech. He had more force and more world-knowledge and everything he said was worth remembering. He was so practical too. They often seemed to me to be a complement to each other.

... Just been interrupted to have a visit: a Miss Freeman, an American girl, was one of them, and she knows you. There were three visitors and only a quarter of an hour for visiting, so not much time to talk.

I can't read what you have written: 'I, etc.,' that Max has put to music. I forget the 'old woman of Beare'. Could it be Ireland? I'll borrow Pearse's work and read it again.

Famines are potent weapons. I would like to read Mitchel's account of the Coalition Government before questions about Russia and Central Europe are put.

Have you ever read *Knocknagow* by [Charles] Kickham? It's not the famine but the eviction of later years, and it's very interesting. Did you ever hear of the Glenveigh evictions in 1861? It's in Donegal, so near home. It makes one's blood boil to read: a high watermark of cold-blooded cruelty!

Thanks for Georges [probably a history of the four King Georges of England from 1714 to 1830; the House of Hanover] and [Arthur] Ransome. I agree about the style of the Georges [book]. You feel that he [the author] is trying to impress you with the amount he knows and that he is not sure enough of his facts to be precise. Ignorance camouflaged by stupidity. However, he is supposed to be a genius. Chesterton now: he doesn't give you many facts, but he has ideas, though he spoilt the book [*A Short History of England*, 1917] in the end by using his marvellously ingenious mind to try and sum up the book against the Hun! He only began seriously towards the end of the book, so it's a failure. Even he found it hard to deny that most of modern England is a copy of things German. If you are writing on religion and start with the theory that the English Protestant Church is a German Mission! – and so it is and beer-drinking and old-age pensions and conscription and the socialism that may eat them all up!

If I were the Kaiser I would make a bee-line for London! It would be glorious before one died to teach the English how to try a King! *'L'appetit vient en mangeant'* [Appetite comes with eating]. I would defend myself and ask for a public trial and for Labour to be on the Bench. Why do the wrong people always get the opportunities? People would not hate the Kaiser if they saw him and saw that he was only a sad and dignified old man, and not a Minotaur.

So glad to hear about Medhbh. What do you think of her playing? Is there any inspiration in it?

Now goodbye and God bless. What a letter I have inflicted on you!

Best love,

Mise i gCuis na hEireann,
Constance de Markievicz I.C.A.
Is Wuss staying with Tina?!!

To Eva   *Cork Jail.*
                                                           5 July 1919.

Dearest Old Darling,

Your letter was most interesting. Thanks also for the books. History is more thrilling than any romance, and so cynical! Do you realise that King Billy of great and glorious memory who fought Popery in Ireland was financed by the Pope? King Billy formed the League of Augsburg to check Louis XIV and to break up the alliance with the English Charles. Billy tricked everyone and collared the swag! I have remembered something about Mrs Fitzherbert and Ireland. The law about Catholics would have been repealed and she would have been accepted as Queen, but this would have involved Catholic Emancipation being conceded to Ireland. There was trouble between Pitt and [Charles James] Fox over it and Mrs F. and Ireland went to the wall. I am much more sorry for Mrs F. than for the Queen! The Queen always had her Queenship which she seemed to attach a great value to, and Princesses never seem to marry for anything else. I dare say she was like [illegible; ink blot]. The whole case seems to me to be somewhat similar.

To go back to style: I suppose I am very Irish for I love Mitchel. Some of his phrases simply bring the tears to my eyes. He always rings true to me, though I don't as a rule like early Victorian rhetoric; but he always seems to me to put a colour and a glow on things that make you see them with your heart.

A book, the wording of which amuses and pleases me, is Chesterton's *History of England*. It is so human and so unexpected and is all written from such an utterly different convention to the ordinary history and there is a great deal of truth in it. Of course he has a style of his own. The modern curt style is, to me, very often telegraphic. We rather like adjectives and symbolic things over here; our speeches are often rather rhetorical but that again is quite different to writing. I know it was a common sneer in England at one time that we could not talk of Ireland in Plain English. It was always 'Kathleen ni Houlihan' or some other unpronounceable name, and her 'four green fields' gave great offence too. Now I like all that.

Another person whose writing I liked was Oscar Wilde, but as a rule when I read books, I just read to get ideas and facts in a great hurry and only disliked the style if it was too obscure and long-winded, so I have really thought very little about it. It has sometimes seemed to me that nowadays people are rather like me, and that the ideas and facts count more than the workmanship. You can find an analogy there in painting but it is all very complex. Correctness is not either truth or beauty and there is always the intangible something that is both, if you can attain to it. Early Victorian artists made a great struggle for absolute correctness in a very scholarly way; to us it is often awfully dull.

To go back to history. Has it ever struck you that in the early days of parliaments when 'burgesses' sent from local councils composed those parliaments, when so much land was common and when religious communities looked after education, sick, poor, etc., that England was on the high road to Bolshevism? I am trying to write that up. It is very interesting work. English politics is so different to Irish but very interesting too.

Why is the *Daily H.* backing Ll. George in a subtle sort of way?

The trades union appeal always seems to be very sordid and very selfish. Until something suddenly makes them realise the value of self-sacrifice, they will never be of much use to humanity, only scrambling for champagne and frock coats in the end.

I am so interested in Medhbh. If she is really clever, I can give her the only thing that she will require to make her a success and that is audiences throughout the world! It sounds a joke but it's true – she can jump into a great career in America any moment she wants to.

Think of Gaga still loving shops! Give her my love. It's not the Georges personally I am interested in but their times – they were such volcanic ones and there was such a shifting of power from one centre to another in their days.

Do you know Mrs [Annie] Besant? She is John Redmond's 'spiritual wife'. I don't know if they ever met. I wonder if the English will adopt the political strike – it's silly not to. They should begin by doing it locally to make a refractory and treacherous M.P. resign his seat. Does that sound nonsense?

Now goodbye darling. Love to you all.

Mise i gCuis na hEireann,
Constance de Markievicz I.C.A.

To Kathleen Clarke   *Cork Jail.*
                                                          14 July 1919.

My dearest Kathleen,
Many thanks for yours – I am not sure that Mr Donough has not done something about insuring things. Do you mind writing to him for me? It will be better as you are on the spot and I'd be very grateful, though I hate being a bother. He has an office with Cosgrave in Dame Street somewhere. I was going to see him about things the day I was pulled.

One big picture is with Mrs Katherine Cruise O'Brien [sister of Hanna Sheehy Skeffington], the rest are all with you. The portrait of Casimir I value at £800 – it's a wonderful picture. My portrait at £200. The triptych (can't spell!) at £300. There are lots of others worth a good deal, but it would be quite impossible to make a list here. I was trying to get them straightened out a bit when I was taken; another thing that should be done is my carpets looked after; they should be shaken and balls of sugar naphtha put on them. *Don't you* attempt to touch them, it's a heavy job. Theo [Fitzgerald] would do it all right – and some such stuff might be stuffed into the top of the boxes where the clothes are. I can't remember the Fitzgerald's number in Brunswick Street, but I don't suppose it matters, they've been there so long. Anyhow I won't write – 'I'll lave it to yer honour' as the cabbies say! But for God's sake be a good little thing and take care of yourself and remember that *nothing* of mine really matters at all except in a small way. Theo has so often helped me in all those sort of jobs, that's why I suggest him.

Carrie [Kathleen Clarke's sister] was here the other day. I was overjoyed and delighted, it was a really pleasant surprise, as I did not know she was in the neighbourhood, as well as being glad for her own sake; it was like seeing a bit of you. It's such a relief that the police won't be asked to guard my possessions! I can quite understand the boys not wanting to go to Ring [in Co. Waterford], when they have you back again; but I'm sorry you haven't all gone somewhere. I'm sure bracing mountain air would do you good. Now good-bye.

Mise i gCuis na hEireann,
Constance de Markievicz
PS: I'll send you latch key that I pinched; *by hand* – the enemy might get it copied. So sorry about brolly, Barney Mellows at 6 Harcourt St would get it to you.

To Eva   *Cork Jail.*
                                                     16 July 1919.

Dearest Old Darling,
Don't you bother about Maunsel [a prominent Dublin publishers] but see about the poems yourself. Nellie Gifford married a publisher. I will write to have their address sent to you tomorrow. So then write to him, use my name, give him names of books and ask him to copyright in the States at once. Somebody may of course pirate them: you will have to come to an arrangement with him. He is very nice and quite straight, I hear. If the copyrighting costs anything much, I'll be responsible. You are sure to make a lot of money if no one has stolen them already. Anyhow, try at once. Ask D. to be your agent. Now do this at once like a dear.

Fancy the Wuss traipsing round after Kings, with a dyed head [of hair]. I had to laugh about Ivan [Lumley Hay; cousin], he was a socialist when last we met.

You did not tell me what you thought about Medhbh's music. Is there a spark in it? I never care for mere technique. I suppose she is in a state of being wildly amused and interested in life. Gossip never bores me, as it's life. To me it is full of character and history. Gaga and Wuss stopped developing mentally before we were born. Gaga anyhow is entirely out of touch with any idea that she did not get through her early associates. Wuss even tries to look as she did then – in her youth, I mean.

Now old Mrs Pearse, who was just a rightly motherly old soul with never a thought or an interest in politics, just kept house for the school and was interested in her sons. Since Easter Week, she has taken to politics, has gone quite slowly and wisely and actually went about speaking in the Election when nearly all the speakers were in jail. She has hair almost snow white! That's an old lady I admire. I often wonder whether we shall ever crystallise.

Yesterday was the first month of my imprisonment. The Enemy celebrated it by putting a barbed wire entanglement under my window. I wonder so why. They are so funny! The Cork people are awfully good to me. They send me in three good meals, cooked already per day, and lots of oddments and all the papers. I feel very proud of being Irish. Our people are so loyal and so affectionate. I quite agree with what you say about any English crowd; it's savagery. The crime record is so terrible and they have so little provocation.

I often wonder what England would be like if they tried to impose the police rule that they have imposed here! Our people are wonderful, under the most frightful provocation. Comparing the English and Irish papers day by day and the way our rulers rule us and the way they rule England is an eye-opener to anyone.

Talking of papers, thanks for *Colour*. I will keep it for you as I know you get it regularly. It is very amusing, though I don't always admire their taste. They seem to get hold of lovely things. They never seem to have any reason for admiring things: I can't get to the bottom of their ideas – if they have any. Are they, the people who run the paper, a club? Or where do they get the strange pictures they publish?

Do send me your article on religion when it comes out. Have you been writing much poetry? Did you see that [Ian] MacPherson [Chief Secretary for Ireland] is saying that his policy was diminishing Sinn Féin? I had a letter today from those in St Patrick's who have been working on the register and they say that if there's another election I should get a still greater majority! You know they passed the P.R. [Proportional Representation] Bill to try to damage S.F. It's going to work out just the other way. Can't explain here, but you watch. The last thing I did was to hustle the constituency to work the register for the municipal elections – to have things ready. Everybody is so ready and eager to work. I have one great girl in my constituency: she is actually President of the S.F. Club. My getting locked up has done more to bring women out into the open than anything else. The shyest are ready to do my work when I'm not there.

Now goodbye, darling. How is your health?

Mise i gCuis na hEireann,
Constance de Markievicz, I.C.A.

To Kathleen Clarke   *Cork Jail.*
                                                 20 July 1919.

My dearest Kathleen,
There will be people coming down for the Oireachtas, probably Mrs W. Power, would you kindly send me my bottle of Jaborandi and two little pots of a sort of cold cream, a little box of powder – also another pair of combinations and grey cotton knickers, and blue ones – and my little bunty scissors, which should be in my attaché case.

How is your health? Do write a line soon. I hope that you are being 'a good little thing'. I heard from Madge the other day, so I got some indirect news of you. Are you still teaching the boys? And are you fascinated by teaching as you have gone on or does it bore you? They sent me in some tomatoes the other day and I was wondering how yours were doing and the grapes too; were you ever able to thin the bunches? It's such hot work and so tiring holding one's arms up. Nothing ever bored me more.

I heard from Fr Albert too, he had been with you in your garden. Two dear old monks with white beards came to see me, they were exactly alike and had great fun puzzling me. I knew one of them before – no one ever knows them apart and they never stop laughing about it. They are letting us half hour visits now, which is an improvement. I find that quarter hour is very trying to the nerves; you feel as if you are catching a train all the time and leaving everything behind you.

I get all the papers I want and find the news very cheering. Dev seems to be making a great stir, God bless him and his work; my visitors all seem to be very cheerful and confident. I believe myself that the whole social system of Europe is going to break up and that we are coming out on top.

There are two books I want very much, if you can see them about anywhere. I was reading both so they would be in the drawing room or my bedroom – a dark red book, I think the name was something like: 'The effect of character on policy'– national character was what it was about. The other was a larger book, dark green, I think 'History of Ireland in the 18th (I think) Century' by [George] O'Brien [The book was *The Economic History of Ireland in the Eighteenth Century*.]. Wasn't it funny of the enemy to celebrate peace when there is no peace anywhere – and to celebrate it as an armed menace. I suppose they wanted to frighten the 'Common People' of England and the 'natives' of Ireland; maybe they are getting a little nervous themselves.

Now goodbye with my love to all the family and more especially to your naughty little self.

Mise i gCuis na hEireann,
Constance de Markievicz I.C.A., T.D.

To Eva   *Cork Jail.*
                                                    22 July 1919.

Dearest Old Darling,
I wish you could do something about poems and am sure he [George Roberts of Maunsel and Company, publishers] diddled

you. He got compensation for burnt stock after Easter Week and I know that since then he has been selling *Egyptian Pillar* for 2/6. [*The Egyptian Pillar* by Eva Gore-Booth published Maunsel and Co., 96 Abbey Street, 1907. Dedicated to Con in remembrance of 10 November 1906.] I believe that he has been turned into a company so you might get satisfaction. Write and ask Susan [Mitchell].

You are mad ever to give that vague 'American rights'. You might try the play. It would not do any harm to write to Donnelly. His wife [Nellie Gifford] is a great friend: she was out in Easter Week with me and is a brick. She ran a kitchen, which is just as important as holding a gun. I agree with you about [Edward] Carson and wonder what he gets for the job. Shares I suppose and to be let into things like the Marconi job etc! It pays well to be an M.P. This is an old English policy – a man whose whole fortune is in Ireland is always dangerous, so they see that he is provided with a stake in England. I've just been reading the following. Sir John Morice was sent over by Edward III to break the power of the Anglo-Irish nobles by removing offices and despoiling English barons who had a stake in Ireland or who had married Irish wives. He (Edward) found that he was better served in Ireland by men 'whose revenues were derived from England'.

There was a list of shareholders of some oil field published in the *D. Herald*. Two Irish names among them and do you remember how Maud's brothers always got good tips? Marconi, etc. Do you remember her yarn about the 'clans' and her wonderful family? Irish chiefs and God knows what? I wish I'd read history in those days and I'd have dished it out to her. They are no better than us!

England seems to be in an awful state, much worse than Ireland. No one will have any control over anybody if they go on much longer, and there will be terrible things happening. If a revolution comes it will be much worse than Russia, for people are so congested. There are no big open country districts, with stores of food. I don't fear a revolution here as many are so disciplined – not that silly compulsory thing which is automatic and breaks down – but disciplined voluntarily, which is quite a different thing.

I loved your poem. Have you written much lately? I am so sorry about 'Broken Glory'. Are you sure that the agreement is binding? Can't you break it, if you get no money? Did you ever get anything out of it? I got £20 for one poem, without American rights. Of course it was not real poetry, only doggerel! But some of your real poetry would have a very large appeal because of the subjects.

I am very interested in family gossip, always. I think Mary knew what she was about when she asked after Gerald. Ivan should pretend to be a Sinn Féiner and then they'd buy him off! There are three cats here; they all play together: father, mother and the ugliest kitten you ever saw: it's just like Mr Balfour – figure, eyes and all. But they are rather superior to an English family, for they don't get cross. Imagine an English *pater familias* following a ball round a field, and what would happen if his young hopeful ran away with it. This old cat never minds.

Thackeray is very dull. It's so colourless and no point of view except the ordinary Child's History one. Whose is the best history for reference purposes? I am getting very interested in it, and one history leads to another. You can't understand the why of things unless you see all round.

Now bye-bye, darling. Sorry about Roger [Roger Fry; Eva's landlord]. He and his work impressed me as 'unclean' but he needn't have been disagreeable. What's happened? They can't put you out I believe?

Best love to you both and to Gaga,

Mise i gCuis na hEireann,
Constance de Markievicz

To Eva   *Cork Jail.*
                                                           28 July 1919.

Dearest Old Darling,
I am so sorry to hear that you have a cold that I must write again at once. I hope you are taking care of yourself. Colds in summer sound so awful. I wish that you were in the country.

I sent you a funny cutting about Cecil Malone. He wrote such a funny advertisement for Pelmanism [a system of supposedly scientific mental training promoted in the early part of the 20th century], it was huge in the *Independent* with his plots! I wondered so much how much he got for it! Write a funny letter to *New Ireland*; say he is my cousin and brother-in-law and get a laugh at him! I am sure one could make it very funny. On the other side of the Paper is a very funny example of the censor's work. The only thing omitted is obviously the word 'President'! But I always knew that Brian Cooper was a bit thick! He's the censor you know.

I was one of the instigators for collecting the money for starving people – 'Cumann na mBan' did it. I believe that the enemy paid the fine, some of the girls would have been here otherwise. No Sinn Féiners would pay a fine. The girls will have been mad. Our women's organisation is huge now and awfully go-ahead. It's great for bringing the girls out of the corner. I quite agree with you about the men doing anything for an extra shilling in England, also to a certain extent with the Daily Liar, but still I think there's a chance of their coming around like the Gadarene pigs.

They haven't learned discipline or self-sacrifice, even their soldiers can't fight clean like ours, or if there is too much unemployment or too many strikers idle and drunk, or demobilised soldiers, or even food shortages owing to foreign strikes, they may start looting and rioting. I always feel lately that very little would stampede a mob into burning London or any other town.

It would be accident and fate, and because they are stupid and don't think. But that kind of crowd is the most dangerous. It's wonderful here how the people think and how they know what they want and what self-control they have and such self-denial too.

The election at Swansea was so odd. [At the by-election of July 1919, David Matthews for the Liberals held on to the seat by a greatly reduced majority in a time of significant industrial unrest in the United Kingdom. Labour would take the seat in the 1922 election.] You could never put our people wrong like that, they vote for the policy and think. They don't go ahead in the blind, ignorant way that the English do, and ours never believe the newspapers, which is so sensible. I am heartily sorry for the English labour leaders, they have a terrible job. Can one buy that Green's history you refer to? Or is it a desperate price? I'm not very flush with cash just now. I've got two small elementary histories here, which keep me well occupied here at present.

Do you know anything about the Act of Supremacy? Henry VIII started it (he to be supreme instead of the Pope). Was it ever repealed? And do English Bishops swear allegiance when they are ordained? And parsons? I am always coming across it in histories but they only refer to it and don't tell you what it was or if it was ever repealed.

Just had a visit from two friends. I do wish you were in Cork. It's so warm and mild, with just a nice sea-breeze coming in. It would do you a world of good.

The moths here are so lovely. They come fluttering in through the bars at night, every shade and every shape: such big ones all splotched over with orange and red, great white soft things and wee ethereal ones, all opalescent and shimmering, moonlight colours. One I got today was like the waves of a pale, twilight sea. Another was like a creamy shell. I try to save their lives.

Is there any chance of your coming over to Ireland this autumn? I am so sorry for you, being hunted by Post-Impressionists. But I don't believe you can be evicted for a year at least.

Now, darling, I must stop this. I have just had a visit from two such nice young men from the neighbourhood. The Cork people spoil me dreadfully. Such fruit and flowers all the time.

Best love to Esther as well as yourself. I hope that she won't get your cold.

Mise i gCuis na hEireann,
Constance de Markievicz I.C.A., T.D.

To Eva   *Cork Jail.*
                                              2 August 1919.

Dearest Old Darling,
So delighted to hear that you are better and that you are contemplating going to the play. Mind you write and tell me about it. I saw a very silly English review of it.

Do you know [Joe] Robinson? He's very nice and a Republican. I never knew it 'til I met him in the Clare election cheering Dev. If you like the play, you should write and tell Lennox Robinson to go and see you; he's very nice.

Of course there are endless possibilities in the economic situation in Ireland. The difficulties are not from us but from the English enemy. You can't even open coal-mines or sell butter or export anything without being faced up with bayonets. Every board in the country is run by a man whose salary depends on his putting English interests first. If they build piers, they build them in the wrong place. The education in the schools is hopelessly inadequate to Ireland. Since the war, all kinds of new regulations against Ireland's trade and commerce have been started. In fixing prices, Ireland always gets less for the same or even superior goods. The old Sinn Féin organisation started on this, but you can do so little with an enemy in occupation of your country. Directly we get the Republic into working order we shall do a lot. I expect Cecil is paid a lot by Pelman.

Is the *Daily Herald* trying to please everybody? They seem to love Ll. George and the King! A knave and a fool. I wonder what would happen if a crown held brains. To me it seems so odd that with all the genius the English have for compromise, no Labour leaders can find a compromise that will make the workers of different sections work together or evolve a policy that will carry the country. English labour always prefer to vote Conservative or Liberal. I wonder if it's because they are such snobs that they don't like the name 'Labour'. They should try another name, something high faluting and romantic – say Trebizongski or Eleonoras! In Ireland, the people have more brains and sense and what is more put their ideals first and you can't buy them with a shilling a week rise.

I am so glad you are going to Miss [Helen] Neild. It will be heavenly in a garden after London. Cork is very warm and very dry. We don't seem to have any rain, though you often see thunder clouds rolling round the prison. The rain often seems to miss this.

That blockading and starving the enemy's children is an old trick of the English. I have just been reading about [George] Carew

[1555–1629] in the reign of Elizabeth, who destroyed harvests with machines and killed cattle with the avowed purpose of starving women and children. They are an awful people.

It's a real pity for me that you are not in the neighbourhood. I had three visits last week. One of my visitors has been arrested since. Such good news from America. Nothing is allowed to be printed, but we always hear from travellers. I think it is a very good sign that Canada wants a representative in the U.S. There are many signs that the tide has turned at last and that we are on the incoming wave, if only we can stick there. It's awfully hard to hover in the air – as it were – and do nothing. But if we can do it we must win.

Now goodbye and heaps of love darling. How I long for an endless talk.

Mise i gCuis na hEireann,
Constance de Markievicz

To Eva   *Cork Jail.*
                                                                 8 August 1919.

Dearest Old Darling,

I simply howled when I read of you a prisoner. 'Gott Bewarhe' [God forbid] that you should even be one in the flesh, it would finish you. You want to be an old scallywag like me to keep hale and hearty through it. I was amused too about Violet D.P. [Douglas-Pennant] I am not altogether sympathetic. If the girls did their work, surely that was all that she or anyone else had a right to ask of them. Mind you I don't approve of the jails, but I do want equal moral codes for both sexes, and no-one interferes with men outside their work.

What's all this yarn about Lord Michelham [a prominent philanthropist who died in January 1919] that has all been kept out of the papers? Who was his father? And why did he marry a child? It sounds like a novel by Miss Braddon: 'Lord Michelham's Millions' – not a bit like real life. I am still scoffing at the *Daily Herald*; my opinion of the English press gets worse and worse. What did they mean by promising Labour's support to the unfortunate police? Now Labour even sends back those few decent railway men who came out. I think that the way that they play with the idea of a general strike is too wicked and utterly senseless.

If they had called it for three days [on] the day the police came out first when I was in Holloway, they would have won and very little damage done. Now with all the soldiers about and idle, God knows where it would end. They always advertise all they are going to do, and talk and talk and talk! The enemy then prepare most carefully and easily 'divide and conquer'! Labour should choose a dictator for six months if they don't want to be beat all round. I send you a cutting of girl pipers, quite a new thing. People used to say that they could never pipe, I never quite knew why, it doesn't seem to require much strength.

It's a pity that Cecil did not get his question arranged in a more comprehensive manner. If he couldn't be shut up under the Treason Felony Act of '48, he could be under the 'Crimes Act'. I got my four months under that for pointing out to people that the police were not fit company for them. I wonder would I have got more if I had threatened rebellion. Most of the Southern Police are Home Rulers, Carson was declaring war on them! Which was more than I did. Of course it amounts to nothing, but C. would have had a better run for his money if he had been more in the know. I wonder how far he will get, perhaps he'll be another Ginnell! He has begun early but Westminster is very demoralising. There are so many plums to be handed out, all to be got in a rather shady manner.

Miss Albinia Brodrick came to see me yesterday. I had long wanted to see her, she wrote such a good letter to the paper when I was in Holloway; and she seemed so nice. Her people were also friends of Gaga's youth, I was there during the 'Grand Tour'! Of course I quite forgot to ask her about it, we only talked about the present. I actually heard the pipers' band here, I think that they must have come as near as they could to give me a treat.

Papers have just come and remind me of another grievance against the *D.H.* It puts in all the horrors! Our 'mosquitos'

[Republican newspapers] never do. Horrible details about murders etc are a waste of time.

You must have had such a funny time with Gaga. I imagine she is very captious and does not like pacifism.

Joss must have been so mad at my capture! Do you remember what a silly fuss he was in because someone invented a lie about me and a policeman in Easter week? And I only laughed and wouldn't contradict it – you'd have your hands full if you were once silly enough to begin contradicting the lies that the English enemy circulate.

I was so glad to see your poem in Figgis's *Republic.* Why don't you send him some odd bits? I'm sure they'd be much appreciated. He's a bit literary – of course they could not pay! But few do pay for poetry. If you only would publish things like that it would sell your books, for people would get a chance of seeing them.

Now goodbye darling, write me a line as to your health. Did I ever thank you for *Colour*? I always forget.

Best love,

Mise is gCuis na hEireann,
Constance de Markievicz I.C.A., T.D.

To Eva   *Cork Jail.*
                                          14 August 1919.

Dearest Old Darling,
I am so glad you are out of London just now and I hope you will remain so. It sounds so heavenly to lie on a sofa in a garden and just enjoy flowers and sun and air. It's hot enough here just now, but luckily for me it is never really oppressive in Ireland.

Don't you mind what [Thomas] Cassidy said in Drogheda [at annual congress of Irish Labour Party and Trades Union Congress]. In some parts of Ireland, we would welcome a Labour candidate, and no one with 'Westminster' on his programme would get a chance outside a few counties in the North and Waterford. Anywhere where S.F. is not it would be a great advance on the right road and would mean an additional shrinkage of Carsonism.

It seems to me that England is gaily riding to ruin, unless there is some wonderful secret policy somewhere. I can't see where it will all end. The futility and brainlessness of all leaders in every camp. With the exception of a few clever 'doctrinaire' socialist people who can state a case, they seem to be devoid even of common sense. The only way for an unorganised majority is to rush them into doing things and to tell them what to do.

Everybody seems to be splitting hairs about 'direct action' and other phrases, while one bit of liberty after another is taken from them. Lloyd George puts off and throws sops to Cerberus [a bribe to placate troublesome people. Cerberus, the hound of Hades, guarded the gates to hell in Greek mythology.] and every clique in England follows suit. They would sell their own souls for a few pence. I get rabid, this hot weather, you perceive!

Walton Newbold was in Dublin before I came in here and I told him what I thought of them all! These English men get very much surprised at what we say to them. They think themselves such 'God-Almighty' fine fellows and they can't understand that we don't admire words: they are so good and so cheap here that we only admire deeds and the willingness to suffer and deny yourself for a cause.

Nora Connolly came to see me today; she was delighted with Drogheda. Do you know that we, Cumann na mBan, have already sent £500 for the starving in Europe? Mostly collected in pennies all through Ireland, without permits? Every collector risked jail! Mind you, it was entirely a rank-and-file collection. Just the girls. I call it so splendid.

Mrs Skeffington has been awfully knocked about [at meeting in Kilbeggan, Co. Westmeath]. She interfered with the police who continued to hammer an unconscious man with clubbed rifles and she was clubbed over the head. She lost a lot of blood and will have to keep quiet for a bit. You probably saw it in the *Independent*.

I have nothing to say today. It's too hot to think, except about you, darling. Write and tell me how your health is and how everyone is going along and would there be any chance of your getting over here [from London] in the autumn (I don't mean to jail!) but to the Republic.

Bless you, old darling.

Mise i gCuis na hEireann,
Constance de Markievicz

To Eva   *Cork Jail.*
17 August 1919.

Dearest Old Darling,

Many thanks for the *New Age*. Labour is very complicated over here and it's very difficult to expound on four censored pages! In the first place, it's supposed to be non-political except on Labour issues and as yet has not debated the question of abstention. Even the 'Transport' contains some who are not Sinn Féiners, though the bulk of Irish workers are with us. Sinn Féin is composed of both labour and capital, mostly of course labour, but there are some 'rotten' capitalists in it. They would use S.F. to damage labour if they could and to boost themselves. The Unionist and Redmondite crowd would in their turn use labour to bust S.F., and Carson would use each to break up the other! So far, labour and S.F. have acted loyally towards each other. Their disagreements have been open and without any spleen, and as long as they continue to do so, they will both be for the good of Ireland.

All sorts of mysterious people are trying to make mischief in a very clever way: sometimes by getting a trades union to believe that S.F. is anti-labour, sometimes by declaring that S.F. is Bolshevism! But so far it has not mattered. It's a bit difficult to side-track Irish people and we just go ahead. I belong to both organisations, for my conception of a free Ireland is economic as well as political; some agree with me, some don't, but it's not a sore point. Easter Week comrades don't fall out; they laugh and chaff and disagree. It annoys the enemy considerably. Of course no labour leader would get in in place of a present S.F. member unless he forswore Westminster. It's so obvious that I don't think anyone would try.

I feel equally sure that any labour man who pledged himself to abstention would be accepted by S.F. in a Labour constituency and not opposed. S.F. is not a solid, cast-iron thing like English parties. It is just a jumble of people of all classes, creeds, and opinions, who are all ready to suffer and die for Ireland, and as long as it remains that, there is nothing to fear from labour. Do tell me everything you hear about Violet D. P. I don't see English capitalist dailies. Her enemies are to judge her I see; that's rather like us! She ought to come out a Sinn Féiner once she realises how pleasant it is to be ruled, accused and judged by people whose morals and principles are diametrically opposite to yours. In Ireland, she would get endless sympathy. Try also to find out about the Michelham case. It sounded so odd.

I enclose you a funny cutting from the *D.H.* in case you did not see it. You know the author. I simply roared over it and would like to congratulate E.S. It would be an excellent idea for a scene in a play. Did you see Lennox Robinson in the end? Nora Connolly is in Cork and has been to see me twice. She is very well satisfied with the Congress.

Can Maunsel prevent you publishing a complete edition yourself? Try and get his leave, don't say for where, but just vaguely to publish, and then write to my friend. I'd put the Easter Week ones in one chapter and those to me in jail in another, each with a little explanation and write a short account of what you saw in Dublin that time: say something about Skeffy's ideas; pacifism and war, and I believe it would go like hot cakes. I am sure you could find some of our crowd going across who would look after it for you. I don't mean political envoys! But there are always people going and I could help in this even here. Some of the priests are very interested in literature, and they are always going across. Anyhow, get leave to bring out a book as soon as you can, and then we'll try.

I know an American poetess – Teresa Brayton. I believe I could get hold of some people to review it too. I forget if you know [Padraic] Colum, who is there; Ernest Boyd, a journalist, and a friend have gone lately. Anyhow, we must get a hustle on now. I must talk to Nora about it too. I am sure my drawing would sell a few copies too.

Now good-bye, darling and best love. How is Esther? You have given me no news of her nor of Clare[Annesley].

Mise i gCuis na hEireann,
Constance de Markievicz I.C.A.

To Hanna Sheehy Skeffington   *Cork Jail.*
                                                21 August 1919.

My dear friend and comrade,
I was indeed grieved to see that you were still suffering from the clubs of inhuman brutes – what a terrible rucking about you must have had. I never realised how much you were hurt from the censored report and only gather it from a line stating that you were still suffering and that you were with your sister. I do hope that you will soon be better. But you must know it's great for the cause and I'm always proud when a woman makes a fine stand. This stand of yours and what you are suffering will put so much courage into our girls and help so many of them out of the old-fashioned corner of slyness and submission.

You would laugh if you saw me here. I often wonder how much I cost them per week for soldiers, police, etc. I've quite a large cool room, which keeps me in good health. I do so sincerely pity all who are in those airless cells this weather. Some of our country boys used to an out-of-door life must suffer so terribly. I had to laugh when I read Col. [Arthur] Lynch's latest [book; probably *Moments of Genius*]. He evidently has not got what he wanted for his job! Thanks for sending me the *Citizen*, your little 'par' on me was very neat. Certainly mine was an extraordinary sentence. Until quite lately anyhow all 'respectable' unionists would have agreed. I know a lady who sacked her nurse because she came on her suddenly in a country lane with a policeman walking on either side of the pram.

What is going to happen to the world at all? Everything, everywhere – except here in Ireland – seems to be heading for ruin. Labour in England seems to have neither plans or courage –

nothing but frothy talk that can always be quieted for 3½ pence. Do ask someone to send me a line as to how you are, if anyone can spare time for even a P.C. It was such a joy to me here to think of you in No 6 [Harcourt Street; HQ of Sinn Féin]. It's splendid to have a woman in your job! Women so rarely get a chance, and it's so gratifying when the one woman who should get it gets the chance.

And now goodbye and God bless you.

Mise i gCuis na hEireann,
Constance de Markievicz I.C.A.

To Eva   *Cork Jail.*
                                                           23 August 1919.

Dearest Old Darling,
Was delighted with Strindberg's poem, please thank Reginald. I agree with you about Dickens and I think his further choice very materialistic. I would have preferred three poets though the others have certainly given us all something to talk about. I shall never stop thanking Darwin for the delightfully funny idea that we once swung out from the tree tops by our tails.

I hear that Molly is again speaking around! At least Bella says so. Who was I right about? Do tell me – I can't imagine, unless it's a labour woman and even then I'm not sure. Such a blessing to hear that you are getting better; such a pity that you can't live in a suburb instead of right in the middle of London. Perhaps it will turn out a blessing that Roger F. is evicting you. London is so pestiferously unhealthy – so low. You should give it up for a year.

If I ever get out of this, I might get over, if there was no chance of getting you across to Ireland. I had been thinking of going to Bella. It's so lovely there; couldn't you come too? I'm sure she'd love to see you. I could look after your food, but they have lots of hens and garden things. Glendalough is close and it's so beautiful. The lake is grand and then the sun most obligingly sets in the right place and the ruins are awfully attractive.

One place I always long to bring you to is New Grange, near Drogheda – it's most inspiring. A great mound as big as Lissadell House: you go in by a narrow passage and come to a huge chamber: great pillar stones roofed over with flat slabs. Here and there dim chisellings are to be seen; circles and spirals. It's like something out of a dream. No one knows its history.

Nora Connolly has just been again. She is going to write to you about publishers in America, and says that you would do better with a more regular publisher than my friend, who is more of a printer, who publishes occasionally.

You will see that Liberty Hall is raided and that they have arrested the caretaker! I simply yelled when I read it. Do you remember how someone carried off his wife's photo? You got it in the end – and another English soldier stole his dog. I think that the police must have brought the gun in with them. They are very given to that sort of trick, and I know that the committee would have made a row if anyone had brought in a gun. I see that another regiment objects to going to Russia – where there is no war! And that again Labour, with a very big 'L', is behind them. I would advise them to remember the police!

Did you ever read a book called *Human Nature in Politics*? It's awfully interesting [by Graham Wallas]. Every would-be leader of revolution should read it. It is the sort of thing that comes instinctively in Ireland, and though we never philosophise about how to run a movement, we do it by faith or luck or instinct.

There is such a nice dog here, a 'Poppet', only bigger and black, but so friendly. The soldiers are nearly all so small and so young that you feel they ought to be at school, instead of idling about with iron hats and fixed bayonets. It's an awful life for a young man; I don't expect any of them will ever settle down to a quiet life again. They all want to be demobilised, but if they were they'd hate it, and there is not enough work already, so Lord knows what they'd do. I suppose they'd starve and that there would be a revolution!

I think one of the reasons why they are making wars is to dispose of revolutionary man-power. They have made an awful world of it, and in the meantime Dev is in America and the oppressed peoples are joining forces. There's a vicious crop of dragon's teeth sprouting in many lands.

Much love, I must stop.

Mise i gCuis na hEireann,
Constance de Markievicz I.C.A.

To Kathleen Clarke   *Cork Jail.*
                                                          28 August 1919.

Dearest Kathleen,
I was so delighted to get a nice long letter from you, so full of news. I'm awfully interested to hear about Daly [son]. I'm sure he is on the right road; the first thing any man should want is work that he can enjoy. It does not matter how hard it is, if he is interested in what he is doing, time flies and it becomes an occupation and ceases to be work which is drudgery – as you say, if he wants to, he can still go to college for many years to come.

I know an electrician, a Mr Paul, who went through Cambridge and took a degree; I knew him when he was there and he must have been well over 30. He started on the practical end like Daly and worked in England and Egypt; wanted to go further and came home to study the theoretical end with a view to inventions and to getting a better paid job with more leisure for experimenting. You must be awfully lonely these days with no boys. I wonder so what the little ones will do and if Tom will develop his talent for drawing. If he ever comes to love it enough, I'm sure he has enough talent to be a fine artist, but without the real love they never work hard enough.

Why did you not make Medhbh show you the drawing room? The dining room is a pokey little room but I like the way she has it, and I love the colouring of the hall. I'm a great believer in change for rheumatism; travelling to some place where you can take a course of waters. I wonder if the treatment will do you good after a bit, this hot summer ought to help. I hope the other ailment is not bothering you and that your heart is behaving. I have suffered very little from the heart as I have a decent room facing east. The jail is on a hill, facing south, a lovely situation for a sanatorium – of course the innumerable walls are disagreeable and block out what otherwise would be a fine view, but some of it is very nice; from the gate up to the prison is very fine, up steps with gardens on either side and in front of you the picturesque castle with two wings making three sides of a square open to the south.

So glad the chickens were so successful, they will be worth a lot when they start laying. I can't make out about the American – he must have clashed with others, as I now have 8 [visitors] (or 3) a week. Of course there are always people from all parts of Ireland, and naturally friends would get in first.

Theo [Fitzgerald] has been knocked up with teeth and I suppose he is recovering in camp. I heard from Cassie last week. Eva has been very ill with influenza; she has luckily got away to the country at last. I read and write nearly all day and my pen is getting much more fluent.

Do you remember suggesting to me in Holloway that I should work out schemes of government? I could never put my mind to it there; but I remembered and started on it directly I got in here. I am absolutely absorbed in it now and have learnt a lot and thought a lot. One is a bit held up by not always being able to get the books one wants, but even so, that throws one back on one's imagination. So here I am from day to day trying to build up an ideal Republic in my mind and getting great value for myself out of the work. I think I shall try and get the socialists to start debates on different branches of government services when I get out.

Now the paper is running out and I have lots more to say – but I'll content myself with asking you to send me thick old shoes with American laces, some of the thick stockings, velours hat – I think it's in the middle drawer of chest of d. with marble top, big blue and mottled silk scarf; it's a dirty grey blue colour with some sort of vague pattern.

Much love from,

Mise i gCuis na hEireann,
Constance de Markievicz I.C.A.

To Eva
Cork Jail.
1 September 1919.

Dearest Old Darling,

I do hope that you are having the lovely weather over in that most awful country that I am having here. This is Sunday and I spent most of the morning sitting in the sun without a coat.

Are you writing any poems? I'm enclosing a 'comic' I cut out. Did you get the caricature? I am still raging at the paper [*Daily Herald*] – without a policy and wondering what its use is. [George] Lansbury ought to know how to run a paper by now. If they can't work out a principle to live for and a policy by which they can hope to attain it, they had much better leave things alone. The English labour leaders are just like so many children with lighted matches and fireworks playing about in a factory where new and unknown explosives are stored. Some day someone will start off something and then God help them all! And in the meantime, everything goes on as if they did not exist. Their silly strikes and bluster are just as ineffective as were the 'Blockateers' or any of the poor south of England labourers who were just brave enough to break machines and nothing more as a protest against enclosing the commons. Some got hanged and hundreds transported and the commons were all stolen by the landlords and enclosed.

I advise them most strongly to sit tight unless they develop a little more nerve. Never start a racket unless you are prepared to face a revolution ought to be a wise man's motto today.

I do long to see you darling, it's always such a rush and such a gasp when I do. I can't of course make any plans for sure as you never know what's going to happen from one day to another if you have the great privilege of living under the Union Jack. The leaders are so like a lot of old cormorants speaking over the carcass of a dead whale. Do you think Italy will become a socialist state with a king at its head? Such funny things do happen these days, they certainly were effective in controlling their rulers lately, they got their hands off Russia anyhow. English labour wanted some of the Liberty Hall crowd to go over and speak for [Arthur] Henderson! They were quite surprised when ours quietly reminded them that he was a member of the cabinet when Connolly was murdered – they did not publish this in the *Herald*! The fur would fly if ever I met that man – we'll leave him to 'T. P.' and his like.

I should like to make a bet that we'll soon have a Labour government with a Northcliffe or a Harmsworth person as prime minister. Will someone explain why the English love those that they are always tripping up in lies? I never want to talk to anyone again if I catch them out. It's so dull to be deceived. Now I ramble on, you see there is so little to talk about in jail; you have to be careful all the time not to say anything that might be helpful to the 'English Enemie [*sic*]'. I am very well and quite cheerful, we have certainly made things very hot for them everywhere. I wish things would hurry up though, I do want to see a little peace in Ireland before I die. Think what fun we could have if the army of occupation were gone. Nobody would grudge me a good holiday. Even now the republic is a happier country than any other.

Now bye bye and best love. You are staying with the kind people who befriended Mr P., aren't you? In the garden where he was so happy and recovered from his arrest.

Mise do chara i gCuis na hEireann,
Constance de Markievicz, I.C.A., T.D.

To Anne Devlin   *Cork Jail.*
5 September 1919 [censor's mark, 5 October 1919].

Dear Anne Devlin,
Yours is such a grand name that I take the pleasure for myself of writing the whole of it. I was so glad to get your note and only wish it had been longer. You must be having very trying times just now in Dublin with this English strike, they seem to be managing it very well.

I shall soon be out now, please God, and among you all again. Do you know I have not heard a word of either Perolz or or Emer [Helena

Molony] since I was in, except I saw that Emer was acting and several wrote that she was good. The Cork people are awfully good to me, it makes all the difference when you are alone if you get lots of things sent in to you, it quite prevents you feeling lonely.

Now goodbye and good luck,

Mise do chara i gCuis na hEireann,
Constance de Markievicz I.C.A., T.D.

To Jennie Wyse Power   *Cork Jail.*
                                                    12 September 1919.

My dear friend,
Many thanks for yours. Mrs Wilson wrote me that Maisie is the mother of a boy. I was so glad. Please send me her address, I would like to write to her. Friends of mine in Dublin seem to think it's all a plant about the bicycles; it certainly reads like one.

One never knows what the enemy will do next. Did I ever tell you that the famous 'Malone' M.P. is a cousin of mine – his real name is L' Estrange. He is doubly related for his sister married my brother. I am still reading away and quite cheerful and my health is good. The Cork people are wonderful, they look after me so well. When you are alone, it makes all the difference if you get things in. They never missed the chance of a visit either and I know what it must have been to toil up that hill in the awful heat.

Did you ever come across Miss Brodrick? I took such a fancy to her. She told me that down her way they have a tame and civilised policeman who was converted. She runs a co-op too. It was a great joy seeing Father Augustine, looking so well and so cheerful after his trip; he is full of hope and had a lovely time. Everybody writes me such good news. I quite see what you mean about Carson – I always believe that it would take very little to bring the North over to our way of thinking, the opposition among the rank and file is mainly artificial and created by the enemy. Do you know anything about a Katie McCormack, who was on the run and taken at last; I can't place her and have a friend of that name, but don't suppose it is her.

Give my love to the Misses C. S. I hope the new premises are good for business. Now goodbye with love to you and Nancy [daughter].

Mise do chara i gCuis na hEireann,
Constance de Markievicz I.C.A., T.D.

To Eva   *Cork Jail.*
                                        19 September 1919.

Dearest Old Darling,
So delighted to know that Staskou is alive; do, do write quick and tell me what you know about him.

I am so sorry for him. I don't suppose he is a Bolshevik and I daresay he is in a rather awful position. He hated politics and wars so, poor boy. I wonder who he'll live with and what he'll do. He was such a child when I saw him last. I've not heard of Casi either for so long, he was in Kiev, rather a bad place just now and he might just as easily be a Bolshevik as anything else. Fine ideas always attracted him, and he would be quite capable of being enthused into thoroughly enjoying wearing a big beard and waving a red flag. He was always torn in two between his artistic appreciation of the rich and princely people and just as strong an appreciation of the wrongs of the people and the beauty of self-sacrifice.

Even here he was a bit of an anxiety, for he could lunch with the enemy and sup with the enemy, and between the two make a wild rebel speech. He was absolutely sincere all the time; here it was only rather compromising, in Russia both sides would be stalking him with guns.

Do try and find out from J. [Joss] what happened to them; I don't like to write. In the old Russia, it would have got them all on to a black list even to correspond with a rebel like me. Do you remember that time you were interested in a Russian society in Manchester? And how serious Casi was about it? He was not exaggerating.

Can you understand the English Labour Party? They seem to be so utterly foolish. I can't make head or tail of what they want. The war should have made them a little shy of government control of industry; likewise the poor police. I suppose somebody stood to gain something by the nationalisation of mines, but it does not seem to me to be the rank and file. Do you bother about these things at all? Or is it only the women's end that interests you. Of course they came into their own a lot during the war and now are being put out again.

Do you know of any book about labour dealing with the time between 1832 and the 20th century? I've been reading [J.L.] Hammond who stops at '32 [*The Skilled Labourer 1760-1832*; written with Barbara Hammond]. The part about child labour is worse than I ever heard of anywhere.

Labour in England has just as much material for propaganda in her past history (that is since steam was applied and machines invented) as Ireland has, and they never use it. They just go on trusting the same old kings, capitalists and clergy who built up fortunes on their enslavement and the lives of babies from three up. Do children work at all in the mills nowadays? I don't believe they do in Dublin, at least I never heard of it. But they easily might in the North. I must find out if ever I am at large again; and if so, it shall be a great point of attack. Aren't Bullitt's [American diplomat] revelations amusing? And just at the right moment for us too. It's a pity Parl. was not sitting. They will be forgotten by the time it meets again. What will they do about a general election? They don't want it here and in their own country it would probably give them a new lease of life. I've no belief that Labour would be true to itself. L.G. is so extraordinarily clever about electioneering tactics that he'd probably carry his country again.

They are such fools over there. You couldn't catch our country with monkey cries – and the last thing we trust is an M.P. If we didn't go straight the country would soon let us know, and they might get a move on. Now bye bye darling, you don't put Clare's address, give her my love.

Mise do chara i gCuis na hEireann.
Constance de Markievicz I.C.A., T.D.
Is it against the 'D.O.R.A.' [Defence of the Realm Act] to put T.D. (Irish MP) after your name do you think?

To Hanna Sheehy Skeffington   *Cork Jail.*
                                                  24 September 1919.

Dear Comrade,
Very many thanks for the American papers. They were a great
relaxation. It's so pleasant when you are in jail to get something
that looks on life from a totally different point of view. The different
mentality of the writers to anything that one meets in the writers
here is very interesting. I never noticed it so much before.

So glad that you are better. It's a good thing to be tough these
days. The enemy are real brutes. I can't help smiling at their
hypocritical miauls. I don't suppose their leaders publicly denounce
the soldiers or police for attempting to pound you to death – and
poor Mr Grace who was so badly shot near Terenure. I wonder will
the man who did it get a medal! You'll want to take care of yourself
for a long time, I'm sure.

I don't feel it matters them suppressing the papers as long
as the jails are full! That keeps the heart in the people – Ireland
always hatches a plentiful supply of Phoenix eggs! And of dragon's
teeth not a few! I shall be so glad to see you and my rebel comrades
again. The winter will be a very trying time for all. Now goodbye
and good luck and my love.

Is mise i gCuis na hEireann,
Constance de Markievicz I.C.A., T.D.

To Countess Plunkett   *Cork Jail.*
                                                  26 September 1919.

My dear Countess Plunkett,
Mrs Clarke told me in a letter that came this morning that you have
undergone a serious operation and been very ill. I am writing to
express my sympathy and to hope that you are on the high road to
recovery.

It's so wearisome for an active person like you to be laid up, I
always think of your flying around on your machine and taking part

in everything like myself. I know that, pain and suffering apart, you must suffer more than most from the monotony of lying up.

She tells me the good news that Maisie is the mother of a son; I will write to her in a day or two. You must be overjoyed. As her President in C na mB, I feel quite a sort of relationship and am longing to see it. I am sure that our proclaimed organisations are all delighted my time is coming to an end soon unless they find some excuse for holding on to me! You would laugh if you saw the soldiers and police around me here. They don't like it at all in this weather – I wonder how many of the Police will blow themselves up with the new bombs they are getting. I must say I can't see them throwing them effectively.

Please remember me to all in Fitzwilliam Place [Plunkett home]. I used to be reading the Count's poems lately until the papers were suppressed.

Now goodbye with love and my best wishes for your speedy recovery.

Mise i gCuis na hEireann,
Constance de Markievicz I.C.A., T.D.

To Eva   *Cork Jail.*
            30 September 1919 [censor's mark, 30 August 1919].

Dearest Old Darling,
I ought to get out on the 16th October but that means nothing, and I would never dream of counting on it.

If I do get out and am not re-arrested on the doorstep, I will wire to you. English law in Ireland is but legalised oppression. Police law is very comic, if you consider: they accused me, they gave evidence against me, their magistrate condemned me, and they are allowed to garrison the jail with guns in their hands to see that I don't get out. It would be awfully funny if everyone was allowed to guard their own prisoner.

The gas has gone on strike here which supplies variety! But they have let me have two candles, so I can see alright without hurting my eyes.

So amused about Muncaster [cousin]. Do you ever see Rhoda [Carlisle; cousin] now? Such a curious life. She missed everything she wanted. I wonder if she is as great a cat as she used to be.

Don't be in any hurry about book, wait and hear more about American publishers. Of course my friend might look on it as a great advertisement and give it a great show, but in my heart I rather think that some regular old established publisher would be better. Anyhow don't be in a hurry and don't send any precious M.S. by post unless you have a second copy. 'The English enemie' would for sure steal it. It's quite easy to get things taken over. The Cat caricature made one laugh so I cut it out and enclose. I believe I have fathomed the English government. L[Lloyd]. G[George]., with soap on one side, Harmsworth on the other and surrounded by oil and rubber is not like to be such a fool as outsiders think. They are not going to be ruined though the workers may starve. I believe that capital is going abroad as fast as it can (Persia, Egypt, etc) and that the lack of employment at home is a deliberate plot to throw men up against destitution and get them to join up. They want huge armies to protect cheap labour abroad and there is no other way to get them. I would suggest that the next time a factory closed down, all the workers and their families went to the workhouses and that they continued to do so. But they are such fools in England and can't see an inch ahead.

The labourers' strike here has been won hands down. I rejoice in the bad weather when I think of Denikin [a Russian White Army officer] sticking in the mud of the Ukraine. Armed cars, lorries and tanks – in a clay country without roads! A motor car is useless there except in the summer – there are no bridges and the fords are often impassable. It's all deep sticky clay. The lightest carriage takes four horses to pull it, and can only crawl. You never saw such a country for getting about in in the autumn! There is nothing for aeroplanes to be attacking it's hardly worth even a Cossack's or an Englishman's while to bomb small villages to thatched mud cottages. So maybe Lenin will win through after all. God speed him – and poor Russia – I wonder on whose side Casi is.

Poor Reginald! I always think that the drips of rain on a tent and the smell of sodden leaves make a very depressing atmosphere.

Have you heard any more of Sidney [Czira]? And how has Bridget turned out? Poor Maud, she missed all she wanted in life. I used to be quite envious of that pretty place and nice house. She had improved it too and had such ambitions. When I think of the family I am quite sure that I am both luckier and happier than most of them even in jail! It's very funny – if Bolshevism comes to England, I don't know what will happen to them all, it would be terrible!

But it would be all right over here. I would love to see the Wuss having to work a kitchen floor and not able to dye her hair – and people like the Ramsdens living in a tenement.

Do you think that the *D. Herald* is honest? Or is it out to keep things quiet? It's so painfully lacking in a policy and one can hardly credit that its editor does not realise that the way to demoralise your followers is to continually bluff and crawl down and never to face up bravely to a situation. The occasional articles are good but the rest! Well, it's very English. How's Esther; you haven't mentioned her lately? Give her my love.

Now darling goodbye and do take care of yourself. I do wish I was ever with you. Revolutions take up so much time and energy. Would you be fit to come over here do you think?

Best love darling.

Mise i gCuis na hEireann,
Constance de Markievicz I.C.A.

To Eva   *Cork Jail.*
                                                        1 October 1919.

Dearest Old Darling,
Your letter just arrived – such a joy, as I thought we were cut off. Fancy you painting cupboards! It sounds quite well, though it did give you a headache. There is something quite poisonous in some

of those made-up enamels. I once made myself deadly sick painting a bath.

I thought there was something queer about the [national rail] strike too. But it may be that [Jimmy] Thomas could not put it off any longer because of pressure from the rank and file. Do tell me more about [Woodrow] Wilson. I don't think the enemy would mind my knowing that! I think that his patent is very nearly up in America. I hear lots of news from there.

Dev is simply splendid. He's not made a single mistake. So straight and honest. Walton Newbold came to see me last Friday. I like him and we had a very interesting talk. He was going to London, but of course, he can't yet, and he promised to give you the latest news of me. He is pretty exercised about how to get a move on. I advised him to 'park'. He wants me to go over and speak for him at Motherwell. Of course, that depends on whether I can be spared. I got a long letter from Joe Robinson and I must go over to Scotland to see him when a visit is due. That is, if I am out of prison myself and if there are any trains and Britain is not 'revolting'.

That's another thing about this strike; the people may take control and everything go with a rush. I have not at all the opinion that the English people could not run amok. They very nearly did about a hundred years ago and neither army nor militia could be trusted. The soldiers don't seem to be a bit well disciplined and I think could be easily carried away. I think the Government must be afraid of this, as they are so down on any discussions of Bolshevism, socialism or even co-operation.

I would have liked to have tried a new experiment in the way of strikes and that would be to run the trains, that is a certain number, with food, coal and a limited number of passengers, collaring the money and paying the staff. It would be great if it could be done. Of course, the clerks would have to join up.

The one great thing about the strike is that they won't be able to keep up supplies to Kolchak and Co. That I think will be the one great gain and that makes me doubt if it's a plot. They do so want Russia to be reduced to slavery again. This may just save the Revolution. The blockade and starvation sound so awful: just the same policy as was adopted over here as early as the time of Henry

VIII. Among the State Papers are letters from English officials in Ireland to Secretary [Thomas] Cromwell, telling that they were destroying the standing corn and killing the cattle.

Philip Sidney's description in Elizabeth's time of the starvation is awful. They never stopped doing this until after Oliver Cromwell's day, and after that 'til quite lately they starved the people whenever they could by legislating so as to produce famines.

There is a great move on at present among the English enemy to influence the Pope against Ireland, but they have not the remotest chance of succeeding. They tried hard to get a pro-English Cardinal for Australia! The Pope wisely refrained from appointing one at all, owing to the 'strained political situation'. There was also a move on to get a Nuncio appointed from Rome to London to have authority over the Catholic Church in both England and Ireland! A very cute move on England's part, for of course he would have to be partial to England. But – I don't think!

Have you heard anything of this? I got it from America. Our people here tell me that a lot of this sniping of police is done by themselves, either for private vengeance or sometimes for money. Most poor young men would think £500 easily gained by a bullet through their arm or leg. Some of the stories are so absurd: it's certainly not any of our crowd.

I'm supposed to be out quite soon now. It will be a great bore if the strike is still on. Of course I wouldn't travel in England if they were on strike: I would always back Labour – even English! And would not put my foot on a blackleg train. I could get to Dublin easily on a bike or walking; give me time enough! I wonder what you will do about food. I see you are being rationed.

You never told me about Staskou, do try and remember; perhaps you didn't get my letter asking you. You put no address, so I write to London and hope that you will get it. Have you fixed up about the flat?

Now good-bye and best love to you. What's Moira like to look at?

Mise do chara i gCuis na hEireann,
Constance de Markievicz I.C.A., T.D.
Thanks for the cuttings.

To Eva   *Cork Jail.*
                                                  8 October 1919.

Dearest Old Darling,

Such a joy to get yours. If you only knew what a joy it was to hear
about Staskou. I feel I never know from day to day whether he is
alive or not. What on earth does he want over here? He wouldn't
like it if he got here. Of course if it's true that he's married a rich
wife, he'd be all right, but if not, I don't know what he'd do. I dare
say, though, that he'd be safer over here.

I am very much amused at the Wilson yarn. Do write me the
truth about Violet D.P. and Miss O'Sullivan. The latter's yarn
sounded awfully funny. Sworn enquiries are only machines for
whitewashing officials valued by the government of the day.

I think you are right about the strike being engineered by those
two. But I believe that the men could have won. They were very
strong and Government would have had to pay the miners under
D.O.R.A. A lot were already idle owing to shortage of trains. The
Irish railwaymen had to be paid too. These two items were quite
humorous, they were kept in to draw Government money to finance
the strike. I suppose you saw that there was a desperate strike
in Mountjoy jail again. I quite agree with them – all politicals are
perfectly right to strike at being put in with other prisoners. Lots
of the politicals are quite children, it's wicked to put them with the
terrible people that get in for crimes.

The eternal smutty talk of some jailbirds is an appalling thing to
be forced to listen to. I wonder what your C.O. would say about it. It
makes me rage to think of our nice boys put to work with the awful
degenerates one meets in English prisons.

Do you see that the police have shot another boy? In the North
this time. I hope Carson will denounce the outrage. I can't make
any plans until I get out. I will write when I do. Would your health
be fit to come across? I am sure it would do you a lot of good
once you got here. It's still like summer, a queer summer, with
lovely autumn tints and birds singing – like fairyland. 'In Tir na
nOg summer and spring go hand in hand in the sunny weather.
Brown autumn leaves and winter snow come tumbling down
together [from poem by Ethna Carbery].' It's just as mad as that

here at present and quite delicious. The cloud effects in Cork are wonderful.

To go back to the strike: I don't quite believe that the middle-class crowd could have run the country for long. They could never have tackled coal: they would have been all right for a bit. But they ought to have struck during the 'season'. It would have been much more inconvenient for the idle rich and much more difficult to feed them. It seemed a very trifling thing to risk a strike for, but wages are the only thing that will move an Englishman.

The Government are counting on establishing an 'aristocracy' of labour, well paid and satisfied, who will go to parliament, compromise, sell every cause, scab with the police, and trample on the underdog.

Now goodbye, dearest. Love to Esther and to you. I suppose that you have settled with the landlord as you have taken a tenant! Bless you darling.

Mise i gCuis na hEireann,
Constance de Markievicz I.C.A., T.D.

To Eva   *Cork Jail.*
13 October 1919.

Dearest Old Darling,

Yours just come, and I am so glad to hear that you are better. I wish to goodness you weren't staying in London for the winter, it's so unhealthy. Why don't you go on a trip to America? To a warm part. It's so odd you're getting a sore throat. I never remember you getting one: you used to get colds on your chest.

If I get out, I will try to find out about folklore for you. I only know the usual things – fighting and making love, like all primeval savages. I have been reading a lot of history here, but more modern, and, like you, have been hunting for the things we have thought and done differently from other nations. The one thing that stands out is that we never produced a tyrant. There was something that prevented any man or woman ever desiring to conquer all Ireland

– a sort of feeling for 'decentralisation' [modern 'soviets']. Brian Boru was High King, but he never interfered with his under King, and so on down until now. It's very curious, for in a way it was that that prevented the conquest of Ireland, 'til the English enemy got rid of every family of note: at the same time it always prevented the Irish getting together under one head for long enough to do more than win a battle. This makes me have such faith in the Republic. The country is now all organised and can do without leaders, but has learnt that it must act together. I have no fear of the North; it held out much longer than the South by some hundred years, and it's only a bit behind the times. It's begun to move at the fringes.

I don't know what this new book of MacNeill's is: it might help you. If it's any good I will send it. Have you *Ossian*? Or shall I send it to you? You pick up yarns locally that are awfully good but I never can remember them. Also let me know: does the *Book of Kells* inspire you? Do you remember about O'Daly, the blind poet of Lissadil [*sic*]? He was the originator of Mrs Clark and Co. There were great stories about St Brigid and other women of that date too. They were very powerful and I believe that is rather a feature of Irish history. There is something coming out in the *Bulletin* about them; I must send it to you.

I don't think I told you about a Peeler in Ballingeary who was being transferred North. No one would even bid for his stock of turf, just saved and ready for the winter, so he burnt it and scattered it and then swore an information! He got compensation levied on the district. It was headed up in the papers: 'Another S.F. Outrage!' Another man in Clare fired into his own house to get money to pay a debt! Surely the English code of morals is a queer one.

Best love to you both. I must try and arrange to get over and see you in London and Joe [Robinson] in Scotland if I get free.

Mise i gCuis na hEireann,
Con de M

'On the Run', October 1919–September 1920

On 18 October 1919, Constance was released from Cork Jail. That evening, Constable Michael Downing was shot dead in Dublin, with the authorities claiming a link with her release. Referred to by Dublin Castle as 'that pestilential harridan', the authorities attempted to deport Constance as an 'alien' because of her marriage to Casimir.

December saw further crackdowns on republican activity; both the Dáil H.Q. and the Mansion House were raided as was the Clarke household. Alderman Tom Kelly was one of many arrested and deported. With tension high, the annual Aonach Christmas Fair was cancelled.

To Eva   *[Undated; probably December 1919].*

Darling,

I was so glad to hear from you. What on earth is the meaning of their latest move? It's such a funny selection. Ald. Kelly always describes himself as a 'Man of Peace' [arrested 11 December 1919; elected Lord Mayor of Dublin 30 January 1920], and it is an admirable description. Irwin is quite unknown to most people.

Was it not lucky that I was away? I hear that Mrs Clarke asked to see the warrant and that the detective in charge said there was none. She then asked what I was charged with and they said they did not know. They had orders to arrest me and that was all. There were some police and a lorry-load of soldiers and they searched the house to her amusement. She made them look everywhere and waste a lot of time! If you see Cecil, you might try and inspire him to find out with what awful crime I am charged this time! It's enough to make any one curious.

I've a sort of feeling that it may mean strained relations with America and nothing more, for of course we'd all be with the Yanks if they started to fight England. We have created a delightful situation in America for the enemy, thank God! Grey's return with his tail between his legs is rather significant. It was wonderful, when you come to think of it, how few were caught. Of course we are on the run most of the time, and no one who respects themselves lives much in their homes.

Wasn't it a shame to stop the Aonach? It was just a fair and nothing more: you hire a stall and sell. Shopkeepers and industries count on making a nice few pounds, and manufacturers hope to get Irish goods on the market through it. It's political to the extent that it is organised to help Irish industry and trade to hold their own against English, German, or any other foreign industry or agencies. It gets customers for the shops that are willing to put themselves out in their efforts to help their country's struggling industries. Of course this is treason, as the enemy wish all Irish men and women to emigrate or starve. McPherson attributed all the trouble in Ireland to the stoppage of emigration during the War.

I believe the 'English enemie' are trying to goad us into another rebellion, so as to murder a large number of intelligent and brave patriots. Everything that is done points that way, but I hope that the country is too well in hand for anything of the sort to occur. The people are wonderfully steadfast, under the most ridiculous persecution and provocation. No one knows at what moment they will be arrested on some vague charge, and any house may be raided at any moment.

The police are employed entirely as an army of occupation, and I believe that there are several gangs of English thieves making themselves very busy. This does not of course get into the papers, but our own crowd are constantly held up and robbed, both in their houses and on the streets.

One of Theo's [Fitzgerald] sisters married Seán McMahon the other day, and as they were going home one night last week from her people's house in Brunswick Street to Queen's Square, they saw two soldiers and a civilian hold up a man with revolvers. They ran! The robbers had white handkerchiefs over the lower part of their faces. Next day they found that quite a lot of people had been stopped and relieved of their watches, money and jewellery.

This is an everyday occurrence just now, and invariably some of the assailants are soldiers. It is generally supposed that Barton the detective was shot by one of these gangs [on 29 November 1919], as he was employed for years in hunting down the cross-channel thieves, but of course it's put down as a 'Sinn Féin Outrage'.

No one can see any sense in the motor permit order, except to cripple Irish trade. Motors have been very little used by us, except in Elections: we have not the money! Of course, S.F. traders can be hit that way and their businesses ruined. All this fuss may be to upset our organisations for the elections, and to prevent our people in the slums learning the intricacies of P.R. [proportional representation], but I don't think that the enemy will gain much. The situation appeals to the imagination of the people, and they love the excitement. They are not afraid and they have a great sense of humour. It gives them endless joy when they out-wit the Hun, and vast and pompous military raids result in the arrest of a couple of harmless pacifists.

How is your health? I hope that you are none the worse for your exertions during my visit. Did I leave a striped flannelette blouse (dirty) behind? I think that I did. It was one I got in Holloway and I wore it on the journey over. I am going to keep quiet for a bit and then go about as usual and dodge them, as there is much to be done.

Now goodbye old darling and love to Esther and to your dear old self,

Yrs,
C de M
PS: I have been about Mrs Evans' shirt, also free stockings! I hope that both will be attainable. How does your lodger spell his name?
Con

To Joseph McGarrity   *c. December 1919.*

A Chara Dhil,
Very many thanks for the newspapers. It is great to read of all you have done and are still doing in America. To be candid I was never a bit sure – not of the Cumann people – but of [Woodrow] Wilson and the big businesses and the ruling classes of America.

I never do believe in the top dogs of any country; international finance holds so many temptations and generation after generation of politicians and rulers in every country in the world always seem to succumb to them.

So I think it's wonderful how you and the others have succeeded in getting such support for Ireland; it must have been a desperate job, thinking of it over here it seems like a miracle. I have been 'on the run' for the last week and so have not much time for thought and leisure to write, as I must lie low in daylight. I cannot help wondering if last week's suppressions and oppressions mean that they realise that they have failed in America and are not bothering about public opinion over there any more; if so, it's only the beginning for us.

All here are very confident of ultimate success and prepared to face anything. I am going to try and write you a little account of things over here; up to this it was hard to find time. Now good bye and with all good wishes for Xmas and the New Year to you and all friends in America.

Mise i gCuis na hEireann,
Constance de Markievicz I.C.A., T.D.

To Eva   *'Somewhere in Ireland'.*
[Undated].

Beloved Old Darling,
I have succeeded in getting *Ossian* at last: it was evidently second-hand, as it was cut. P.S. O'Hegarty has been looking for it since before I was on the run. Awfully funny things are happening, and

we manage to have many a good laugh. The enemy raided Mrs Fahy and found only two women in the house. They tried to terrorise her into telling them where her husband was. In the middle of the altercation the lights went out. It was a penny-in-the-slot meter. The officer ordered her to put in a penny. She refused point-blank. 'Put it in yourself,' she said, and watched them relighting the gas. They went away empty-handed, the officer saying that they would get him in spite of her.

I have not been able to get either grey stockings or yellow shirt. Maybe they will turn up when we have forgotten all about them as two places said they would try and get them for me.

Now bye bye darling.

Best love from,
C de M
PS: Did I leave a very untidy manuscript with you when last seen?

To Eva   'On the Run'.
                                                           [January 1920].

Dearest Old Darling,
You were an angel to send me such an interesting parcel. Thank you so much, and Esther too, for her book.

I sent a hamper between the two of you. I hope you got it all right. I had to get someone to choose the contents, as I was taking no risks before Christmas, as I did so want to have one at liberty. I told them to put in a turkey for Esther and other carnivorous friend!

It is awfully funny being 'on the run'! I don't know which I resemble most: the timid hare, the wily fox, or a fierce wild animal of the jungle! I go about a lot, one way and another, and every house is open to me and everyone is ready to help. I fly round town on my bike for exercise, and it's too funny seeing the expression on the policemen's faces as they see me whizz by! There are very few women on bikes in the winter, so a hunted beast on a bike is very remarkable.

Things are going ahead alright, so it does not much matter. People are subscribing to the [1st Dáil] Loan, in spite of, or perhaps because of, the fact that it has been made a jail-able crime by the enemy.

I wonder how you are getting along and how you spent Christmas. I had two Christmas dinners at the two extremes of Dublin and had quite a cheery time, everyone congratulating me on not having been at home!

Poor Alderman [Tom] K. [Kelly]! No one can understand why he was taken. He is a pacifist and he was never mixed up with anything violent. The housing of the poor and building up industries was his line. His nickname, given to him by himself, was 'the Man of Peace'. Some of them think that a 'plot' is being fabricated to prove that everyone who has been keeping rather quiet was engaged in secretly conspiring to shoot policemen! But I think that this is too absurd a lie, even for Lloyd George, McPherson and Co.!

You can write to me at any friend's address or at Liberty Hall. I always keep in touch when I move around, and my letters get to me all right.

Best love to you both.

Mise do chara,
Constance de Markievicz I.C.A., T.D.

On 15 January, municipal local elections were held using proportional representation for the first time; many seats went to Sinn Féin. A total of forty-three women were elected.

To Eva   *'On the Run'.*
February 1920.

Dearest Old Darling
A thousand thanks for your letter and lovely gift, which actually got to me in time! I was delighted and overjoyed and surprised. It's wonderful to have a birthday 'on the run'. It's an awfully funny experience. Mrs. C. will tell you some of it.

I spoke five times for various women in the elections and had some very narrow shaves. At one place I spoke for Joan [Hanna Sheehy Skeffington], and they sent an army, just about an hour too late. At another, I wildly and blindly charged through a squad of armed police, sent there to arrest me, and the crowd swallowed me up and got me away. The children did the trick for me.

Of course I don't keep quiet, and the other night I followed some of the army of occupation round about the streets. They had a huge covered wagon, and they seized some fellows and put them inside and searched them. They charged the crowd with bayonets too, and children were knocked down and terrified and women too.

Shawn [Seán MacBride] and some boys were held up by detectives last night when they were leaving the public library. One of them said he thought there was a detective watching the people reading, when two men stepped past them and poked revolvers at them through their pockets, in the American way, and said that they were talking of them, and demanded to know what they were saying. Of course they just humbugged, and the two men finally moved away.

With regards to Staskou's box: I already told you that it was looted by the enemy; some of the things I have, but there is nothing that he could possibly wear. So instead of sending him rubbish, I will give them some. Write him and tell him that the box was looted and tell him to send measures and list of what he would like. I could send stuff unmade or get a suit made here – I would go to £20. Stockings, underclothes or anything that he would like – tell him that things are dear here and not to expect much. I would like to send the little wife something too, if I knew her size.

Now best love darling and many thanks. Mrs C. is starting a day sooner than she intended so I could get butter for you.

Love from,
Con

To Eva   *[No address, no date; c. late February 1920].*

Dearest Old Darling,

I was much relieved to read the list of things that Staskou wants! It does not look as if he were in any great straits to live! I had quite a happy laugh when I read the list of 'frivolities' that he wants. Evidently he can't be in serious want, or any real danger. Such a blessing. I doubt if one could get all he wants for £20! Of course he has no idea of prices. Do you think that anyone could be found to bring him sweets? Stockings, handkerchiefs and sweets and tobacco are the only things that would be practical to send. There is no use sending hats, gloves or shoes on chance. I can't get at any of his things at present, and I think it really would be folly to send him things like English novels just now. I fancy that the camera, handbag and footwear, etc., were all stolen. The clothes were all too small. He exchanged his cabin trunk for mine and it has vanished.

Of course I will send him things in place of them in time, but just now seems rather a bad time. When I was on the Continent, English cameras were a great nuisance, for you could not get plates to fit and it would probably be better for him to get a French or German camera. Would not the person who will take clothes bring a business letter (open) just to tell him these things?

I am sorry, too, that there was no woman in the Albert Hall. I suppose that Mrs Skeff. could not get away. She is president of the Court of Conscience, Mrs Clarke of the Children's Court, and Mrs Wyse Power chairman of the Public Health Board, so the women have done well in the Corporation. It was very difficult to get women to stand for municipal honours; it was part of our policy to run women. I could not get any woman to stand in either of the wards in St Patrick's. I got Mrs Clarke who, of course, headed the poll, and Mrs McGarry, a stranger to them, but the committee, mostly men, worked hard for her and it was given out that they had selected her because I was not qualified to stand myself, and more than all she is pleasant and has a good personality and the right kind of brains. But most of the people who got the votes got them because they were known personally to the voters, and men as well as women who were on our ticket did not get in, not being known.

Iseult is engaged to be married; a Mr [Francis] Stuart, cousin of Capt. White's. No money and no prospects; poetical and nice. I have not met him. Medhbh [Maud Gonne] of course is rather distracted as they want to get married at once and Iseult is both helpless and extravagant. She always had every pretty and luxurious thing she wanted and knows nothing about housekeeping and housework. Shawn is working hard to get into College, and Medhbh herself is very busy. She seems quite fit and well and is looking lovely, though thin.

It is rather wearying when the English Man Pack are in full cry after you, though I get quite a lot of fun out of it. Even the hunted hare must have a quiet laugh sometimes. You don't know what a joke it is sometimes to speak at meetings and get through with it in spite of their guns and tanks and soldiers and police.

I had some very narrow shaves. The other night I knocked around with a raiding party and watched them insult the crowd. I was among the people and I went right up to the Store Street Police Barracks where the military and police lined up before going home. Night after night they wake people up and carry off someone, they don't seem to mind who. Some of the people they took lately did not belong to our crowd at all. When they could not find Mick Staines, they took his old father, aged 60, and his baby brothers!

Mrs [Margaret] Crofts had a very funny scene with them. They found a pair of socks in her old room and asked whose they were in a most insulting manner. Of course, she gave it [to] them hot! She wound up by saying that even Sinn Féiners occasionally put on clean stockings, when they still continued to believe that they were not her husband's. Of course I can't tell you how people escape and where they all are because of the Enemy's thrice accursed spies who open our letters.

We all have very cheerful news from Dev and we feel sure that we are at the end of the British tyranny over here.

I was so glad to see that you were at the meeting in the Albert Hall. I wish I had thought of going over for it and having a glimpse of Joan.

Poor old Mrs C. – she very nearly died. She's a nice old thing, but such a flop. I don't know how she ever worried through, but people like her always are propped up and supported by strenuous friends. Now bye bye darling. I am going to try and look for some things for Staskou. Sweets would be better got in London and first one would have to find out if anyone would be good natured enough to bring them.

Yrs lovingly, i gCuis na hEireann,
Constance de Markievicz I.C.A., T.D.

In March 1920, Constance went to stay with the O'Carroll family; 'Auntie' remained for eight months. Also that month, Sir Neville Macready was appointed as Commander-in-Chief of the 20,000-strong English Army of Occupation in Ireland. The 'Black and Tans' and, later, the fearsome 'Auxiliaries' arrived. By August, Ireland was under martial law, yet anarchy reigned and 'Big Houses', including Lissadell, were targets for republicans.

To a Friend

[Fragment].
May 1920.

My latest news regarding myself is that I have just received what is commonly called a 'Death Notice from the Black Hand Gang in the police'. On paper they had taken the precaution to steal from us they had typed:

An eye for an eye
A tooth for a tooth
Therefore a life for a life.

I think there is no doubt that they are plotting to murder us and before doing so they are taking precautions to manufacture evidence to prove we assassinated each other. No action is too mean or low for the present government and its officials. Luckily we are not nervous and have the strength to go on just the same as before. One is a little more careful to try and be ready to die and that is all.

We heard our Aeriocht on Sunday – the annual commemoration of our Fianna Martyrs, and it was a tremendous success. The boys made Aunt Sallies in the form of hideous caricatures of police and soldiers painted on boards – these were a great attraction as well as being an educational form of amusement. It gives a boy a great sense of his own capabilities to shy sticks at a Peeler even if it's only a wooden effigy.

To Éamon de Valera in the USA   [Fragment; c. May 1920].

Just a few words to wish you luck and congratulate you. In spite of everything we go on just the same, and if they are clever we can always manage to go one better. The situation has brought such splendid boys to the front, such courage, brains and discretion, a rare combination.

You've done wonders. I expect great things but your tour has been beyond my wildest imaginings. We've all just received death notices from the police, on our stolen note paper too; but no-one seems to mind much.

Mountjoy Prison,
September 1920–July 1921

On 26 September, Constance, as a member of the renegade Dáil, was arrested after a trip into the Dublin mountains with Seán MacBride and Maurice Bourgeois, a visiting French journalist; they were detained in Mountjoy. Her Department of Labour continued its work first with Joe McGrath in charge and, after he was arrested, with Joe MacDonagh.

To Eva
'Remand',
Mountjoy Prison.
5 October 1920.

Dearest Old Darling,

Have just got a card from you, forwarded from Liberty Hall, which wonders most appropriately what I am doing! It must have been written somewhere about the time when I was laid by the heels again. It was very bad luck. I went for a weekend holiday with Seán [MacBride], and the motor car he was driving kept breaking down all the time. We had to spend Saturday night at a place somewhere among the Dublin mountains: I at a farm house and he and a French journalist at an inn. Coming back the same thing happened. Engines, horn and lamps all being out of order. The police pulled us up because of the tail lamp not being there: they asked for permit; he had none, so they got suspicious and finally lit a match in my face and phoned for the military.

All the King's horses and all the King's men arrived with great pomp and many huge guns and after a weary night in a police station, I found myself here on remand, 'til – to quote their own words – they 'decide' whether to bring a charge against me or not. It sounds comic opera, but it's the truth!

Your card, talking of heat and sunshine, sounds so delightful. It's bitter here. Storms of rain and a light frost. A hurricane two nights ago.

Did you see they [the IRA] raided Joss? I heard a very funny account. He met them in the hall and let them look everywhere with a broad grin on his face telling them that everything had been handed over to the police. They trotted around the house and looked everywhere and found nothing and they were all very friendly; but when they'd finished, they just went through to the garden and dug and unearthed all they wanted. I would like to have seen his face. The whole performance must have been so funny. I wonder so what Molly thought of it all.

I saw such an appreciative note on a book Esther wrote the other day: something just published about Art and the Renaissance. It was since I was here, so I could not keep it for you.

I wonder whether you will ever get this. How long are you staying in Florence? It must be heavenly. I wonder if you love all the places I loved. I suppose it is all getting spoilt and modern. Half its charm was its old-worldness, and the absence of the English with their Baedekers, bother and bad manners. There used to be only a small and select colony, which we avoided. Do you know any Italian people? I believe they are very exclusive and don't like the English too much. I'd love to see the front of the Duomo and go up to San Miniato and look down at the sunset. I wonder where your hotel is. We stayed in a pension in the Piazza Cavour. Poor old Squidge. I wonder how she is. She was great value in Florence as she knew all about everything, and was nearly as good as a guide book! How she loved Savonarola! I could never quite forgive him his bonfires of vanities, so much beauty must have been burnt.

I've been working so hard these last few months, and quite successfully. Nothing is held up, even for an hour, by my removal. You'll be glad to hear that I am not on hunger strike at present.

Now goodbye darling, best love to you both.

Your loving Con

To Eva   *Mountjoy Prison.*
                                                  16 October 1920.

Dearest Old Darling,
I have no facilities, alas!, for sending postcards and obviously
my last letter must have been stolen or you would have got it by
now, as three cards took three and four days to come. Post marks
(Italian) were very legible. I never thought of noticing letter. I will
only say that I am well and cheerful, as usual, and that I should
wish that I was with you, only that I know I am more useful where
I am.
    So goodbye and all my love to you both,

Mise do chara i gCuis na hEireann,
Constance Georgine Gore-Booth Dunin Markievicz

To Jennie Wyse Power   *Mountjoy [Female] Prison.*
                                                  16 October 1920.

My dear Friend,
    I want you to send a P.C. (picture) to my sister –
    Hotel de Grande Bretagne,
    Lung'Arno,
    Florence.
    Just to say I am all right and well and cheerful. I don't think she
could have got my letter, and post cards have a knack of getting
through all right.
    I was very glad to see Mrs McW. She is so charming.
    I wonder whether Nancy will come next. I won't take any visit
unless I am sure, on the chance of missing her. Isn't it extraordinary
how I am being kept? I don't understand it at all.
    Now goodbye.

Mise do chara i gCuis na hEireann,
Constance Georgine Gore-Booth Dunin Markievicz

To Maud Gonne MacBride *'Remand',*
Mountjoy Prison.
20 October 1920.

My Dearest Medhbh [Maud],
Very many thanks for the delicious fruit you sent me. It is so refreshing and pleasant to get fruit and flowers in a jail. I am spending my time trying to get ahead with Irish, but it's very difficult without a teacher. I wish you would send an odd picture card to Eva, Hotel Grande Bretagne, Florence, and tell her that I am all right. It's so bad for her to be worried, and she does so worry about me.

I saw that Seaghan [Seán MacBride] got out all right. I was so glad. The police have finally given me back my clothes and toilet things, and all the contents of the bag are safe. I suppose someone is busy trying to concoct a charge against me. It takes a long time. I was wondering if anything would be planted in my bag!

Now goodbye and best love,

Mise do chara i gCuis na hEireann,
Constance de Markievicz

To Eva *Mountjoy Prison.*
27 October 1920.

Darling,
Just a scrawl to tell you that I'm very well and 'quite calm', as Wee Ga used to say. There's no use putting anything in about myself, as it would never reach you if I did!

Clare sent me two lovely cards from 'somewhere in Europe' – a great joy. I hope the 'flu is better. Do take care.

Where is the lovely picture of Florence taken from? The one with the high terrace in the foreground? So glad you like San Miniato. I loved it best of all, I don't quite know why, but all through the years I keep the memory of it, San Marco and the Campanile dearer than anything else.

How I'd love to go to Italy with you and see all those wonderful places and things again! I suppose it is very much changed, but it must always be beautiful. I hope that you are not going to come in for trouble there. Things seem to be boiling up and now my beloved darling, goodbye and God bless you. Love to Esther.

Your loving,
Constance de Markievicz

To Eva   *Mountjoy Prison.*
                                                                5 November 1920.

Dearest Old Darling,
Still you find me here and still untried. I was arrested on September 26th. My friends all try and console me by saying that I am safer here than anywhere! And I suppose it's true. So glad that you heard from my two friends, I asked them both to write and give you news of me. I think that you are very wise to stay in the Riviera, it's a pity though that Esther has to go, so you will be lonely.

Isn't the British parliament a disgrace to civilisation? I don't understand the English people at all. The governing classes seem to be such unmitigated brutes and the rank and file such unmitigated fools, and slaves. I sometimes think the pushing scheming hypocritical and godless crowd are of a different race, that they have inherited the inhuman nature of the Norman conquerors who conquered so sorely and tricked and lied and burnt their way down the centuries and that the common people are the simple futile and cowardly Anglo-Saxons who were conquered in one battle and never heard of again becoming slaves, hewers of wood and drawers of water for their conquerors, changing their religion for them, fighting their battles, and building up wealth for them.

Haven't the miners made fools of themselves! After all the talk they collapse like a pin pricked tyre at the first jab from the enemy. Sylvia [Pankhurst] seems to be one of the few progressive sorts. I think there must be a drop of Celtic blood in her. I am quite proud of my cousin-brother-in-law [Cecil L'Estrange Malone]. He'll soon be locked up if he goes on; how respectable the family is getting. I laugh when I think of the heavy respectability of Joss. His last speech in the English House [of] Lords was the speech of a 'hairy Bolshie'.

Now goodbye darling.

Very best love from yours lovingly,
Constance de Markievicz

To Josslyn Gore-Booth   *'Remand',*
Mountjoy F. Prison.
8 November 1920.

My dear Joss,
Have you got any papers concerning the letting of St Mary's? Mr Cochrane has referred me to you, if so please send them to Mr Noyk esq (solicitor), Star Buildings, 12 College Street, Dublin.

If you remember you saw after the letting of it in 1918 to a Mr Ellis, who now wants to buy it and I am thinking of selling it as with the increase of rates, it only brings in £11 per year and I can do much better with the money he is prepared to give.

Yrs,
Constance de Markievicz

To Eva   *'Remand',*
Mountjoy Prison.
26 November 1920.

Dearest Old Darling,
Do you get your letters forwarded on from Florence, because Dulcibella was writing to you just as you were leaving?

I have now been locked up for two months. However, I believe it is all for the best. I love your postcards. They are such a lovely little bit of colour in this dismal place. Medhbh [Maud] Gonne has just been to see me and was most pleasant. I do hope they'll let her alone. She looks very ill and worn.

I have just finished working three little blue birds on a black riband for you. They are very gaudy. Do you remember the picture I sent you out of Holloway Jail? I must see if I can send you the riband when you come back, but maybe they'll think it a 'plot' if I ask to do so! My time here is spent in working and in learning Irish. It is impossible to paint under present conditions.

Aren't you delighted with Cecil [Malone]? Of course he missed a chance at his trial, but still, he's made a good start. It is curious how thirty seems to be an age for people to start on arduous and dangerous paths. I only hope he goes on. One almost pities Joss with his relations. Cecil was the white-headed boy of his family. I wonder if they will be decent to him or if it will be the unpardonable sin. People are so odd and mixed in their ideas nowadays. To live up to the principles that everybody preaches and teaches seems to be the only crime for which there is no forgiveness.

Mr Nevinson [British journalist] is over here again. I hope to see him. He is one of the real, nice, honourable men who are so often found among the English. What puzzles me with most of them is that they never want to hear the truth, and that the most they expect from their rulers is to conceal all disagreeable and unpleasant facts and dangerous, new ideas. It must be so dull to go on and on like that.

Now goodbye my darling.

Much love from,
Constance de Markievicz

On 21 November, another 'Bloody Sunday', the IRA, under orders from Michael Collins, shot dead fourteen people, most of them alleged undercover British agents and many still in their beds. Later that afternoon, members of the feared Auxiliary Division, along with the police, opened fire on the crowd at a Gaelic football match in Croke Park, killing eleven and wounding at least sixty with three more dying later. Constance could hear the shooting from her cell in nearby Mountjoy Prison.

At her court martial, which finally started on 2 December, she was charged with organising Na Fianna ten years earlier. On 24 December, she was sentenced to two years hard labour.

On 11 December, Cork city centre was set on fire by Auxiliaries, causing outrage. Twelve days later, on 23 December, the Government of Ireland Act was passed, legislating for two Irish parliaments; one in Dublin, one in Belfast. Michael Collins took over as acting president following the arrest of Arthur Griffith, and de Valera returned to Ireland after his eighteen-month sojourn in the USA. The War of Independence continued.

To Eva   *Mountjoy Prison.*
                                              6 December 1920.

Darling,

I was delighted to get yours and paper re prison reform. Like most things, of course, the man who is able to start it and carry it out is the one indispensable factor, and such men are rare. Under the present English system of making such appointments, it would be very unlikely that such a man would ever get the job.

You are quite right when you say things are lurid here! The Croke Park affair lasted 40 minutes by my watch and there were machine-guns going. It felt like being back in the middle of Easter Week. Croke Park is quite close. It's a miracle that so few were killed.

I haven't given up the Bolshies yet: I believe that they will greatly improve conditions for the world. Of course, I agree with you in disliking the autocracy of any class, but surely if they have the sense to organise education, they can abolish class. While they are menaced by the moneyed classes of the whole world, their only hope lies in the success of a strong central government: a tyranny in fact, but once the pressure is relieved, if Lenin survives, and he has not lost his original ideals, we may hope.

Of course, they may go mad with the idea of Empire, and go out with their armies to force the world to come under their ideas and do awful things in the name of freedom, small nationalities, etc. But even so, they have done something. The French Revolution gave France new life, though all their fine ideas ended in horrors and bloodshed and wars. The world, too, gained. Nothing else would have given courage to the underdog and put fear into the heart of the oppressor in the way it did. I believe all the reforms at the beginning of the nineteenth century have their roots in the Terror.

I don't agree about people being sheep. I don't find that here, except among a very small crowd indeed. Everyone wants to know, and reads and thinks and talks, especially the young. In Belfast you have the other thing – a mob of fools, 'thug'-led – but the rest of the country is wonderfully self-controlled, patient and heroic. I have always used my influence towards decentralisation, and to make people think and act independently.

How are the women doing in Italy? This is being an education to them here. Their heroism and spirit of self-sacrifice is wonderful, but outside the towns they want their initiative faculties developing. There has been less physical restraint on the actions of women in Ireland than in any other country, but mentally the restrictions seem to me to be very oppressive. It is hard to understand why they took so little interest in politics as a sex, when you consider that both Catholics and Dissenters (men) laboured under all their disabilities and yet remained politicians.

I am so glad you are staying on in the sun. Do look after yourself, and whatever happens, don't come here. You are too like me to go about safely. I loved your long letter. Any foreign gossip is interesting. You must be very lonely without Esther. I am well and quite warm and cheerful.

Best love old darling and take great care of yourself.

Lovingly yours,
Constance de Markievicz

To Eva

Dearest Old Darling,

D.[Dulcibella]'s address is: Glendalough House, Annamoe, Co. Wicklow. How I would love you to see it! It's tucked away amongst the hills and lakes, behind a little village. A low, straggling house of grey stone with a porch – quite unlike the usual kind of Irish house. Some of the windows open on to the lawn, which is a steep slope down. You go up a lot of steps into the Hall, and there are lovely fir trees and woods behind the house. You climb up onto the moor in a few minutes and look across the mountain tops. In front, the ground slopes to a mountain torrent. The place is a sun-trap, in the midst of the bleakest mountain scenery.

I was awfully interested in your bit about prisons, and I am sending you a bit of the *Irish Times* in exchange. I wonder if you'll get it. They see danger in the most extraordinary things these days.

Nora Connolly has been to see me and is full of Russian news. Glowing accounts as to organisation of railways and industries, in face of almost insuperable difficulties: but says they are terribly ruthless to anyone who is 'an enemy of the Republic'. I hope they won't treat Lenin as the French treated Danton.

Do you remember my talking to you about my 'special' work and all my difficulties and doubts? Well, I got it so under way that it goes on just as well without me. That wasn't too bad work for an untrained fool, was it?

I suppose now that I can tell you that I was tried by court-martial for 'conspiracy', and that the 'conspiracy' was the Boy Scouts! They have not made up their minds just what they'll do with me. I think they dislike me more than most. The whole thing is Gilbertian, for we have carried on for eleven years. Anyhow, it's a fresh 'ad.' [advertisement] for the boys!

I am now working hard at Irish. It's awfully interesting. There are such an extraordinary number of shades of sound in it. The people must have had wonderfully subtle musical ears. I wonder how much of the history of a race lies in the language.

Best love from,
Constance de Markievicz

To Eva   *'Pending Sentence',*
                                          Mountjoy Prison.
                                          11 December 1920.

Dearest Old Darling,
Your almanac has just come. It's a joy to see all that lovely colour in the midst of this greyness. To appreciate colour, one wants to do without it for a bit.

I am so sorry that you are ill and I wish to goodness that I was with you. I learnt a lot about minding the sick when I had my two invalids in Holloway Jail, and I didn't make a bad hand at it at all, in spite of the many disadvantages I was born with.

Don't bother about me here. As you know, the English ideal of modern civilisation always galled me. Endless days of exquisite food and the eternal changing of costume bored me always to tears and I prefer my own to so many people's company. To make 'conversation' to a bore through a long dinner party is the climax of dullness. I don't mind hard beds or simple food. None of what you might call the 'externals' worry me. I have my health and I can always find a way to give my dreams a living form. So I sit and dream and build up a world of birds and butterflies and flowers from the sheen in a dew-drop or the flash of a sea-gull's wing. Everyone who has anything to do with me is considerate and kind, and the only bore is being locked up, when there is so much to be done.

I have just read the lives of Tolstoy and of Danton. I rather love the latter. The former I don't pretend to understand. He was so imbalanced, and he compromised with all his principles – like an English trades union leader. I am now reading *Eothen* [A. W. Kinglake's account of a trip to the Middle East]. What an oddity

Lady H. Stanhope was! Jail is the only place where one gets time to read.

I am interested in what you say about Italy. It has gone through such vicissitudes that one feels it must have learnt a good deal. Co-operation is good, but by no means a panacea. The old problem always remains: how to prevent all the money and power, etc., getting into the hands of a few, and they establishing themselves as a ruling tyrant class.

I'm beginning to believe that everything must begin from the schools, and that only when all children of a nation have the same education will they have the same chances in life and learn to look after the people as a whole. Of course, education will have to be different, but now, in England, a few are trained to bully and rule, and the mass is brought up and educated to be fit only to be slaves. In Ireland we are not so bad, as local and family history educates the children, so our minds are more receptive and more free.

Now I've written you a long letter of rubbish and I have come to the end of my paper.

Bless you darling.

Yours lovingly,
Constance de Markievicz

To her mother, Lady Gore-Booth   *Mountjoy Female Prison.*
                                             11 December 1920.

My dear Gaga,
What a lot of gossips you all are! I didn't answer Joss, because I did not want to write a cross letter, and I resented his interference.

The letter he wrote to the tenant put me in quite a false position. I have made up my mind that if there is any more bother, I shan't sell St Mary's. Perhaps I will live there some day. It will go down in rates every year as the lease shortens and the rates go up. But that can't be helped. I was thinking of buying another house later – but only thinking. They say that prices are going to go down [at] rather a run.

How you all must be talking about Cecil! Truly he is wonderful. I can't say how I admire his self-sacrifice. It is quite heroic when you think of the career and riches that he must have renounced for his principles.

Now bye bye,
Best love,

Yrs,
Constance de Markievicz

To Eva   *'Pending Sentence',*
                                                 Mountjoy Prison.
                                                 15 December 1920.

Dearest Old Darling,
I do wonder how you are and whether you are being looked after properly in Bordighera [Eva was in Italy]. I wonder where Esther is lecturing and on what. I should love to hear her.

I suppose you saw all about Cork – also the explanations! Some men have a wonderful capacity for lying! What puzzles me is why they don't do it better. For instance, it was silly to assert that the City Hall caught fire from Patrick St. I know the city well, and a broad river and many streets lie between the two areas. An ordinary human being like myself is puzzled when the cleverest liars in the world state things that are so easily contradicted. The extraordinary policy of lying and perjury surprises me anew every day. I'd no idea people were so bad.

Italy seems to be rather lively still. I hope you won't come in for trouble. Greece makes me laugh, also Armenia. I think that they must at last have realised the capacity for lying on the part of Western politicians. I have been hearing first-hand news of Russia. They have had a terrible lot to contend with, but they have done some wonderful reconstructive work. Of course they, the workers, were horrified with the number of executions, and thought them horribly cruel and drastic, but, comparing them to the French Terror, said that these were just, according to their own laws, and said that accusations had to be proved, and were proved, quite honestly; but that anyone proved to be acting against the interest of the new regime was remorselessly executed. Nothing approaching the orgies of appalling murders that Robespierre indulged in has occurred, although the circumstances, in many respects, are similar.

India seems to be getting pretty warm too. I see that volunteers have been 'proclaimed', according to the papers, and they don't do that for nothing. Ours were only proclaimed about a year and three months ago.

How one longs for peace. The silly old League of Nations is talking pompous rubbish (for the benefit of Democracy, I suppose) about reductions of armaments, and each one of them is only intent to find out what his neighbour is going to do in the way of navies, etc., and tip his boss to go one better.

Tell me, do the Italians go in for polished brown leather boots and gaiters? The legs of the English Army of Occupation were one of the things that struck me at my court-martial. Such a lot of time must be wasted polishing them!

Now goodbye darling and best love. Clare sent me a P.C. of such a lovely mysterious track up a deserted and rocky mountain valley.

Constance de Markievicz

To Hanna Sheehy Skeffington   *'Pending Sentence',*
                                       Mountjoy Fem. Prison.
                                       17 December 1920.

A chara dil,
Many thanks for yours. I would love to see you – also to get my sister's gift. Could you see Mrs Power about coming to visit me? Or Miss L. [Lily] O'Brennan? Otherwise you might get here and find someone else in! I had to make some arrangements about visitors because of things that happened in Cork. I saw that you have been very busy in England.

With kind regards from,
Constance de Markievicz

To Eva   'Pending Sentence',
                                             Mountjoy Prison.
                                           20 December 1920.

Dearest Old Darling,
I am enraptured with the blue bird. I think it is just perfect. It was
sent into the jail for me to-day.

I wonder so what you saw in the papers. It's no use trying to
write the truth to you. The papers here were not too bad at all.
I can't see myself how any one with a sense of humour could
seriously regard a child's organisation as a 'conspiracy', but any
stick does to beat the Irish rebel with!

I long to see you. If I ever get out, we must have a week together,
somewhere warm and pretty. You'll have to wait for a present!
There are complications. My love and thoughts and good wishes
and prayers are with you all the time. Take great care of yourself,
and run no risks.

The world seems to be in an awful state. One wonders so about
Japan and America and England. My belief is that the English would
not mind another war. They don't know what to do with their
unemployed. I am sorry for the poor in places like Manchester
these days.

I am now reading the *Conquest of Peru* [by William H. Prescott].
It's so modern. All those atrocities were done in the name of
Christianity and of all the noble virtues – just like to-day. A nation
of quiet, peaceful people was wiped out and their civilisation
destroyed because the Spaniards wanted gold. The only hopeful
thing is that the Spaniards went down, and if corruption drags
a nation down and breaks up an Empire, we ought soon to see a
debacle such as has never been seen before!

Best love darling and good luck for the New Year.

Lovingly,
Constance

To Eva   *'Pending Sentence',*
Mountjoy Prison.
24 December 1920.

Dearest Old Darling (Pen gone wrong),
Your brooch is the greatest joy. Colour and design both perfect. The lovely card and long letter have just reached me, and both are a joy.

You have no idea of the awful things that are happening here and how wonderful the people are, so determined and so self-controlled. The enemy have found more than they expected. At other times, when they got rid of 'leaders', the country sat down, but today leaders count for very little. They are mouthpieces and keep order, and there are rank after rank of men and women capable of taking their places. It is wonderful how they understand the international possibilities – isolation, etc.; everyone realises too that it is by suffering, doing and sticking out that we will win. Great attempts have been made to divide us, but nobody differs about fundamentals, and everybody has their own ideas about details of policy, which they discuss quite amiably and openly. There is no jealousy, and no one is out for self.

The whole world situation is extraordinary. The triangle – England, America and Japan – is to my mind the most exciting thing of all. Against whom is the American Fleet being built? I met an Indian prince this summer who told me of his ambitions to form a great Asiatic Empire! Imperialism gone yellow and brown. Then there are the Bolshies, who are working for yellow and brown communes. One feels that both sides would want Australia. Harding [William G., elected president of the USA on 4 November 1920] was the candidate we most favoured of the possible two, though all were sympathetic, and Dev, etc. naturally would not take sides in a purely American political campaign. I think those who rule in America must want anti-English feeling stirred up, or they would have locked us all up, as they did the Bolshie crowd.

I heard one tale about the Vatican. Balfour and Co were very anxious to get a 'nuncio' (I think that's the word) for London, who should have jurisdiction over the 'British Isles'. A cardinal they would have liked [Cardinal Francis]; Bourne [Archbishop of

Westminster] I'm sure. But it didn't come off. Instead they found the Vatican singing 'The Soldiers' Song' and flourishing the Tricolour.

Did you hear that Ll. George arranged with [Jimmy] Thomas for Labour to prevent munitions being shipped for use against Bolshies? He wanted to trade with them, and keep in with the other crowd by promising them war material. I quite agree about the [blacked out by ink blot]. We must puzzle him so when we won't be bought.

So glad you saw the *Irish Times*. It was much the best. What appals me so is the tricky [blacked out by ink blot] I can't understand how they get so many to play their game. They swear on oath again and again that they can account for every cartridge in a barrack and know when one is missing. And they swear just as often that they can get no information when half a dozen lorries full of men shoot off hundreds of cartridges [blacked out by ink blot]. But, of course, you see the papers.

It will be three months come St Stephen's Day that I was arrested. Isn't it Gilbertian to pretend that the Fianna is a conspiracy? It was started in 1909, and has always been open and never secret. I asked them could they point to one 'cowardly attack' on the armed forces of the Crown by little boys. It was an awful performance: after being shut up alone for two months to be suddenly brought up before eight 'judges', plus prosecutors, be-wigged barristers, enemy witnesses, etc., and surrounded by bayonets! It was very bewildering. I'm glad you thought I did not do so badly.

Now bye bye and love and good wishes to all friends. How I wish I was one of the crowd.

Yours lovingly,
Constance de Markievicz

To Eva   *'Two Years Hard Labour',*
                                        Mountjoy Female Prison.
                                              30 December 1920.

My dearest Old Darling,
A happy New Year to you all. You should see how gay my cell is, with all the lovely cards stuck around. Don't forget to thank Clare for two lovely P.C.s she sent me from Germany. Tell her she should

come over and help the starving Irish children, though we are not as yet so distressful as Central Europe, thank God.

I am so engrossed by my Irish studies. I know you'll say 'Jack of all trades!' but anyhow, if I can only go on for two years, I will be master, and I began as a duty, not as a pleasure, but luckily find it most entertaining and quite different from any other language I ever dabbled in. The letters have so many different sounds each that it is as if you had an enormous alphabet. Then the words have sort of inflexions in front as well as behind and, above all, it's a language of idioms, and corresponds little with any other language. There is no verb 'to have' (I think national character is shown in a language, and that shows that we are not a covetous and aggressive race). It seems to have developed along the lines of the softest and most subtle sounds and to be capable of very definite and subtle expression of shades of thought. I wish we were together. I'm sure it would appeal to your poetic instincts, and that you'd get all sorts of ideas from it. It often seems to me that Yeats got most of the charm of his writing from it.

I have just been reading *Celtic Twilight* [by W.B. Yeats] again, was surprised to find it so bad. Egoistic and frothy bubble, but a lovely poem in front. The subject is so beautiful too and he seems to make it so common, like Andrew Lang's fairy tales.

Things seem to be moving slowly here. Do you realise that Æ prophesied all this and worse and that a great 'Avata' (I don't know how to spell – it might be Avatar) is to come out of the mountain country round Fermanagh and lead Ireland to victory. He should be about 20 years old now. He told me this years ago when blood and flames seemed incredible and of the dark ages. We'll hope the end will come true as well. I believe myself that it is only a question of holding out, and that it is by sacrifice that we shall win. The people are so wonderful in their steadfastness. English labour leaders might open their eyes to our willingness to starve, suffer or even die for our ideals and our willingness to forgo the extra pence they are always following for themselves.

Love darling to you and all friends.

From,
Constance de Markievicz

To Eva

H.M.F. Prison,
Mountjoy.
New Year's Day 1921.

Dearest Old Darling,
I was so delighted to get your P.C. yesterday. I have written you twice since I got the lovely bird. Mrs Skeffington brought it over and sent it up at once. She was so afraid of its being stolen in a raid. It's a real joy. I also got an almanac and a triptych card. Both beautiful. I can't remember how to spell 'triptych'. Where the 'y' should go is a mystery to me. I wonder so how many of my letters you get. The post seems to be awfully unreliable; one Christmas card I got took five days to come from England.

It rather amused me to see that for starting Boy Scouts in England B.[Baden] Powell was made a baronet and I've always heard that he did not really start them and that it was a woman. I suppose, though, that he more or less ran them and made them a success. I bet he did not work as hard as I did from 1909 'til 1913.

It's been so warm here the last few days that some of the birds started singing, and pigeons were carrying bits of straw about in their mouths, and cooing and bowing to each other in the most absurd way.

I see that D'Annunzio's reign is over [in Italy] and that he says he would like to come to Ireland! I don't think he'd like it if he got here, at least, judging from the only book of his I ever read. I think that he'd find us too strait-laced. You could certainly write the most thrillingly exciting books of adventure, telling of hair's breadth escapes and daring deeds, but for love affairs people have little time to spare. Kathleen comes first, though people get married on the run, and go on 'running'. This last year many babies were born, whose fathers were on the run. It's awfully hard on the mothers. Curfew, too, is terrible, for you can't get a doctor. However, the women are as brave as brave, and though they suffer terribly both mentally and physically they put on a brave face and you'd never guess.

Now good luck to you and E. and all friends in the New Year.

Best love from,
Constance de Markievicz
Cheerful though captive!

To Eva   *Mountjoy Prison.*
                                              7 January 1921.

Dearest Old Darling,
I hope that you have got some of my letters by now. This will be the
last for some time! Don't you worry about me, though. I am all right.
I have written three times to thank you for the lovely brooch. It's a
joy and came quite all right and in time for Christmas. I am working
very hard at Irish. If I can learn at my time of life, I think it will be
a record. I wrote you a lot about it in my last letter, which you may
have got by now. One thing I like in it is the liberty. Now English ties
you down; if you are going to be considered educated, you must
speak and spell in the same way as those who are belonging to the
ruling clique. They clip words and talk slang and it's all very ugly.
Now in Irish, localisms are not like English accent, but they add
expression and beauty. Spelling varies and words vary, and most
of the changes seem to be made to soften and beautify the sound;
while in English much seems to be sacrificed to speed.
    I think that probably the language had a good deal to say to the
development of the pretty soft Irish voices one hears everywhere. I
often wish that the Irish musical scale, with its quarter-tones, had
not been civilised out of existence. I feel that there is some faint
echo of it in the innumerable vowel sounds that glide into each
other and seem almost interchangeable. I am so full of it all that I
must write about it, though maybe it's dull to you, but there's not
much to write about in here. I am sure we are going to have some
great authors, once the younger generations get in on the language.
    Are you writing anything much? I wish we had you here for
a laureate! I'd love to see you writing to order of the Republic!
Though I'm afraid you'd only get tragic themes, with now and then
a dash of broad farce.

Poor Sylvia [Pankhurst] seems to be in a bad way [convicted of sedition in January 1921]. If her friends played their cards well, at any rate, they could get her made a 'political' after the release of *The Freeman's Journal* men here. I'm afraid too that she has very little tact and makes it much worse for herself than it needs be

I wonder what your plans are and I do hope that you will stay in the land of the sun for the present. I think that England is getting into a very bad way and anything might happen there. After the Napoleonic Wars, they met the trade depression by shipping off hundreds of jailbirds (political, labour) to convict settlements. They have not got that outlet now, and goodness knows what a more educated proletariat will do when starving. It's an awful lookout everywhere. Ll. George is still busy screwing down safety valves.

Now darling goodbye and much love. When I get out, we must have a holiday together, and Esther too, somewhere beautiful and peaceful. Perhaps in the great New Republic! Who knows? Don't come over here just now. It would not be safe for you.

Yrs lovingly,
Constance de Markievicz

To Josslyn Gore-Booth   *Mountjoy Female Prison.*
                                             18 January 1921.

My dear Joss,
The question you ask is exactly the one that I consider you have no right to ask – with respect to your position as administrator, I understood that you were given certain powers to deal with my affairs for my convenience and that those powers ceased automatically on my release. If this is not so, it is rather curious that you did not inform me of it, but by ceasing to interfere in my affairs led me to believe that I had control of them. Otherwise I should certainly have taken steps to find out my position and if I had not, I still do not believe that you have the power and you certainly have no moral right.

Have you any other documents of mine? Copy of marriage settlement, or will? If so please forward at once to Mr Noyk, Star Chambers, College Green.

Yours,
Constance de Markievicz

To Josslyn Gore-Booth
Mountjoy Female Prison.
'Without Prejudice'
31 January 1921.

My dear Joss,
I am very sorry to hear of Cousin Fran's [Josslyn's mother-in-law] death. I am sure that Molly feels it very much.

You say that you are not a lawyer, neither am I, but I have as much common sense as most people and I'm prepared to assert that in equity. You would find a great many lawyers take the following view – that an administrator appointed to administer the property of a person undergoing a 'life sentence' is appointed for the convenience of those with whom that person had business relations and to safeguard the property of that person for the use and enjoyment of that person at the end of the sentence (which is usually of 16 years duration). In this an administrator would differ from a trustee, who holds property in trust for the next generation, etc. I do not believe that any law would justify an administrator deliberately blocking a good sale of property and causing money to be lost because they wanted to force the owner to invest the money according to their own wishes. This is what you must have done; and more, for you have not only lost me the sale but you have lost me the tenant, who was only buying to sell again and who had got another house in the meantime.

If I had not trusted you absolutely I should certainly have gone into the matter on my release from Aylesbury. I believe that on my unconditional release that the powers you had automatically passed away, but that it would be necessary to go through some formal proceedings. I put this off because of the expense and it did not seem to me to be important as I trusted you and believed that you would never have abused the powers that you had acquired over me to act against my interests and cause me to lose money. I don't know how you reconcile it with your conscience.

I don't know what you meant by instructing your solicitors to act, which would be very expensive; as I don't know what more you can do than you've done, unless you mean that I will have to pay them. If that is so, I protest again, that the only responsibility you have to me is for my property, which is absolutely my own and not held in trust, and that you have no right to spend my money against my interests.

To repeat – you were appointed to protect my interests; i.e. my property not held in trust – from the sharks of the world while I was in prison, not to prevent my improving or increasing it after I should be released and though technically you may have the power to do so, I don't know how you justify yourself morally in using it in this way.

Yrs,
Constance de Markievicz

To Eva   *Mountjoy Prison.*
                                                                   1 April 1921.

Dearest Old Darling,
Just had a visit from Clare, which no doubt you already know. It was delightful and we had such a pleasant talk and she is such a joy to look at, all shimmering blues and soft, pretty draperies. I did not expect her, so you can imagine the excitement.

I grub away at my plot here and have got quite a lot of things in. It was a desert when I began and I don't believe it had been honestly dug. Few people share my love for digging deep. I have a few sweet-peas quite four inches high, which is a triumph. Most people are only sowing theirs. The eating peas are just coming up and the starlings and pigeons make war on everything.

How I envy you in the land of flowers! I wonder are there starlings in Italy? I remember things they called 'uccellini' [sparrows]– at least it sounded like that – but I don't know what they looked like with their feathers on as I always saw them, almost daily, in stews.

I am working hard at Irish and more and more interested every day. It is so picturesque and so utterly unlike anything else and much more difficult to learn. No other language helps you and it is all idioms and exceptions to every rule. I can write compositions and letters and I can read, of course, with a dictionary, and I think I could get what I wanted if I were stranded, but I can't really talk yet. I wish I knew why grammarians always search the world – or dictionaries – for the words you want least in a language, and give them to you to learn, and leave out the words you want every day. I can talk about hawks and flails, scythes, rye and barley, magicians, kings and fairies; but I couldn't find out how to ask for an extra blanket or a clean plate or a fork. I suppose I shall find out some day!

Have you been writing much poetry? I forget; did I ever send you a little book by Austin Clarke? He is the latest minor poet over here and he is quite unlike a modern. He is heroic and writes long yarns about kings and historical magnificence, which is very original, in this country, where the poets wander in dim twilight mixed with turf smoke, peopled with peasants and mystic beings with pale hands. Do you ever write what the writers call *vers libre*? To me they seem the last resource of the lazy and incompetent. Send me something of yours next time you write.

Italy certainly fills one with hope, Greece too, and Poland. We are the only people left in chains. Our people are wonderful; there is little fear of death among them, and heaven is so real to them that they look forward to meeting their friends there. The present persecutions seem to have brought the living and the dead into such close touch, it is almost uncanny.

It all makes one feel that they must win. The spiritual must prevail over the material in the end. We suffer, and suffering teaches us to unite and stand by each other. It also makes for us friends everywhere, while the policy of our enemies is leaving them friendless, and more ominous still it is utterly demoralising themselves and setting all the decent of their own people against them, as soon as they find out the truth.

A volley has just gone off suddenly, quite close. It has ceased to be a novelty or to make one jump, but it's an awful bore not being able to go and see what's up. Most nights one hears them and to me it's a wonder that more people are not killed. There were aeroplanes over this yesterday, which is usually a bad omen.

I was awfully sorry about Janey [Coffey, died 18 March 1921]. She was such a dear and there are so few of the old ones left. She somehow never grew old and only gave up bicycling quite a little time ago. A great many people will miss her and I was glad to hear that she was with friends and well looked after. Poor D. [son Diarmid?] will be very lonely, they were great pals. She spent all her life looking after other people.

I was delighted with your appearance in the snaps. I hope Esther is as well as you appear to be. I was awfully interested to hear that Reginald had staged a Pearse play. I wonder which? Now I have reached the limit and must say goodbye and God bless you. Love to you both, and now darling good night with all my love.

Constance de Markievicz

In April, Fr J. F. Sweetman OSB, founder of the Mount St Benedict's school in Gorey, Co. Wexford, attended by Staskou and Seán MacBride, visited Constance in Mountjoy Prison. He brought a gift from Eva of green and silver rosary beads blessed by Pope Benedict XV in Rome. On 24 May, a general election for parliaments in the north and south of Ireland was held, with Sinn Féin returning unopposed in 124 of 128 seats in the south. Constance was re-elected and joined by five other women. Sinn Féin refused to recognise two parliaments for Ireland. A day later, the Custom House in Dublin was set on fire by the IRA; three IRA men died and around eighty were detained. A truce was declared on 11 July after two years and almost six months of conflict.

To Eva   *Mountjoy Prison.*
                                                3 May 1921.

Dearest Old Darling,
It was such a joy getting the rosary and a visit from Father
Sweetman the other day. Please thank all concerned. It is really
beautiful. The combination of green and silver is a treat. Another
great joy is the last P.C. – Our Lady, Botticelli: red dress, blue cloak
and eastern headdress. I have a lot of your cards stuck up and I am
always looking at them.

Such a blessing to know that you are so well. It is a pity you
have to come back just now. How I'd love to see Florence again
and the country round! I did so love it long ago. I remember
catching butterflies wildly across hedges and ditches at Fiesole
and distressed Squidge quite unable to follow. Young ladies hadn't
found their legs in those days, and mine would have been quite up
to the mark – even in these days!

I have had a lot of bother with J. [Joss] about the house. He put
in a tenant and a good one. Tenant made a very good offer to buy
and to sell it again. Wrote to J. for title deeds. He sent them but
wrote to tenant that house under marriage settlement was under
control of trustees and money must be paid to them! Of course
this was a myth. When it was exploded, he declared he was still
administrator! and again blocked sale. Tenant got fed up and left
the house. J. tried to make me let him get hold of money or else
say where I wished to invest it. I don't get the point of it all, as
Adm. are appointed to look after things in your interest and the
place is absolutely mine to do what I like with. Anyhow I got the
great satisfaction of selling! I think I may be able to bring him to
book too, if it's not too much trouble and I wrote him some most
satisfying letters. It's being sold now and all traces of money will
disappear so if there are ever further administrators, there will be
nothing to administer!

In times of war it is better to have at least six different banking
accounts, all under different names! And all in different banks,
though it is awfully hard not to mix cheque books. If I die in a hurry,

there will be a real old treat for heirs. I did not tell you about this before because I did not want to worry you, but it's all right now.

My garden work is beginning to repay. Peas are six inches high and new seeds coming up every day. I've a pink carnation in bud that I am watching every day. We've had a spell of fearfully dry weather and a scorching sun, but today we had a nice soft rain, and the sun is now shining again, so the garden will be great tomorrow.

Irish is going ahead. I am beginning to get hold of more useful words. Half the difficulty comes from there being no grammars or modem literature. Everything Irish being smashed up in each generation since Eliz. of England's reign, the language never seems to have got consolidated into a complete whole. Some of the words exist in four or five different forms, and each little district is wildly keen to stick to its own form. I suppose it will take some time to get something worked out that everyone will accept. I am just through the whole of O'Growney and can write composition and read a bit, also talk a little. Were it any other language I should be able to talk quite well with the knowledge I have of words and grammar, but the idioms and exceptions to every rule are endless. If only the Lord would give us a grammarian who would organise facts like Otto and Arne [German grammarians] did. I rebel at learning bits of Connaught, Ulster and Munster, with a smattering of fifteenth century thrown in. Fancy if a German had to learn Cockney, Yorkshire and Somerset, with Chaucer thrown in.

It was awfully nice seeing Clare. She had such a pretty frock and a lovely Italian jewel and a shawl that was a dream and a treat to the eyes. Surrounded by ugliness and greyness, I delighted in your poem: 'humble-splendid' is beautiful. I wonder have you been reading German. Do send another verse next time you write. Gaga must have been shocked at your seeing the Pope. You must be great at Italian.

Father McGuinness is a delightful person. I made a speech at a party in his honour when I was on the run. 'The run' is awfully funny, I'd love to tell you some of the adventures and hair's breadth escapes. They are (the enemy) very clever about detail, but so often don't see the wood for the trees, and they don't understand simplicity and truth. That is their weakest point and where we score most. If you want to deceive an Englishman, always tell him the truth. They judge others by themselves. Now goodbye darling and best love to you both and do look after yourself.

Mise do chara i gCuis na hEireann,
Constance de Markievicz

To Eva   *Mountjoy Prison.*
                                                         8 June 1921.

Dearest Old Darling,
I had a visit from Mrs Kent today and quite forgot to ask her to write to you, and tell you how well I am. It is so difficult to remember to tell everything in the rush of a monthly visit. She told me that she was raided the other night and that the B. and T.s [Black and Tans] stole a bunch of my letters, written to her and her sister, some time before Christmas, from here, all of which had passed their own censor. I have been puzzling ever since as to their motive, for I can see no point in it at all, unless they mean to sell my autograph! And I never asked more than 6d. for that, and I did such hundreds for various just causes.

I was so delighted to hear of your deliverance from a crisis and wonder so all about it. I suppose I shall hear some day. J.[Joss] has sent me over £100! But I've my money's worth and intend to have more value. I've put my solicitor onto him, just to annoy for the present and when things are settled here, I believe I shall be able to get money back. I love getting at same's timorous priggery! I only hope he understood the letters I wrote.

I long to see your book, and I know I should love it. No philosophy worth speaking of has yet come out of Ireland. Yours sounds as if it might be philosophy, and it might, therefore, be epoch-making. Mind you send me a copy if it comes out before I do. I am sure it will be educational and they let me have educational books.

Just been reading *After the Peace* [H.N. Brailsford]. It's awfully enlightening. I am very sorry for the English working people. I don't think their leaders or their writers ever get to the bottom of the incredible wickedness of their rulers. Brailsford and others of his type seem to think them short-sighted and stupid. Over here we don't. We realise that the stupid blundering good nature of J.B. [John Bull] is the cleverest disguise for refined cruelty and unscrupulous self-seeking that could be invented. At the back of it all, the apparent and obvious stupidity that created famine and provokes strikes, there is a sinister motive. Certain people will always profit by all the misery.

I am wondering if the largest among the coal owners own oilfields and want to substitute oil for fuel and close some of their mines – and if it's a dodge to recruit for the British army! I hear that such a large number of those who signed on for three years are leaving as the time comes around. I hate to think of all the hungry children. England is desperately over-populated and I suppose that the population went up leaps and bounds while the people were not able to emigrate. I wonder how Sylvia is. If you see her, give her my love and tell her I hope she is none the worse. And Cecil – what effect has jail had on him? I fancy that he had a very easy time and was only in the 1st division.

How delightful P. A.'s garden must be! Mine is a great pleasure. Seeing seeds grow into flowers is a great joy. My cooking peas are covered in blossom and sweet peas in bud, pansies are very bright, carnations in bud – and it's all come out of a desert. There are lots of little annuals coming up too but I don't a bit know what they will be like. There are baby sparrows hopping about it today.

The Irish is going ahead fine. I believe I could make a speech in it already and could blunder along about a great many things. I can write much better than I can speak. I could write most of this in Irish. What I find most hard is understanding both reading and talk. There are such infinite varieties of both pronunciation and spelling for nearly every word: then again, there are so many words for some things and none for others. It's utterly unlike anything else and makes me realise for the first time how like each other French, German and English are. The idioms, too, seem to be endless and quite impossible to get at except by memorising. I am wishing for someone to work out the theories and grammar that must be at the back of it all.

So far, all the grammars are based on English and are very scrappy and bad. They worry you to death explaining obvious things, and whole volumes are taken up with unnecessary phonetics and details of the tenses of verbs which are very easy and only a matter for memory. The real difficulties (i.e. the verbal noun and prepositional and adverbial phrases) are never tackled or systematised. I have gone through three grammars and a half, and yet I don't believe I could go through an ordinary story even with a dictionary. With half the knowledge of French, I could read anything in that lingo.

Do write soon – very best love to your old self and to Esther and Clare if she's anywhere about. Best love again and again.

Is mise do dheirfiúr i gCuis na hEireann,
Constance de Markievicz
PS: I almost forgot to wish you many happy returns of the day. 'Bail ó Dhia ort', 'go raibh tu laidir'. These are two Irish wishes for you. Bless you darling.

To Eva   *Mountjoy Prison,*
Dublin.
[Undated; presumably after 8 June].

Dearest Old Darling,
I have just finished my Irish exercises, a task I set myself each night, and it's curious how one works when it's only oneself drives one. The only thing I want at the moment is someone to compare notes with, to find out if I get on as quickly as I ought. I write about 250 words each night for an exercise of composition, as all exercises seemed to be about things I could not conceive wanting to talk much about. Flails are things they are very keen about in grammars: cows and rye, mice and cats are favourite subjects. I do wish a scholar would write an Irish grammar for me!

Your last poem is absolutely perfect. I like it as much as anything you ever wrote. You'll be glad to hear that I have a fellow-prisoner who will appreciate it. It's quite true, too – I mean the poem. Do send me another. The post-cards are a great joy and I often bless the inventor. I've heard nothing about J. [Joss] and your letter filled me with curiosity. I hope he's not being silly, they would stand a lot from him because of me; but, of course, he may go too far. Do explain when you write next.

I long to see your book. Will it be big? If things work out all right here, I will be able to help you publishing it when I get out, as I have a 'job' and will go back to it.

Am very interested in what you say about [John] Scottus Eriugena [Ninth-century Irish philosopher]. I vaguely thought of him as a cleric and a magician but know nothing. What sort of a philosopher was he? But I still stick to it – that we have not produced a philosophy, though we may have produced one philosopher. Look at the French, Greeks, Germans. They tell me that our ancient writings were nature poems and minute family annals, with immense detail of each head of a clan and their relations: wars, marriages, the buying and selling of cattle and such like. Also histories on rather the same lines. Each family or clan had its annals told by its bards, but they don't seem to have written about abstract things much or indulged in speculation, thoughts or theories.

I do hope Dr K. M. [Eva's doctor] will be able to do something for Esther. I know you'll all do what you can. I wish you could see my rock garden. It's beginning to be quite interesting, with little stairs up and down and paths and a sort of obelisk at the top. A most obliging warder, who was bringing me stones, offered to get a huge rock put on the top of it, so I made a flat 'plateau', with a stairway up to it, and he got the two rocks hoisted up. Unluckily, the weather is too dry for anything to be planted. Once it begins to rain, I shall make heaps of cuttings and cover it with things. My peas are not bad, in spite of the drought. The first were ripe about ten days ago.

I can have educational books, and so far I have not got many: Irish grammars chiefly, and Brailsford's *After the Peace*, but it's quite impossible to know what to get when you are shut up. If there's anything thrilling in the line of labour or economics or co-operation, you might send it to me. I do hope that Cecil has not toned down and that the lady is an enthusiast.

I had a visit to-day from Medhbh and from another great friend, Moira O'Byme [Member of Cumann na mBan and IRA]. They both promised to write and tell you how well I am looking. The latter had just seen Bob Barton, who is in splendid health and spirits and can't make out why he was released. No more can I. Diplomacy is very puzzling. Fancy Gaga taking a house in Cumberland! I wonder what the point is – it seems such a queer way of flinging away money unless she has some great friend knocking around, or could have lots of horses and motors. Distances are so great and she doesn't particularly care for loneliness and scenery. Muncaster is a great loss to her. I wonder what the Wuss is doing! I haven't heard anything of any of them for a long time.

There's an ambush going on outside this, and it's most tantalising not to be able to see. I never saw one, and I should love to! We heard a great explosion one day and saw dark columns of smoke. It was very exciting!

Did you ever read *My Life in Two Hemispheres*, by Gavan Duffy Sen.? He must have been a most exceptional man, and a most highly principled and noble one. Fintan Lalor and he were the only real brains among the Young Ireland movement as far as I can see. He seems to have originated and thought out everything we are doing today, as well as the Parnell policy. It's curious how he is not appreciated here.

[John] Mitchel's rhetoric has been like a bible to patriots and is quoted up and down the land. He put out fine phrases, things that the incoherent wanted to say and could not — and so he lived. G. D., who went in for ideas and policies, not phrases, is practically unknown. I think that he must have been one of the noblest characters that ever came out of Ireland and one of the wisest. His weakness, if it was a weakness, was that he could not work with crooks and twisters. I wonder, was he grandfather to our friend? I am always so vague about relationships. He seems too young to be a son.

Clare got a special visit through interest; I don't know whether Gertrude [possibly Gertrude Harding, a Canadian suffragette who worked with the Pankhursts but returned to Canada in 1920 and was normally called Gert] could or not, it depends on whom you know. Pri. knows everybody. Isn't the grit in this country wonderful?

I do feel so proud of being Irish. Now bye bye darling, love to you and Esther and remember me to Reg. 'Debussy' [Esther's brother] and all friends you come across. I could not get a [illegible] shirt, nobody wears them here.

Lovingly and i gCuis na hEireann,
Constance de Markievicz

After the Truce,
July 1921–March 1922

After the Truce ended the War of Independence, Constance was released from Mountjoy Prison on 24 July 1921. At the first meeting of the 2nd Dáil on 16 August, de Valera was declared president, and Constance, though demoted from the cabinet, remained Secretary for Labour. In September, she received a letter from Casimir, now settled in Warsaw, and learnt that her stepson Staskou had been arrested in January 1921 by the Bolsheviks. He would be held prisoner for twenty-five months until 1923; his Russian wife would leave him.

To Eva   *[No date, no address].*
c. July 1921.

Darling,
I have not been able to turn around since I came out [of Mountjoy Prison], with discussions and meetings. I can't tell you anything about what is going on because I am pledged to secrecy, and for the first time in my experience, Dublin is not a whispering gallery.

I was thrown out at about midday on Sunday and luckily found the O'Hanrahan's shop opposite open, from whence I tried to get a taxi. There were none in town owing to some races that were on. At last, I got a car and started off to find where I could lay my head. Nearly everyone is away.

Finally Mr Kent, 44 Oakley Road, took me in for the night. Your cards are so beautiful. I am keeping a lot of them, some I give away as keepsakes. I am sending you two ribbons I made for you in jail.

To Eva   *Dáil Eireann,*
                                          Department of Labour,
                                              Mansion House,
                                                   Dublin.
                                          [Fragment; c. 1921]

Dearest Old Darling,

Just received the lovely brooch from Reginald. The colours are perfect. I don't know what you mean by not being able to find yellow, for the yellow is quite right.

I wish you could get over for a bit during the truce. You'd be quite safe here now. I do hate that old channel between us, but I suppose I ought not to abuse it, as it separates us from England so crudely and so definitely and is such an unanswerable argument.

It is so heavenly to be out again and to be able to shut and open doors. It is almost worth while being locked up, for the great joy release brings. Life is so wonderful. One just wanders round and enjoys it. The children and the trees and cows and all common things are so heavenly after nothing but walls and uniformed people.

It is so funny, suddenly to be a Government and supposed to be respectable! One has to laugh. The Irish Government should publish a new decalogue [Ten Commandments]. Would you believe it, darling, I am in French poetry these days! A man Camille de Mercier d'Erme has sent me a book about Ireland 1916.

To Casimir Markievicz   *Mansion House,*
                                                   Dublin.
                                          [After July 1921].

My dear Casi,

I was very glad to see your writing on an envelope. I don't suppose I should have got your letter except that it arrived in the time of the Truce. It is the first I have had from you since 1916. You ask me 'what are my plans'? Well, I have none, in fact it's quite impossible to make any at a time like this.

Everybody here remembers you. I have come across a great many of the old acting crowd lately and everyone besieges me with questions. Jacky O'C. I met at Mrs Kennedy Cahill's (I don't know if you know that Frances Baker married your friend the actor); also Hanson, and they are full of affectionate inquiries. Since the Truce we have all become popular. It's a funny world. I met Nora and P. J. in Grafton Street, I hadn't seen them since I stayed with them, and they stopped me and asked me to spend the evening. They are just as nice as ever and full of inquiries about you and told me to remember them to you and give their love. Poor Nesbit is shut up in a camp. I'm sure I don't know why. He always used to ask after you.

I never go anywhere that someone does not want to know have I heard from you. 'Sink' is always wishing for you back. I met him at a fête a few nights ago. I am so glad that you have been successful with plays, and only hope that you are fairly comfortable. I've often been very unhappy thinking of all you and your people must have suffered. Did they lose everything at Zywotowka? Is Babshia alive still? And what happened to Stanislas? I'm so sorry about Stas. I wonder why anybody considers it wrong to marry the girl you love! Surely it was not political, he hated politics so. Do write and tell me. Most of the pictures and some of the furniture is safe up 'til this. Lots of things were stolen and destroyed in 1916.

A one-act play of mine was played last night with great success! If this Truce goes on you ought to come over for a bit. I know a lot of Irish now, you will be surprised to hear. Now goodbye for the present and do write to me again soon.

Yours ever,
Constance de Markievicz

In October, the Anglo-Irish conference to settle the Irish problem opened in London, with the Irish delegation led by Arthur Griffith and Michael Collins; de Valera, who had spent weeks negotiating for the conference with David Lloyd George, opted to stay at home.

On 6 December, the Anglo-Irish Treaty was finally signed. The new Irish Free State would have its own parliament and army, but would give up its aspiration to a thirty-two-county Ireland and would swear an oath of allegiance to the British monarch. Éamon de Valera refused to recommend acceptance of the Treaty.

After much fractious debate, the Dáil approved the Treaty by 64–57 votes on 7 January 1922. Three days later, de Valera resigned as president of the Republic on grounds that he would never take an oath to a British monarch and walked out of the Dáil, along with Markievicz and others. On 16 January, Michael Collins, chairman of the Provisional Government, took over formal control of Dublin Castle from the British.

Cumann na mBan became the first national organisation to reject the Treaty in early February, with members who supported the Treaty, including Jennie Wyse-Power, leaving the organisation to establish Cumann na Saoirse. That month, Markievicz, along with Mary MacSwiney and Éamon de Valera, attended the Irish Race Congress in Paris, along with Free State delegates. Tensions were already so high that the two groups travelled separately.

In March, Markievicz took up residence with the Coghlan family at Frankfort Terrace, Rathgar, where she would remain for the rest of her life. May Coghlan aged 14, had worked as a clerk in the Ministry for Labour.

Preparations had begun for an election in June 1922, with Markievicz arguing for an extension of the vote to women between the ages of 21 and 30. De Valera had other plans for her and on 1 April 1922, in Southampton, she boarded the Cunard Line's RMS Aquitania *bound for the USA, along with Kathleen Barry, a sister of Kevin Barry. Their mission was to promote the anti-Treaty cause and to raise funds where they could; a Free State delegation had already visited the USA.*

To Eva [*Fragment. Undated; probably March 1922*].

We are all frightfully busy here, preparing for the elections [held 16 June 1922]. Though personally I should not be surprised if they were put off again. The Register is a farce. Griffith is afraid that if it is revised he will be beaten. None of the Volunteers are on [it]. We brought in a Bill to enfranchise women under 30. Griffith turned it down. Quite spontaneously the demand arose here, women everywhere throughout the country suddenly finding their position to be humiliating, and it was the fight that did it. They say they must have a say as to the Treaty, and that if they are good enough to take part in the fight, they are good enough to vote.

Things are awful here. There are more people being killed weekly than before the truce.

American Tour,
April–June 1922

On board RMS Aquitania
[undated; early April 1922]

I find a ship the next worst thing to jail – and rather like it. Small, stuffy cabin and crowds of people round you that you don't want.

We had some of the usual English at our table, who started abusing Ireland and libelling Dev. the first night. We told them what we thought of them and got ourselves put on to another table for breakfast.

I've not been ill, though things were charging about the tables one day and every one was rushing from wall to wall in their progress across the room. At night, too, I couldn't sleep because of the way I was banged about.

I'm sure I hate a big boat and would never like a voyage. It's so luxurious and yet so uncomfortable and such an inactive, lazy life, with nothing to do but eat, sleep and look at freaks. The only nice thing is the sea, and you are so far from it, it might not be there at all. There are no birds. There were porpoises one day, also a whale which made a fountain that caught the sunlight. For the rest you have miles and miles of dirty water.

I already wish that I was home again. It's awful not to be there at such a moment. The difficulties ahead are colossal, not the least of the problems being that for a very long time (perhaps for always) we shall each and all of us be suspicious of everything and everyone. In fact, I sometimes wonder if the rank and file will ever trust a leader again.

I wouldn't be a bit surprised if the army, or some of it, started out doing things on its own. The domestic enemy are doing a very wrong thing; both wrong and foolish, not only for the sake of the country but for their own sakes. They are conducting a campaign against Dev and [Erskine] Childers, a campaign of mis-statements and innuendo, utterly despicable. It does not matter what anyone thinks about C. but Dev is the one strong, personal influence in the country. He has always used that influence for unity and toleration and sanity, for repressing personal ambitions and for turning people's minds from a desire for vengeance to higher things.

I believe that his influence and his alone has made it safe for the new domestic enemies to flaunt around. I don't like to think of what might happen if they were ever able to get the people, especially the army, to distrust him and to disbelieve in his honesty, his brains and his courage. If they succeed in this I am sorry for them, for their end will be swift and sure, more sure than his.

To Stanislas Markievicz   *Hotel Waldorf Astoria,*
New York.
6 June 1922.

My dear Staskou,
I have just received your letter forwarded to me from Ireland via New York to this place – St Paul it's called. It's on the Mississippi in the wilds of Minnesota. I am on a tour visiting all the Irish centres in the U.S.

I never wrote to you because I was afraid of compromising you but I sent you many messages by Eva. She gave me yours. Do you remember you wrote her asking from some articles of apparel? I was getting them for you and my daughter-in-law when I was again shut up. You know I've had a pretty stiff time of it about three years and a half and some of it was awful. I did what I could to help you. I think some of the people who got to intercede for you might have been a little help. I did not know how it was with you for a long time and when first heard I could find out nothing. Father just mentioned that you were locked up for no reason. Some of poor 'Mixer's' old friends found out all about you for me and have been doing all they could to get influential men among your captors to see a little reason and let you out.

I do long to see you again, you were always as dear to me as if you had been my own son. Also dear Casi; I hate to think of him having to work on a job. Of course we are all frightfully poor just now for money won't buy anything. I wonder if he got the money I sent him from Ireland. He never wrote, at least I never got the letter! Do send me a photo of your wife, Eva showed me one long ago.

When you have time, write and tell me all about yourself and what happened at Zywotowka. I got a letter from John Michael Flick, a fellow sufferer of yours, who is awfully fond of you and knew I would like news of you; I was getting it copied and was sending it to Jim Larkin who had already promised me to try and get certain Bolshie friends of his to try and get you set free. He is in prison here, I think because he was too revolutionary and made wild speeches. But he's awfully decent and promised to do all he could to try and get you out.

Flick is very anxious to get in touch with you if you get out. His address is 1018 Sandler Building, 220 West 42nd St, New York City. He gave me a long account of all your sufferings.

You rail against the Bolshies, I know little about them, but one thing I do know is that our people suffered far worse from the English and what I begin to believe is that all governments are the same and that men in power use that power to get more power for themselves and are completely unscrupulous in their dealings with those who disagree with them.

I'm finishing this letter in the train. We are now in the Rockies en route for Butte, Montana. The scenery is beautiful, wild and rugged with patches of snow everywhere and real cowboys rounding up cattle in the fields.

Mabel is very anxious for you to visit if you get out, so Eva told me. She has been trying to get [Fridtjof] Nansen [High Commissioner for Refugees with the League of Nations] interested in your case.

I have no house now and I was raided and things smashed up. The first time heaps of things were stolen and destroyed by the English. They tied up the kitchen utensils in tablecloths and carried them off.

Again I must say how glad I am that you are out and how I pray that your troubles will be soon over. Of course if we get things fixed right in Ireland, I am sure we should want men like you who know languages that I could get you a good job.

Now goodbye darling boy,

Much love from,
Your loving mother
Address will be Irish delegation, 8 East 41st St, New York.

To Eva   *[No address; c. June 1922].*

Dearest Old Darling,
So far, I've had no time to write to you, it's been hustle, hustle, hustle from meeting to train, from train to meeting, interviews, and so on.

We started from New York to Philadelphia, then Detroit, Cleveland, St Paul, Minneapolis, Butte, Montana, Anaconda, Seattle, Portland, San Francisco, Los Angeles, Springfield, Cincinnati and now we are on our way back to New York.

I often wonder, as I look out of the train window, if you passed the same way long ago and loved the same beautiful length of river, rock or group of trees. The line to-day runs in a valley following the rambles of the Susquehanna River. When we passed over it on our way west, the trees were all bare and wintry. Today, they are all gold and green and sparkling with white flowers. In many ways it is like Ireland, only so much bigger.

Everywhere we go we are feted and get great receptions. Indeed, our only complaint is that we are too much entertained, for our entertainers take absolute possession of us and of our bedrooms even, in the hotel, and we are never allowed to be alone for a minute, and if they can possibly stop me, they don't allow me to walk one yard. We arrived here before the spring had established herself in the East, but found in Detroit to Minneapolis early spring, the first pear trees white, and pink buds on the apple orchards.

I love the way they build cities here. So few rows of gaunt bare houses all joined together in dismal uniformity as we have at home; but each 'home' by itself, with trees round it and on its little plot of green grass, joined onto no other house, and with no paling or wall between it and the street and between it and its neighbours. The houses too are so nice, with their big verandahs. They are so much nicer than the houses at home or in England, and so much more comfortable and much cleaner and better divided-up. The bathrooms are a joy, and even the small houses have them; walls and all of shining white tiles, and cupboards built into the walls, so convenient.

Akron especially took my fancy. We drove out to the suburbs, and even the poor houses stood alone, among greenery. We saw the Mississippi at Minneapolis and a lovely waterfall, by the side of which great piles of unmelted snow lay, melting slowly in the shade of the cliff crowned by flowering cherry trees and shrubs in full leaf. It was very wintry crossing the foothills and the nearer we came to Butte, Montana, the wilder and colder it grew.

Butte was one of the places that stood out for its reception, for they met us with a band and an army. All Sligo seemed to be there! Do you remember Paddy Carty of Kilmacannon? His son called to greet 'Miss Constance' as he called me and he says he'll never call me anything else. He tells me that I 'put the first pair of britches' he ever had on him; it was a matter of 'some plovers' eggs,' he said.

Our procession marched up muddy precipices through a desolate-looking town to the Hotel. All Hotels in America are good and clean. Snow on the fields and snow in odd comers, but you don't feel the cold, I can't imagine why, as it's all muddy and damp. The town is built on the side of a mountain, and motor cars cheerfully bustle up and down mud tracks, and the ruts so deep, up to the axle, that we would hesitate to drive an ass and cart up and down. Looking down into the plain, one held one's breath and prayed that the brakes would hold. But cars don't seem to run away and turn somersaults. Only occasionally the ruts are more than axle deep and they have to wait to be pulled out if the wheel gets in.

We started for Anaconda in a blinding snow-storm. Twenty-eight miles were before us, and the road good at both ends, but unmade for a stretch of over three miles in the middle. Our car was lucky, but the one Miss Barry was in came to grief both ways. Soon after we got on to the mud track it skidded off the track, hurled itself across the ditch and landed somewhere on the mountain among the bog and scrubby bushes. It got back in the end somehow, with a wild jump.

At Anaconda we found a white town and snow over the tops of our boots. In spite of this, the meeting was fine, and we faced for Butte at midnight in deep snow. Luckily, our motor was the second, for the one in which Mr. [J. J.] Kelly was got lost for hours in the snow, and Miss Barry, who preceded us, landed with hers in a ditch and there they stuck. Luckily we had a chain on board and after about an hour's work – snow falling heavily – with much groaning and creaking, we dragged and the men pushed and the beastly thing crawled out. No damage was done.

Next day we went down a copper mine. It was awful! Of course the manager showed us the show parts, the great passages well ventilated and the wonderful machinery, but we saw few men working. I had been put up to things by 'wicked' friends in the [Industrial Workers of the World or 'Wobblies'] and I started to ask awkward questions. I insisted on going into hot places and seeing men working with pick and with drill. I insisted on climbing into a stoop. I saw a man drilling the copper ore without the water appliance to keep the dust down and breathing in copper dust eight mortal hours every day.

This is nothing but murder, as the dust sticks in the throat and eats into the trachea and they die for sure of a terrible form of consumption. The hospitals are full of men suffering from work in the mines. Two men were injured during our short stay, one internally. We saw him at the hospital and they thought him dying. They told us few men live to be old in Butte, Montana.

From Butte we went across the Rockies to Seattle, passing through the waste lands of Montana; weird, unwholesome-looking mountains, slimy rocks and hollows and slimy brown earth with patches of dead grass or sage bush, looking as if the Deluge had just drained off it, and as if each hummock might hide a scaly, prehistoric monster, and each stagnant pool a water snake. For hours and hours we passed through this, like nothing I had ever seen before, until we came to the Cascade Mountains, where innumerable brooks and green pines and great cliffs surrounded us. The railway line is a marvel. Round horse-shoe curves, up and down mountains and over ravines. I wonder that the engineers are not national heroes. They certainly ought to be.

At Seattle we visited an Indian store and went wild over the work, but things were too expensive to get there, so we hurried on into summer at San Francisco. 'Roses, roses all the way' here. We were met by huge bouquets at the station, before the ferry and by a huge committee, and we crossed a calm summer sea and looked at the Golden Gate. When we landed we found a band and a procession headed by two American soldiers, and more roses and children in Irish dress and photographers and press men and women. We got into gaily decorated cars, surrounded by the flags of both Republics, and processed through the city. Roses were thrown at me from the tops of trams. I got an hour to spare and rushed through China Town and we were driven round the resurrected city. You would never know there had been an earthquake and fire so short a time ago.

At Los Angeles we found the tropics. Great palm trees lining the streets and aloes scattered like thistles through the waste stretches of country. We passed through orange groves where the fruit hung ripe on the trees, and saw great piles of golden balls on the brown earth, ready to be packed and shipped away.

Then we passed the desert of Arizona, with nothing but sand and a scanty crop of yellow bent-like grass, and aloes everywhere. We passed day and night through this on our five days' journey to Springfield, where apple blossom, lilac and syringa met us in the full blast of spring. I found a bird's nest there in a friend's garden. At Cincinnati we found summer and roses again. We stayed there with friends and had one day's peace.

I am writing this in the train and it's very jumpy at times. The great meeting is to be in Madison Square Garden on Sunday. We find great sympathy and support here and have got a lot of money. Subscriptions and pledges given at various meetings tot up to over £20,000.

Nobody likes the Freak State [Free State]. They are trying to block us by saying that we are making civil war in Ireland, and I hear that they are organising stunts every night, firing off vast quantities of ammunition at nothing and pretending that we are attacking them!

We stayed with a Mr and Mrs Castellini at Cincinnati: awfully nice people, who have a son, aged fifteen, who is a musical genius. I knew his father in Paris.

Civil War and Final Arrest, Mid-1922–December 1923

By early June, Constance was back in Ireland. In the election, the pro-Treaty republicans came out on top. On 14 April, anti-Treaty republicans had occupied the Four Courts; on 28 June the Provisional Government, under pressure from the British, began bombarding the Four Courts with eighteen-pounder field guns. Fighting raged for a few days in the city centre, with Constance playing her part, though avoiding arrest. Anti-Treaty fighters switched to guerrilla tactics: ambushes, raids and sniping.

In August came the deaths of both Arthur Griffith after a cerebral haemorrhage and Michael Collins, who was shot dead at Béal na Bláth in Co. Cork by anti-Treaty fighters. William T. Cosgrave was declared chairman of the Provisional Government and the opening session of the 3rd Dáil took place in September; anti-Treaty Republicans elected in June refused to attend.

With escalating violence, martial law and military courts became a reality under the Public Safety Act. In November, Erskine Childers was executed for possession of a revolver. After TDs Seán Hales and Pádraic Ó Máille were shot by 'Irregulars', with Hales dying of his injuries, Rory O'Connor and Liam Mellows, along with two other members of the IRA Army Executive, were executed in retaliation. A total of eighty-one 'Irregulars' would be executed by the Irish Free State.

To Stanislas Markievicz   *January 1923.*

Dear Staskou,
You must have thought best not to write before; but it was unavoidable; times are so upset. I got separated from your letter the day after I

received it, and just succeeded in picking it up again. As soon as the Xmas rush and flurry is over, I will try and get Eva to get someone in London to send you the [illegible]. I can't manage it from here.

I am trying to send you £10 for Xmas, but everything is hard for me to manage just at present. I believe that you saw Edmond, so perhaps he explained things. Write to me again and tell me how you are getting on and about your wife.

I wonder have you ever thought of going to America? If she finds it impossible in Poland, it might be wise. If I know what sort of work you like I could write to friends there. I couldn't get you agencies without canvassing around, but if you were there yourself, I believe that if you got a start somewhere you would come out on top and I could give a great account of your powers of work for I saw the way you tackled studying Russian; and also of your very high standards of honour and honesty and these are two rare qualities that help a man to success.

Now good bye and good wishes to you and father for the New Year.

Love to you both,
Your loving Mother
Answer to:
2 Frankfort Terrace,
Dartry Road,
Rathgar,
Dublin.

From January to April 1923, an exhausted and disillusioned Markievicz took a ten-week break in Scotland and England, accompanied by May Coghlan, who, as a teenager, had worked as a clerk in Markievicz's Department of Labour. She spoke at a number of republican meetings and had an enjoyable stay with Eva and Esther in London.

Following the Civil War ceasefire on 24 May, the fourth Irish general election took place on 27 August – the first election since the establishment of the Irish Free State, with all women over the age of 21 voting for the first time. Under the leadership of W. T. Cosgrave, the pro-Treaty side, now called Cumann na nGaedheal, won sixty-

three seats. Despite having eighteen candidates in jail and another thirteen on the run, the anti-Treaty republicans under Éamon de Valera took forty-four seats and Markievicz regained her Dublin South seat. The republicans would again abstain from taking their seats, refusing to take an oath to the King.

Tensions and arrests continued. In late November, Markievicz was arrested while canvassing with Hanna Sheehy-Skeffington on behalf of hunger-striking republican prisoners in Mountjoy. Prison At the North Dublin Union in Grangegorman, a former workhouse converted into a temporary prison, she joined the other women on hunger strike for three days. She was released on Christmas Eve. A rare letter from Eva, carefully reconstructed from torn fragments, survives from this period.

To Mary O'Carroll   *North Dublin Union.*
                                              Undated; c. December 1923.

Dearest Mary,

How clever it was of you to find me in the Bridewell! It was such a cheer hearing that you were outside. Such a horrible dark dungeon of a place as I was in.

Everyone is very cheerful here and full of the joys of coming to life. Poor Baby Bohan [from Ballymote, Co. Sligo; a family known to Constance] suffered terribly and very nearly died. They are now discussing graves in the compound quite cheerfully and really death has so often been so near these last years that it has lost all its fears. Now I'm going to ask you to send me in a bean feast, you're such an angel that I know you will not mind the bother.

I want you first to send a cooked ham. You could possibly get your grocer to cook it; I did twice and to cook me a big apple tart! Two big cardboard tumblers of cream, 1 lb coffee, 1 lb tea, 2 pots marmalade, 2 lb rashers cut very thin, 2 doz raw apples and some bananas. I will send a cheque as soon as book arrives.

I also want my paints, brushes, pencils and blocks and loose rolls of paper, penknife – paints would fit into small attaché case. May would see to this. All paints (2 boxes and one good tin full). Isn't the weather awful? May would see after paints.

The girls are wonderful but still very weak. I did not suffer even from hunger during my three days. It was such a joy seeing Daniel. Love to you all. Do write me a line, I am quite cheerful and feel that the lorry must have been a great success to have got me this.

Lovingly,
Con

Please send enamel saucepan and frying pan. Plus flake oatmeal.

To Mary O'Carroll   *North Dublin Union.*
                                   Undated; c. December 1923.

Dearest Mary,
Thanks so much for all your kindness. It's lovely to have a family of one's own on the spot! I can tell you I appreciate all your loving thought and all the trouble you take. I got your letter and everything all right. I want you to get us a Xmas pudding and to let me know how long to boil it. Get a real rich one for four, not too small and not too big, and send us a pot of cream to make sauce and a small bottle of brandy to burn. I will send you a cheque in my next, it would only delay a post getting book from governor.

What news of Carrol and how is Kathleen? [O'Carroll's son and daughter] Give all nephews and nieces my love. We are gradually getting our digs here straightened up and are not thinking about getting out at all; it's just all in God's hands. We can keep our kettle and the food we get in gives us something to do getting it ready. It was not rolled oats I wanted, I think it was 'blown', a preparation in a tin to be eaten with milk or cream, but the rolled makes lovely porridge. The peaches were lovely, you might send more for Xmas. The India rubber teeth things are like this [drawing]. I've bought them in Lincoln Place several times, also in Glasgow, do try again if you can spare time. My dentist was O'Brien, 2 Percy Place. They only cost 3d per day. Now goodbye again with much love.

From,
Con

To Eva   *North Dublin Union.*
                                        [Undated; c. December 1923]

Dearest Old Darling,
You will have seen how I was arrested and I hope that one of the
two girls I asked to write to you wrote. I was getting on splendidly
with continual meetings to ask people to sign a memorial for the
release of the prisoners.

I started every morning with three girls who gave out bills
and went up and down Dublin and wherever a crowd collected
they said a few words. It was a great tribute to my efforts to stop
them!

I went on hunger strike directly I was taken: they offered me
tea in the police station and I just decided right off. I only did three
days and I was quite happy and did not suffer at all. I slept most of
the time and had lovely dreams and the time went by quite quickly.
I think I would have slipped out quite soon. Tom Derrig came in
and called off the strike and woke me up! One girl is very bad;
she nearly died and it only stopped just in time. She is in hospital
outside now.

Be a darling and send me your book. I meant to order it in
Dublin, but could not remember the long name.

There are three very nice little girls in here with me and we are
quite a cheerful little party. It is a vast and gloomy place, haunted
by the ghosts of broken-hearted paupers. Sea-gulls and rooks fly
around. I saw a piebald rook today; it looked so odd.

Do write a line. I could not write before, as letters are so limited
and I had to get things in.

I have been sketching the girls and have done the work in water
colours.

Now bye-bye and best love to you both.

Do chara i gCuis na hÉireann,
Constance de Markievicz

From Eva Gore-Booth   *14 Frognal Gardens,*
Hampstead,
NW3.
9 December 1923.

Dearest old darling,
It was great joy to get your letter. You can imagine what a fuss
we have been in over this horrible starvation business. Your two
friends kindly wrote – also Hanna and others. I wrote one letter
to you but it must have gone astray as I didn't know your address.
I have been in bed coughing my head off with bronchitis for over
a fortnight. I do hope you are well again and that the rumour isn't
true that the beastly thing has begun again? I can't think why you
aren't out, everybody said you would be quite soon.
　You must have been awfully cold starving like that in this bitter
weather too. What a dreadful state things seem to be in. Joss writes
the people have no turf or potatoes round Lissadell way, it's going
to be very hard for the poor. He wanted to know what I heard of
you. Also the D[illegible] in a fuss to know about you. I am sending
you my book but feel sure it will bore you to tears.
　Every one here is mad about the election. It seems a great shove
on for Labour. The Conservatives *can't do a thing.* By the way the *D.
Herald* is sympathetic and very decent – I think – I do long for Peace.
Also I love the enclosed mountain tops; if I am in a horrid place I
like to imagine the tops of mountains and think of the torrents and
rocks and wonderful air and sky all the time! Esther sends love
and wishes and we both wish if you must frequent those Houses
of Bondage that you were in Holloway again and more get-at-able.
　[What remains of the letter, which had been torn up and stuck
together again, ends here.]

To Eva   *North Dublin Union Internment Camp.*
12 December 1923.

Dearest Old Darling,
I was so delighted to see your dear old fist. The letter came
yesterday, but book has not materialised yet. I expect the first

letter went up in a blaze! A whole row of wooden huts, in which the censor's office was, went up in smoke and one letter and some parcels went up. It was a glorious blaze, we enjoyed it enormously, far better than the pictures! The red shirts and brass helmets of the firemen on the roof, in and out of the smoke and the orange flames, made a dramatic note, and suggested thrills and romance and heroines and the nethermost pit. But all that was burnt was beds and boots and an apple pie of mine and other rather valueless property.

As far as I am concerned, I don't know how long they mean to keep me. There can be no charge against me – that is, anything more than a police-court charge of 'impeding the traffic'. It's just spite and fear of my tongue and voice. My real democratic principles, I expect! This place is crawling with cats, dogs and ghosts, but we are really a very cheerful little party. The hunger-strike did not involve any suffering for me, but it was very short.

Take care of yourself dearest Eva. Love to Esther.

From,
C de Markievicz

Final Years, 1924–1927

To Eva
2 Frankfort Terrace,
Rathgar.
January 1924.

Dearest Old Darling,
Please take as said all the excuses that lazy people make for not answering letters. I think that it is a disease with me.

Did I ever thank you for the lovely bag? It is a joy. And your book and the book of plays? I find your book very difficult for my memory is so bad and I keep muddling your symbolic words (I don't know if that conveys anything to you) but you have a language that I do not know and until I can learn to use it easily I know that I shall not benefit much by the book. But it is very thrilling trying to work it out and every sentence that I read gives me something to think about. Perhaps if we live ten years I shall be able to tell you what I think of it.

The tragedy of Christ's life to me is far greater today than it was during the few terrible last hours of suffering. For every church and every sect is but an organisation of thoughtless and well-meaning people trained in thought and controlled by juntas of priests and clergy who are used to doing all the things that Christ would most have disliked. And yet I don't know how this can be avoided, for without organisation Christ would be quite forgotten, and all organisation seems in the end to go the same road: and if it does not go in for graft and power it just fizzles out.

That is what is wrong too with all public bodies and governments, and what the world has got to think out is some scheme by which power can be evenly distributed over every person in the world and by which the foolish and uneducated can no longer be grouped in unthinking battalions dependent on the few pushers, self-seekers and crooks and made slaves of and exploited. I suppose that all lovers of freedom are looking for this.

I do hope that you are better. I hate you to be in London in the winter. Everything here is very dull. The main thing is the appalling poverty that meets one everywhere, and the enormous increase in the numbers of huge motor-cars that threaten one at every crossing. I am still trying to get somewhere to live in my constituency but there are no houses or flats to be got anywhere. Was not my arrest funny?

'Honour bright', as we used to say, I was engaged in no work that was not visible to the naked eye and all my activities were passivist and within the law. I directed an election, I did lightning sketches at a bazaar each day for a couple of weeks and I went round on a lorry asking my constituents to sign the petition drawn up by the Corporation for the release of the hunger strikers. I always rather dreaded a hunger strike, but when I had to do it I found that, like most things, the worst part of it was looking forward to the possibility of having to do it. I did not suffer at all but just stayed in bed and dozed and tried to prepare myself to leave the world. I was perfectly happy and had no regrets. It is all very odd and I don't understand it but it was so. I had no wish to live and no regrets. I just seemed to be sliding along in a happy sort of dream.

When [Tom] Derrig came to me, he woke me up with a jump and it was like coming to life again and I wanted to live and I wanted the others to live. I am telling you this because you have such a horror of the hunger strike and I want you to realise what it was to me, that for just one moment when I was making it imperative on me when telling the police of my decision, I had the sort of shrinking that one has before taking a header into a cold sea: just a want of faith in the unknown but that was all.

Once I had begun I did not suffer either mentally nor physically, nor did I regret the step that I had taken. And by the way it has cured my rheumatism for the moment. It has done this for a great many of the strikers. Also it has cured quite a number of people who were suffering from stomach trouble. Most of those who were on for only a fortnight seem to be none the worse. One girl who was suffering from an ulcerated stomach has been absolutely cured. Of course some of those who were in for a month or longer have been very bad. One girl, Baby Bohen from Ballymote, will probably never be the same again: her kidneys are affected. She was awfully plucky and suffered a lot.

English politics are very exciting just now – I am afraid that the Labour Party are not strong enough to do anything and that they will be in a position where they can be discredited and from which they will get a big set-back and lose a great many of their supporters who expect them to do something. But one cannot tell.

I hear that it was the Orange lodges of Glasgow and the Protestant hysteria that beat Newbold. He could count on the Catholic (Irish) vote and that fact used cleverly by the Protestant capitalist interest did the trick.

Now, old darling, I must stop. Writing on a machine always tempts one to ramble on and on. I got you a present. I got it before I was locked up, but though it is small, it is hard to pack and laziness intervened. I must try and make an effort.

Love to you both and good wishes for the New Year. By the way, what has really happened about M.'s engagement? Gaga told me a long yarn. I hope that she will steer her own ship the way she wants and will not let anyone push her into doing what she does not want 'for her own good'. The more I live the more I believe in people usually knowing what is best for themselves.

Now bye bye again, old darling. How I'd love to be with you! It was so lovely last summer and it made amends for the long months of exile.

Lovingly,
Con

To Eva   *Limerick.*
                                                        22 May 1924.

Dearest Old Darling,
Many happy returns of the day! As I am in Limerick [for by-election held on 28 May], I am sending you a wee piece of lace.

Work here is desperate but things are going well. The tide has really turned, but it's work, work, work and no rest for the wicked.

Each by-election goes better and we have hopes of this. People's hopes have come to life again and enthusiasm is rising and blowing on every wind.

Did I ever thank you for your 'blue Glory' of a cape? I have a horrible feeling that I did not, but it is such a joy and it was so lovely to get a birthday present, you old darling.

Up 'til recently, we have just been trying to block the stampede of the nation, and now it is all changed again.

I am such a fool about posts. Your Christmas present is still in my room, and I could never get it packed, but you'll get it in time.

To Stanislas Markievicz   *[1924; probably summer].*

My dear Staskou,
Mr Budd gave me your letter, and indeed I felt awfully sorry that I had not written to you before. I waited and waited hoping that something might turn up; but the conditions here are awful and seem to get worse and worse every day. There is starvation on every side, not only among the very poor, but among people who were quite well off.

The terrible result of the world war is felt in every house, except among those who were in the know and who were able to gamble with stocks and amass fortunes for the profiteers. All the small businesses here are heading for ruin, and the farmers are in a bad way. The list of bankrupts is something appalling. The list of highly paid officials for whom jobs are made by those at present in power is daily increasing. To meet these expenses, the old age pensioners have been docked 1/- per week off their pensions, as well as their bag of coal per fortnight.

Taxes are awful, food prices are daily rising and rents are wicked. Heaps of people just as well educated as you are unable to get to America, either because the quota is full or because they have not the money to pay. I have one friend, a professional gentleman, with a distinguished career who had a nice house on Garville Avenue. This man had a job worth over £1,000 per annum. He was dismissed to make room for a job hunter, who had friends in power and he now has to begin life afresh. His sons' careers are ruined and he with a son and daughter have opened a tiny shop in a slum on money that they were able to borrow.

If I ever saw any chance at all, I would say come over and look around, and if things brighten at all that is what we will do. But just now, you don't know what may happen. Anything might happen to me for one thing. I am living in a room in a friend's house and personally have nothing to complain of as the money I have keeps me. I thought, 'til I began to enquire, that there might be some opening for you in America. But there are many here with good qualifications and powerful friends over there who can't get anything. The whole world is so tragic since the war.

Is there no opening for you in commerce in Poland? I mean in quite a small way; £200 I would think would not be necessary, if you worked on your own. I mean for a start, as you would only have yourself to look after at the start. I can quite understand and sympathise with your dislike of being dependent on your father for your living. It must be dreadful and most humiliating to a man of your independent character. You poor old darling, I feel bad being so powerless to help. Father probably told you how he was done out of the price of his picture here, and how most of the old gang are scattered.

This is rather a doleful letter, but it will just let you know that I have not forgotten you, and you will always be one of those people whom I love most, for you really became like my own son, and I loved you for your honourable and upright character. But I'm a fool at writing letters as you know. Goodbye with much love from,

Your loving,
Mother

For Markievicz, the highlight of 1924 was a visit to Dublin by Casimir; his first since 1915. She was thrilled to see him again. His visit revived her interest in the theatre and she organised the Republican Players' Dramatic Society as a fundraiser, putting on a

dozen plays in the next year, including two one-act plays of her own
– The Invincible Mother *and* Blood Money. *During the summer,
her pamphlet 'James Connolly's Policy and Catholic Doctrine' was
published by Sinn Féin.*

*In 1925, she was co-opted on to the Rathmines and Rathgar Urban
District Council and began working on a full-length play.*

To Stanislas Markievicz   *Frankfort House,
Dartry.
[Probably autumn 1925].*

Dearest Staskou,
I was so awfully glad to get your letter from Miss Smith the other
day. She came here and saw me and I felt quite in touch with you.
I did not know that you had a job and I am so glad to hear it. Of
course what you earn is little for one of your education and ability,
but, as you say, in these bad times, it's good to get anything.

The shops here all seem to be in a bad way, you would be
surprised to know how many old firms are gone, either bankrupt
or sold over to foreign big businesses. Don't know if you remember
Brown Thomas, a big shop, one of the biggest and oldest places for
clothes etc., in Grafton St. Selfridge, a huge company with houses in
America, London etc. has taken it over. Roberts, another big place,
has gone bankrupt, Switzer's even is supposed to be in a bad way.
There is always some shop either being sold out, or empty and 'to
let'. I don't know what's going to be the end of it all.

There is an awful shortage of houses for all classes and rents
have gone up leaps and bounds. I never remember so much poverty.
The unemployed tramp the streets and there's little help for them.
There are also hundreds of unfortunate men who were thrown
out of the Free State army who are mostly only fit for labouring
work and who are in a sorry plight. When Larkin came back from
America there was a row between him and the men who had come
to control the Transport Workers Union. They split, and now both
parties are more concerned with fighting each other and trying to
ruin each other than in helping the workers.

The only people who have done well for themselves are the relations and supporters of influential Free Staters and well paid jobs are being created everywhere for these, paid out of the taxes! So much for conditions here. We can only hope that the worst moment has come and that things will mend.

What a lovely and vivid description you write me of the place you live in; reading it makes me wonder why you don't try writing seriously about it. An article describing it in coloured words and giving some of its history would be awfully interesting. It would also make an interesting background for not only one, but many stories. Talking of stories, a girl I know got £15 for a short story in an American magazine and an offer of £20 each for two others; this is a small price for stories in America. There are a great many Poles and Russians in America and anything that would appeal to them would I feel have a good chance of being taken. I am awfully glad that you are translating. It will teach you form, also increase your vocabulary.

You want to be very careful about the words you use. In general, it's a golden rule to avoid words derived from French or Latin sources and try and express yourself in words with Saxon derivations. The Latin and French words are more complicated and a little affected and should be kept in reserve for sentences dealing with things rather out of the common, or as a little remote from the common events of our daily life. I tell you this because this particular wrong use of words is a mistake which writers who are not 'Native Speakers' of English always seem to fall into. We might possibly be able to help you place things in London; here there is very little opening for a writer, most authors publishing in London, I'm sorry to say.

Do send me something you have written soon. Do you remember once beginning a story? It was quite good and I was always sorry that your love of outdoor amusements did not give you time to go on writing and developing the very obvious talent you had.

Those occult cabalistic things seem to be all the go in America now. You probably remember Nora Connolly, poor Connolly's girl, she wrote a story on those lines and the *Atlantic Monthly* gave her £20 for it. She sent it there just on chance. America seems to pay very well. It's quite right if you sent it there. Please don't think you're troubling me to be trying new schemes all the time, and I love to hear from you, and would do all I could to help. I wonder whether it would help you to have some standard modern books to read? I don't read much these days but could easily find out what the sort of stuff [is] likely to help you in forming a style of your own. The local colour over where you are should be a beautiful novelty.

I wonder can you typewrite? I'm quite fairly good these days and have a little portable Remington of my own, on which I do all my writing. I think I told you that I lodge with a very nice woman. It's very much cheaper than any other way of living. She has 8 nice children, and is always pulling the devil by the tail. The garden is left to me to do what I can with, it's quite big. The room I have looks out on it. I could always get you tucked in here, I know you don't mind living simply, and you'd be quite at home.

Did [I] tell you that I had bought a second-hand Ford car; an old 'Tin Lizzie' they call it, but it carries me along all right, and I can drive all right and do my own road repairs. I keep it in an old stable in the garden, and spend most of my spare time driving out and sketching. I have been struggling to teach myself watercolours these last few years, and am just beginning to express myself a little in them. Oils were too expensive for me to continue, unless I gave up politics and tried to earn real money by them, also they take more time and are more trouble to cart around. I began water colours when I was in prison in England, and it would not have been possible to paint in oils there, because of the smell, and being in such quarters with the other prisoners, one of whom was very delicate. I didn't like to even suggest inflicting the smell of oil on her.

I wonder can you drive a car? My Ford is very easy and anyhow you will be able to learn if you like when you come. I met the McMurdo girl in a tram the other day and she was asking after you; but I forgot to ask her where she was living. It makes me very sad to hear what you tell me about your wife. You should take whatever steps you refer to soon, and find out what has happened to her. Possibly she never got your letters. But you must remember that you married very young and that all you have both gone through has probably changed you both very much, and that she is probably quite a different person now from the girl you married. If you ever again meet, you will almost be like two strangers meeting.

Fancy you being nearly 30? I suppose I should not recognise you if we met by accident. I remember so vividly the little boy so thin and fragile with a crop of golden hair and the most pathetic little face I ever saw; and later on the big healthy lad just growing into manhood with the same huge tragic blue eyes. I often think of you and long to see you and wish I could do something for you. But the letters you write are quite the same old you I used to know and love.

I have been very sick ever since I got your letter and only felt fit to write today. Nothing is really wrong, but just the worst attack of 'flu I ever had and growing old. But my health is wonderful, also I don't get old very quickly, thank God, and can still do a good day's work at the garden or car without getting unpleasantly tired. I am sending this letter back the same way. It's much safer. I wonder where Bialowieza [on Belarus/Polish border] is.

Best love,
From Mother

To Frank McHugh   *Frankfort House,*
Dartry.
1 December 1925.

A Chara,
Many thanks for your subscription to Fianna. We are working very hard building up the organisation and have to start again from the very beginning, with nothing; but thank God, we are getting on and subscriptions like yours are what are enabling us to do so.

We are running a memorial concert on Sunday week for Liam Mellows and the others. This Sunday, we are holding a ceremony at his grave.

Things here seem to be on the turn at last. The rescues from Mountjoy have given us all new life and hope, it was so well done, not a hitch anywhere. I suppose I should drift over to Glasgow

again some day when I will hope to renew my acquaintanceship with you.
With best wishes for the season and many thanks.

Do chara i gCuis Phoblacht na hEireann,
Constance de Markievicz

A few days after this letter was written, twelve Fianna boys were arrested in Wexford under the Treasonable Offences Act of 1925. Constance gave evidence at their trial.

To Staskou   *Frankfort House,*
Dartry.
14 January 1926.

My dear Staskou,
I was so delighted to see your friend who kindly came to see me, and to hear how well you were getting on. You were right about books, I was in a fix what to send, as I have so little time to read and when I came to think it over I only knew of old books that you probably know.

So I am sending you four of Conrad's, and two others that struck me as rather remarkable. They both made a great hit. *Romantic* is rather nasty I thought, but it is awfully interesting as a character study very well put together and the conversations very natural. It's very modern and what you might describe as a book that strikes the note of the hour. *When Winter Comes* is not quite so much a book of the period, but more a book that might have been written at any period, and be counted good as a novel, natural and sincere and well written. I liked it very much. Do write and tell me what you think of them.

I have been very busy, we are in the middle of endless conventions and the re-adjustment of all our political activities, which takes up a terrible amount of time [paving the way for the establishment of Fianna Fáil]. Also some fools took out my car without leave or license and to add to the worry a child of the house got scarlet fever. She has mercifully been carted off to hospital, where she is doing well.

Maeve spent a day here on her way to Sligo and helped me pull the car to pieces. She loves machinery and is very clever at it. She is very tall and pretty and full of life and charm.

You will laugh when I tell you that I have cut off my hair! It's so comfortable and I don't see why old women should not be as comfortable as young.

Every one here is wearing Russian boots, and it will amuse you to hear that the red pair that your aunts got made for me at Zywotowka had survived the looting and that I fished them out and am wearing them every day, and they are far the smartest pair in Dublin.

As this letter is going by hand, I can tell you that I have been over three years in jail. I was in five different prisons. One year in an English convict prison herded with murderers and prostitutes quite alone.

I was a year in Holloway jail in London with Mrs Tom Clarke [Kathleen] and Maud Gonne. I was in solitary confinement in Cork jail, with others in Mountjoy. I was released from there at the time they were negotiating the Treaty and arrested again by the Free Staters and put in the North Dublin Union, which they were using as a prison. I went on hunger strike there. We are constantly raided here, but have been very lucky, as they found nothing. I am very lucky to have escaped with my life as both Black and Tans and Free Staters are out to murder me, but I went around disguised in various ways and had wonderful escapes.

My whole life since Easter Week has been one round of hard work and danger, but my health is wonderful and I am quite cheery and hopeful.

Joss I never see, and never want to see. Gaga I see whenever she comes to Dublin as I am useful to her. The rest of them live in England and I only hear from and see Eva from time to time, who is the only real relation I have left. She is a wonderful old darling, and always looked after me when I was in jail and came over and fussed around when I was condemned to death after Easter Week and helped save me from being shot.

A friend went down to Sligo to get Joss, but he would not come up. I saw him once since, he came to see me just after I was released the first time here in Dublin. I don't mind, I never worried, I only tell you so that you know, if I blow across any of them, I shall be quite amiable to any of them. They are no worse than anyone else, and I suppose it's very embarrassing to have a relation that gets into jail and fights in revolutions that you are not in sympathy with.

I'd love to see you again, and of course where I am would always be home to you, except of course if I was in jail!

Now good bye, dearest boy, and do take care of your health. You know you were rather delicate as a kid. I wish I could look after you and spoil you for a while.

Your loving mother
And a happy New Year to you!

In early March, Éamon de Valera resigned from Sinn Féin after an extraordinary general meeting rejected his proposal to join government. De Valera had discussed the formation of a new Irish republican party with Markievicz, who had already resigned from Cumann na mBan. On 16 May 1926, Markievicz chaired the inaugural meeting of Fianna Fáil. She was unaware of her sister's deteriorating health; Eva had been diagnosed with terminal cancer in mid-1925 but kept the news to herself.

To Eva   *Frankfort House,*
                                                      Dartry.
                                      [May or June 1926].

Dearest Old Darling,
I don't suppose that you have been wondering why I hadn't written before, because I am such an awful slacker at writing and I am always so full up of work of all description.

I've been writing a play [*Broken Dreams*]! I don't quite know what started me, but somehow a situation came into my head and

I wrote a scene and then I simply could not stop. Wherever I went I had an old copybook and whenever I was not actually using my hands I wrote.

I had to go and drive for an election in the middle – such hard work – and one day I got my car out at 7 o'clock and never stopped driving round until weary and sleepy I rang up a house at 2.30 to beg for a bed. But every minute I had to wait for someone outside a house – out with my old book, and anyhow the play is finished at last. Of course it is not literary, only just a thrilling story during the Tan war and in Sligo, but I think it is human and natural.

I loved the book you sent me. I got it in the middle of the election. It reads like truth, and one gets so fond of the hero that one longs to know what happened to him in the end. After all his adventures, it seemed so sad that he was back again into exile and slavery.

How are you? I wonder so where you are and if you've been abroad. Poor D. [Macardle] has been operated on again and is so brave and patient. She misses her father very much. I saw her last night at a little gathering at a friend's house. I am sorry that she has left this [house], for she was great company. She has a lovely flat. Her father had just fixed it up before he died.

I wonder what you think of us all? I sometimes think that people get rather mad when they go in for politics. The latest has made me laugh since it began. Dev, I say like a wise man, has announced that he will go into the Free State Parliament if there is no oath and this has caused an unholy row. I myself have always said that the oath made it absolutely impossible for an honourable person who was a Republican to go in, and that if it were removed, it would then be simply a question of policy with no principle involved, whether we went in or stayed out.

Dev thinks the moment has come to start out attacking the oath and demanding its removal. Some illogical persons are howling. They stand for principle and for the honour of the Republic and prefer to do nothing but shout continually 'The Republic lives!' It was as good as a play to hear the self-righteous fools lauding their own stand as being a stand for principle and honour and then trying to 'throw flowers' at Dev. It was Mark Antony's oration. They don't want to quarrel with him; they know he's an honourable man. Such a queer lot of people who are taking this stand. It's quite surprising. I think the ordinary man and woman in the street will agree with us. I don't think that we'll get the oath removed, at any rate for a long time, but anyhow it is something to go for with a chance of success, and something outside Ireland might help.

Maeve blew in on her way to Sligo and commandeered the car. I love the queer little musical instrument she has and the way she has of lilting to it all sorts of silly little songs without any pretension at all but very attractive. Is there any chance of your coming over this year at all? It is such an age since I saw you, and the beastly [Irish] channel and the long, long journey costs such a lot and I never have any time or money somehow.

Is there going to be any real trouble in England with the miners? There is no work here at all. Crowds are starving all over the country. I wonder if it is as bad over there.

I would like to see you laugh at my bobbed head. I have it quite short at the back and parted at the side, covering my ears. It is quite smooth and straight as a rule, for I seldom curl it.

How is Esther? Give her my love. I often think of the time I was in London 'on the run'. I loved it. I wish they'd send me again. Perhaps they will someday. It was rather a pity after all that I was not caught that time for I would have got a nice round sum and it would have been worth it.

They raid this place an odd time and get nothing, but I suppose they want to keep their hand in. They have nearly gone mad, looking for the eleven prisoners who escaped so supernaturally. They looked here.

There is nothing the least interesting to tell you about. I garden and drive about. One blessed thing about this row is that I have got out of a great deal of awful meetings.

Now goodbye, old darling, and best love,
Con

This was the last letter Markievicz would ever write to her beloved sister. On 30 June, Eva died of colon cancer.

To Esther Roper   *Frankfort House,*
Dartry.
July 1926.

My dear Esther,
It was very good of you to wire. I simply can't realise it. I know how
I feel and I know how much worse it is for you who were with her
the whole time.

There was no one ever like her. She was something wonderful
and beautiful, and so simple and thought so little of herself. I don't
think she ever knew how much she was to me. I am so vague and
stupid and can't express myself.

But her gentleness prevented me getting very brutal, and one
does get very callous in a war. I once held out and stopped a man
being shot because of her. And she was always there when I was
down and out, she and you.

I was writing to her in answer to a letter she wrote me the other
day, when she told me she was playing with 'glitterwax'. Her letter
seemed well and happy and she was full of interest in us and the
strike. Other letters had often rather frightened me, but this was
quite a jolly letter and firmly written.

I was frightened too when I read her book on Saint John, [*A
Psychological and Poetic Approach to the Study of Christ in the
Fourth Gospel* (London, 1923)] for it seemed to me almost as if she
had done the work she was destined to do: that her whole task in
life was finished and that she had just gone on living while some
strong force was working through her and in her. I can't explain.

I'm not coming over, because I simply could not face it all. I want
to keep my last memory of her so happy and peaceful, and nothing
but love and beauty and peace. I sent a wreath: white and her own
blue.

Write to me when you feel you can and tell me how it happened.
I got the wire when I got home. It had been here for a day or so,
while I was with a friend at the sea, and it gave me a terrible shock.
Everything seemed to go from under me: sometimes I could not
realise it. I had been awfully depressed and I did not know why, for
days. People noticed it and I thought I was seedy.

I had always had a funny habit, since Aylesbury, of referring anything I was doing to her. Every sketch I made I wondered how she would like it, and I looked forward to showing it to her. If I saw anything beautiful, I thought of her, and wished she was there to enjoy it.

I was always dreaming and planning to take you both along to some beautiful places in the car. I was writing a play and doing a copy to send her, and so on, through everything, though I didn't write often. And then everything seemed to be cut off all at once.

But lately I've begun to feel and see her often. When I'm painting she seems to look at me and help me from the cloud. I wake suddenly and it is just as if she was there. Last Sunday at Mass, when I wasn't thinking of her at all, she suddenly seemed to smile at me from behind the priest, and I know it is real and that she, the real Eva, is somewhere very near.

I know too that you will feel this in time. It is only that you were so much in touch with her human form that you miss it so, and your mind can't rest: but it will find rest, and her, only it will take time.

I'd love some personal relics of her and a photo, if a good one exists. I have no good one. My things were destroyed so often. I want to come over and see her grave.

I always looked on you as a sort of adopted sister, Eva's twin. And you're all I have now, in that way.

To Esther Roper   *Frankfort House,*
                                                  Dartry.
                                                  1926.

Dearest Esther,
I would like to come over to you, and any time after the second week in September would suit me. I do hope there is nothing serious wrong with you, and that you are better than when you wrote.

I love the Spanish wrap. Eva always wore it latterly when I saw her. It is so associated with her in my mind. I should love the cross:

our granny left it to her years ago and it was a thing she loved and wore so much when we were girls together.

About the Celtic Cross: they are very commercial here. I might be able to find someone: don't hurry. Let's consult first. I think something rather simple would be nicest and on the lines of some of the old ones, not too finished and correct but rather rough and bold.

Patricia Lynch called with her husband [R.M. Fox] on Saturday to show me an article he had written on her in the *Millgate Monthly*. It is really a beautiful appreciation of her, and he seems really to have understood and loved her, [Eva] and to have got a far deeper knowledge of her than many who knew her better.

I had a collision in the car the other day – it just escaped being a very bad accident – and when I saw the other car rise suddenly from behind a corner wall, I just had an extraordinary feeling that Eva was there and that it was all right. I can't explain.

I am longing to sit in the room where she lived and worked again, and I know she left the feeling of peace and love that was her gift there more than anywhere else.

To Esther Roper   *Frankfort House,*
                                                              Dartry.
                                                              1926.

My dear Esther,

I was very glad to get your letter and to hear that you are bringing out another book of Eva's poems. The one thing we can do to honour her is to make her work known and help her to immortality here in this world through the ideals she lived for.

It seems to me that it is almost a test of a person's soul-worth, if – reading her – they understand. So many more do than I ever dreamed of. I met a woman among the International Peace women [at a 1926 conference in Dublin, 1926], who had been at the Kemp's school and had acted in Eva's play. She came to me and told me how she had loved her writings, and so many others have said the same.

She has left a spiritual inheritance to those who can understand, which will never die.

I don't feel lonely as I did at first, and I know you won't, after a bit. It is only natural that you should, who was so much nearer her body than I was, for her human presence was so beautiful and wonderful; but with her the spirit dominated every bit of her and her body was just the human instrument it shone through.

It's so hard to put things like this down in a way that one can understand. When I was in Aylesbury, we agreed to try and get in touch for a few minutes every day, and I used to sit at about 6 o'clock and think of her and concentrate and try to leave my mind a blank – a sort of dark, still pool – and I got to her and could tell how she sat in the window and I seemed to know what she was thinking. It was a great joy and comfort to me.

When I got out, I lost this in the bustle and hurry of life, but now, just the last few days, I seem to get in touch again.

To Mrs L'Estrange [Leah Kaye]   *14 Frognal Gardens,*
Hampstead.
1926.

My dear Mrs L'Estrange,
I feel very sad leaving this house, probably for the last time.

Every corner in it speaks of Eva, and her lovely spirit of peace and love is here just the same as ever. And Esther, too, who is her spiritual sister, I hate leaving. She is wonderful, and the more one knows her, the more one loves her, and I feel so glad Eva and she were together and so thankful that her love was with Eva to the end.

To Josslyn Gore-Booth   *Frankfort House,*
Dartry.
22 Jan 1927 (received).

My dear Joss,
Many thanks for yours. Poor old Gaga, I do hope she won't suffer and that she is happy. Maeve tells me that she is worried because

she believes that you and I would quarrel if we met, and I hate to think of her dying and thinking that, and perhaps not writing to ask me to come because she is afraid of it.

The last time I was there was just after you had blocked my selling St Mary's to a good customer and lost £100 over it as houses were falling in price and it was only an encumbrance and I wanted to get rid of it quickly and did so. I was very cross when you came to see her and bolted through the window as I could not trust my temper and did not want to make a row. Now this is all years ago and I've long ago ceased to bother about it but believe that she took it so to heart and got so nervous that she never asked me there since. I never bothered as I didn't particularly want to go, I was so busy always.

Now only you can put this right with her and make her feel that if she'd like to see me, she can ask me and no danger of a row. I should not write this, only I feel that she is the only thing that matters – poor old dear. What I should suggest is this; that you just said in an ordinary way that you had a letter from me. You need make no explanation. You may have things against me, but I think nothing should stand in the way of putting her mind at rest if this worries her.

You could tell her that I said it was awfully cold in Dublin and that I was very busy helping to get up a jumble sale for our 'Child Welfare Centre' in Rathmines and I was out all day collecting rubbish in my old tin Lizzie.

I can only add, as I think it best to be quite frank, that I've always felt you had something against me, and was prepared if I met you to take my cue from you. I would have been glad if you'd been pleased to see me; and if you had appeared to wish to avoid me, I wouldn't have forced myself on you.

I think that's all I can think of to say, and I also hope you'll not misunderstand me. I don't want to bother you, but I *do* want Gaga made easy about it.

Yrs,
Constance de Markievicz

A day after this letter was received on 23 January 1927, Georgina Gore-Booth died. Markievicz attended the funeral and met her brother Joss for the first time since 1917.

In the June general election, Markievicz was one of forty-four Fianna Fáil candidates elected to the 5th Dáil. Despite looking frail and nursing a broken arm, she walked to Leinster House with de Valera to seek admission to the first session of the newly elected Dáil on 23 June. When the Fianna Fáil TDs refused to take the oath of loyalty to the British monarch, they were denied entry.

On 7 July 1927, Markievicz was admitted to Sir Patrick Dun's Hospital with peritonitis. When she took a turn for the worse, her family was notified. Casimir and Staskou arrived in the days following; her daughter Maeve was already at her side. Joss sent a bunch of beautiful roses that delighted her. Early on the morning of 15 July, she died peacefully.

To Hanna Sheehy Skeffington from Esther Roper   *14 Frognal*
Gardens.
Friday.

My dear Mrs Skeffington,

I am quite overwhelmed with the sudden end to all our hopes. Before I left, I made sure that both Sir William Taylor [the surgeon who attended Constance] and Dr Kathleen Lynn thought she was getting better or I never would have left her. I don't even know who was there or what happened, but I am sure in the end they gave her all the skill and affection they had. I fear none of you were with her.

If you think it will make any difference to the feelings of any one of her friends, I will come. Otherwise I shall not. Funerals do not mean anything to me. I would rather have the memory of her as she smiled and said how happy she was the other day. I never saw anyone more brave and undefeated than she, bless her. But I think she would have wished not to live if she had known that it would have been to a crippled life she would have returned, and I feel sure it would have been. You were all angels to her and she loved you. You were her friends and Dublin her home and nothing else matters. Did I tell you she said Eva had been with her all the time by her side and 'now you are the other side of me', she said, 'it's all right'?

I would be most grateful if I might have a telegram saying if you think I should come. Also if you would let Miss [Moira Kennedy] O'Byrne read this and ask her to tell the others of Con's friends who were there on Saturday night what I have written as I have so many letters to write. But I should always feel a great bond of sympathy and friendliness for all of those with whom I lived through those days.

Yours sincerely,
E. G. Roper

Telegram from Esther Roper to Hanna Sheehy Skeffington, 15 July 1927.

Reginald and I are coming tomorrow. Disregard letter. Roper

**Draft of letter by Mary O'Carroll
to Casimir Markievicz**   *[Undated; after 1927].*

Dear Count Markievicz,
We were going on our holidays when your letter to my husband arrived. He has been very busy since our return so I have decided to write to you about Madame. There is really nothing political that I can tell of. She came to us in March 1920 disguised as an old lady. Only the older members of the family knew who she really was and so that her identity would not become known, we called her auntie, and continued to do so until the day of her death.

During her stay here (8 months) she took a great interest in the garden. She loved flowers as you know and was very happy amongst them. When she was not caring for them, she was sketching. During the time she was here, Mrs O'Carroll told her a true story on which she built her play *The Invincible Mother* which was short but very effective. She began Irish taught by Carroll my eldest boy and made short speeches in it.

The poor too concerned her. I saw her frequently take pound notes from her purse and give them [to the poor] after having brought them to my kitchen to be fed. One day when out with her, she was stopped by a poor woman who smelled heavily of drink. She gave her a large silver piece and when afterwards I remonstrated with her and said that woman would spend the money in a public house, she said, 'Poor thing, it's probably the only enjoyment she gets in life.'

Constance's funeral on Sunday, 17 July 1927, was one of the largest ever seen in Dublin, with the poor of the city lining the streets to bid their 'Madame' farewell on her final journey to Glasnevin Cemetery. Eight motor tenders were needed for the wreaths and flowers.

Éamon de Valera gave the oration at the graveside: 'Madame Markievicz is gone from us – Madame, the friend of the toiler, the lover of the poor. Ease and station she put aside, and took the hard way of service with the weak and the downtrodden. Sacrifice, misunderstanding and scorn lay on the road she adopted, but she trod it unflinchingly.'

He applauded 'this wonderful outcrop of Irish landlordism and Dublin Castle, this brilliant, fascinating, incomprehensible rebel'.

'She now lies at rest – mourned by the people whose liberties she fought for, blessed by the loving prayers of the poor she tried so hard to befriend. The world knew her only as a soldier of Ireland, but we knew her as a colleague and comrade.

'We knew the kindliness, the great woman's heart of her, the great Irish soul of her, and we know the loss we have suffered is not to be repaired. It is sadly we take our leave, but we pray high heaven that all she longed for may one day be achieved.'

Dramatis Personae

Annesley, Lady Clare (1893–1980). Born in Castlewellan, Co. Down, the daughter of Hugh Annesley (5th Earl Annesley) and Priscilla Cecilia Armytage Moore (a friend of the Gore-Booth family). Was briefly engaged to Hugh Lane. She attended the Slade School of Art (like Markievicz) and became active in social work in the East End of London, and in the suffrage movement, alongside her sister, Constance Malleson. She was a pacifist, a vegetarian and anti-hunting.

Ashe, Thomas (1885–1917). Commanded the Fingal battalion of the Irish Volunteers, which won a major battle in Ashbourne, Co. Meath during the 1916 Rising. He was sentenced to death, but this was commuted to life imprisonment. After undertaking a hunger strike, he was freed from Lewes Prison in June 1917. In August 1917, he was arrested for sedition and sentenced to two years' hard labour in Mountjoy Prison, where he went on hunger strike demanding prisoner-of-war status. His subsequent death became a rallying call for Irish republicans.

Baden-Powell, Robert (1857–1941). Founder of the Boy Scouts in 1909.

Barton, Robert (1881–1975). Born in Co. Wicklow, he was an officer in the British Army during the First World War. During the 1916 Rising, he resigned his commission and joined the Republican movement. He was a delegate at the Anglo-Irish Treaty negotiations of 1921, along with his cousin Erskine Childers. His older sister was Dulcibella Barton.

Barton, Dulcibella (1879–1956). Known as 'Bella'. A friend of Markievicz's, she would stay in Surrey House when she came to Dublin and looked after Markievicz's dog Poppet while she was in jail. Her brother was Robert Barton; they lived in Glendalough House, nestled in the Wicklow hills near Annamoe.

Besant, Annie (1847–1933). British socialist, theosophist, women's rights activist and supporter of Indian and Irish independence.

Bibby, Fr Albert (1877–1925). A Capuchin priest based in the friary at Dublin's Church Street. He and Fr Augustine ministered to the rebel prisoners in Kilmainham Jail after the 1916 Rising. He was sent to the USA in 1924 and died five months later.

Boyd, Ernest (1887–1946). Writer. He settled in the USA in 1920.

Braddon, Mary Elizabeth (1835–1915). Popular novelist of the Victorian era.

Brailsford, Henry Noel (1873–1958). A prolific writer, his *The Russian Workers' Republic* (1921) was one of his many books.

Brayton, Teresa (1868–1943). Poet with republican sympathies. She was a native of Kildare who spent many years in the USA.

Brodrick, the Hon. Albinia (also Gobnait Ní Bhruadair) (1861–1955). From a privileged background, Brodrick lived in Caherdaniel, Co. Kerry and in mid-life joined the republican cause. Like her friend Mary McSwiney, she opposed the Anglo-Irish Treaty and in April 1923 was arrested and sent to the North Dublin Union where she went on hunger strike.

Bullitt, William Christian (1891–1967). An American diplomat working for the American president Woodrow Wilson at the 1919 Paris Peace Conference, he resigned when Wilson refused to support American rapprochement with Bolshevik Russia. He later testified to the American senate against the Treaty of Versailles.

Carney, Winifrid (1887–1943). Northern Ireland-born republican who was James Connolly's secretary before and during the 1916 Rising. In the 1918 general election, she stood as a Sinn Féin candidate for Belfast Victoria.

Carson, Edward (1854–1935). An Irish Unionist politician born in Dublin who campaigned against the introduction of Home Rule for Ireland from 1911 onwards.

Cassidy, Thomas (?–?). President of Irish Labour Party and Trade Union Congress. He presided over the 25th congress in Drogheda 4–7 August 1919. Under his leadership, Labour abstained from the 1918 general election at the request of Sinn Féin to avoid splitting the nationalist vote.

Cavanagh MacDowell, Maeve (1878–1960). Older sister of the political cartoonist Ernest Kavanagh, who was shot dead on the steps of Liberty Hall during the Easter Rising. She was a talented poet.

Childers, Erskine (1870–1922). A bestselling novelist, Childers had used his boat the *Asgard* to smuggle guns into Howth in June 1914. He was secretary to the Irish delegation at the Anglo-Irish Treaty negotiations of 1921; his cousin Robert Barton was a delegate. In 1922, he was executed by a Free State firing squad for possession of a small hand gun, given to him as a gift by Michael Collins. His son, also Erskine Childers, became President of Ireland in 1973.

Clarke, Kathleen (1878–1972). Born in Limerick; widow of executed 1916 leader Thomas Clarke and older sister of Ned Daly, also executed for his part in the 1916 Rising. She was a founder member of Cumann na mBan in 1914. In 1919, she spent eleven months in Holloway Prison with Markievicz, who lodged with her and the three Clarke boys after her release. She was a founder member of Fianna Fáil and later the first female Lord Mayor of Dublin.

Clarke, Thomas, 'Tom' (1858–1916). One of the seven leaders of the 1916 Rising. A believer in armed insurrection all his life, he spent fifteen years in prison for his part in the Fenian dynamite campaign of 1883 in England. After his release in 1898, he moved to the USA and married Kathleen Daly, twenty years his junior. The couple returned to Ireland in 1907.

Coffey, Jane (*née* L'Estrange) (1857–1921). A cousin of the Gore-Booths. She founded the Dublin Workingman's Club through which she met her husband George Coffey (1857–1916). Their son Diarmid was a writer and public servant.

Cole, George Douglas Howard (1889–1959). An English political theorist and historian who was an advocate of the co-operative movement. He wrote biographies of William Cobbett and Robert Owen.

Collins, Beatrice (?–?). Taught art at Homerton Teacher Training College; a pacifist.

Colum, Padraic (1881–1972). Irish poet and writer; leading figure in the Irish Literary Revival. His wife Mary (1884–1957) was also a writer. They emigrated to the USA in 1914.

Connolly, James (1868–1916). Irish republican and socialist leader. When living in Belfast, he lodged with Markievicz at Surrey House on his visits to Dublin.

Connolly, Lillie (*c.*1867–1938). Married James Connolly in 1890; mother of Nora and Ina. She stayed in Markievicz's Sandyford cottage during the 1916 Rising.

Connolly Heron, Ina (1896–1980). Younger sister of Nora and daughter of James and Lillie Connolly. She stayed in Markievicz's Sandyford cottage during the Howth gun-running.

Connolly O'Brien, Nora (1892–1981). Daughter of James and Lillie Connolly. She established a girls' branch of the Fianna, called the Betsy Gray Sluagh, in Belfast, through which she met Markievicz.

Connolly, Seán ('Shawn') (1882–1916). Actor and member of the Irish Citizen Army who shot dead Constable James O'Brien at the gate to City

Hall in the first skirmish of the 1916 Rising. Within an hour, Connolly himself was shot dead by a British sniper. His sister Katie Barrett joined the Irish Citizen Army at the age of 17.

Crofts, Gerard (1888–1934). Musician and member of Irish Volunteers. Markievicz refers to a raid on the family home and to his mother Mrs Margaret Crofts in a letter. Her illustration of Dora Sigerson Shorter's poem 'They did not see thy face' made in Aylesbury Prison was a wedding gift for Crofts.

D'Annunzio, Gabriele (1863–1838). Italian literary figure who became a war hero in the 1914–18 conflict. An ultra-nationalist, he seized the city of Fiume after the Paris Peace Conference and attempted to set up an alternative League of Nations for oppressed nations, including Ireland. He surrendered the city in 1920.

Daly, Madge (1877–1969). A sister of Kathleen Clarke and of Edward 'Ned' Daly, who was executed after the 1916 Rising, along with his brother-in-law Thomas Clarke.

Derrig, Thomas (1897–1956). An Irish Republican who fought in the 1916 Rising and, after he was arrested by the Irish Free State Army, helped organise the 1923 hunger strike of prisoners. He later served as a Fianna Fail Government Minister.

Devlin, Anne (1780–1851). Housekeeper for the rebel republican Robert Emmett, she refused to inform on her employer after the abortive rebellion of 1803.

Dickenson, Sarah (1868–1954). Manchester trade unionist and suffragist. A friend of Eva Gore-Booth.

Douglas-Pennant, Violet (1869–1945). Commandant of the Women's Royal Air Force but later dismissed. She demanded an inquiry into her dismissal, claiming that it was part of a cover-up of 'rife immorality' by other WRAF officers. She was successfully sued for libel by two of the senior WRAF officers.

Dryhurst, Hannah, Ann, 'Nannie' (1856–1930). Dublin-born nationalist and anarchist thinker. She had a long affair with the journalist H. W. Nevinson, who became a regular visitor to Dublin.

Dunne, John Patrick, 'J. P.' (?–?). Secretary of the 1798 Centenary Committee; later he was a member of the Wolfe Tone and United Irishmen Memorial Committee.

ffrench-Mullen, Madeleine (1880–1944). Member of Inghinidhe na hÉireann, where she met her lifelong companion Dr Kathleen Lynn. She worked in the Liberty Hall soup kitchen with Markievicz during the 1913 Lockout. A member of Irish Citizen Army, in the 1916 Rising, she took charge of the first aid tent at St Stephen's Green and in the Royal College of Surgeons. Her brother Douglas also fought in the Rising. With Dr Lynn, she established St Ultan's Children's Hospital in 1919.

Figgis, Darryl (1882–1925). Sinn Féin activist and writer who edited *The Republic* newspaper, later *An Phoblacht*, for a short period after 1918.

Fitzgerald, Theo (1899–?). Long-serving Fianna member, who painted 'Irish Republic' on the green flag hoisted over the GPO by the Irish Citizen Army on the opening day of the 1916 Rising.

Foran, Thomas (?–1951). Labour activist. A member of the Irish Transport and General Workers' Union; he was elected president of Irish Trade Union Congress in 1921.

Forbes-Robertson, Eric (1865–1935). A British artist who was based in France and married a Polish art student, Janina Flamm, in 1897.

Fry, Roger (1866–1934). English painter and critic. He rented the top storey of his house in Bloomsbury to Eva Gore-Booth and Esther Roper when they moved to London from Manchester in 1913.

Gavan Duffy, George (1882–1951). Irish politician, barrister and judge; he was the son of Sir Charles Gavan Duffy, the writer and nationalist politician who became governor of Victoria in Australia. He defended Roger Casement in his trial for high treason after the 1916 Rising. In 1918, he was elected a Sinn Féin MP; in 1921 he was a signatory of the Anglo-Irish Agreement. His sister Louise, an Irish language enthusiast, taught in St Ita's, the school for girls established by Patrick Pearse in Dublin.

Gifford sisters: Katie, Nellie, Ada, Muriel, Grace and Sidney. Nellie, born 1880, was a socialist and ICA (Irish Citizen Army) member and married Joseph Donnelly, a publisher, in 1918. Muriel, born 1884, married 1916 leader and poet Thomas MacDonagh in 1912; she tragically drowned in 1917. Grace, born 1888, was a gifted cartoonist and famously married Joseph Mary Plunkett at Kilmainham in the hours before his execution in 1916. Sidney (or Sydney), born 1889, wrote for *Bean na hÉireann* as 'John Brennan'. She married Arpad Czira and moved to the USA, but the marriage failed.

Ginnell, Laurence (1852–1923). Irish MP from Delvin, Co. Westmeath; a member of Irish Parliamentary Party who transferred his allegiance to Sinn Féin in 1918. When in Dublin, Ginnell and his wife, Alice, stayed with Markievicz at Surrey House; after her first jail stretch, they shared a house in Dublin.

Gonne MacBride, Maud (1866–1953). English-born political activist, suffragist and actress, who was interned with Markievicz in Holloway Prison. Her children were Iseult (1894-1954) and Seán (1905–1988). She suffered from TB as a young woman.

Gore-Booth, Augusta (?–1906). Older unmarried sister of Sir Henry, who lived at Lissadell House. She was known as 'Wee Ga' because of her small stature.

Gore-Booth, Eva Selina (1870–1926). Younger sister of Constance. A poet, trade unionist, pacifist and suffragist, she became an active campaigner in the UK, mostly on women's issues. She fought for the reprieve of her sister's death sentence after the 1916 Rising and for the improvement of her prison conditions. Always of delicate health, she died in 1926; a broken-hearted Constance did not attend the funeral.

Gore-Booth, Lady Georgina Mary (*c.*1842–1927). Mother of Markievicz; known as 'Gaga' to her children.

Gore-Booth, Sir Henry (1843–1900). Father of Markievicz. Landlord and Arctic explorer.

Gore-Booth, Josslyn (1869–1944). Brother of Markievicz; a progressive farmer and horticulturist. He married his second cousin Mary 'Molly' L'Estrange Malone; they had eight children.

Gore-Booth, Mabel (1884–1955). Youngest sister of Markievicz. She married Charles Percival Foster on 1 December 1900; they had two children. She remained close to her step-nephew Stanislas 'Staskou' Markievicz.

Gore-Booth, Mordaunt (1878–1958). Youngest brother of Markievicz. An Oxford graduate and later the manager of Vickers Tyre Mill, Doncaster, England. He married Evelyn Mary Scholefield in 1906; they had three children.

Gray, Betsy (d. 1798). Irish peasant girl from Co. Down, who was killed in the 1789 Rebellion. The subject of many folk ballads and poems.

Grey, Edward (1862–1933). Long-serving Liberal politician. British ambassador to the USA, 1919–1920. He wanted British troops pulled out of Ireland.

Harmsworth, Alfred, 1st Viscount Northcliffe (1865–1922). British newspaper magnate, born in Chapelizod, Co. Dublin, who founded Associated Newspapers, publishers of the *Daily Mail* and the *Daily Mirror*, with his brother Harold. He was director of propaganda during the First World War.

Harmsworth, Harold Sidney, 1st Viscount Rothermere (1868–1940). A pioneer of popular journalist along with his brother Alfred, who took a controlling interest in Associated Newspapers after the death of his brother. He was president of the Air Council during the First World War.

Henderson, Arthur (1863–1935). Elected leader of Labour Party in 1914. In 1915, he was appointed the first ever Labour cabinet member in Asquith's coalition government and became a member of a small war cabinet when Lloyd George replaced Asquith as prime minister in December 1916. He resigned in August 1917.

Hobhouse, Stephen (1881–1961). Prison reformer, peace activist and religious writer. A conscientious objector, he was jailed in 1916 for refusing to fight in the First World War. He was finally released in December 1917 after a sustained campaign by his mother. He wrote a number of books on prison reform.

Hobson, John A. (1858–1940). English economist and critic of imperialism. Author of several books read by Constance while in prison.

Humphreys née Rahilly, Nell (1871–1939). A sister of Michael Rahilly, better known as The O'Rahilly; he was shot dead during the 1916 Rising. Mother of Dick and Sighle, both active Republicans.

Kavanagh, Ernest (1884–1916). Political cartoonist, who worked in Liberty Hall as a clerk to the Irish Transport and General Workers' Union. On 25 April 1916, the second day of the Easter rebellion, he was shot dead on the steps of Liberty Hall. Maeve Cavanagh MacDowell (who adopted a different spelling of the family name) was his sister.

Kelly, Alderman Thomas (1868–1942). Long-serving member of Dublin Corporation and later a TD. He was a founding member of Sinn Féin

Kent, Áine (Áine Ceannt) (1880–1954). Her husband Éamonn Ceannt was one of the seven signatories of the 1916 Proclamation and, like the other six, was executed. After 1921, she helped found the Irish White Cross which distributed funds raised in the USA for needy Irish republicans. Her son Ronan is mentioned in a Markievicz letter. Her sisters, also republican activists, were Lily and Kathleen O'Brennan.

Kolchak, Alexander (1874–1920). Leader of the White Russian anti-Bolshevik government based in Omsk, Siberia, who was captured and executed in 1920.

Lalor, James Fintan (1807–1849). A writer and a leading member of Young Ireland, his words 'Remember this – that somewhere and somehow, and by somebody, a beginning must be made' were much quoted by later Irish rebels.

Lansbury, George (1859–1940). British politician, pacifist and social reformer. He was editor of the *Daily Herald,* founded in 1912.

Larkin, Delia (1878–1949). A trade union activist, she was the younger sister of James Larkin with whom she founded the Irish Women Workers' Union. During the 1913 Lockout, she worked with Markievicz in the Liberty Hall soup kitchen. She left Ireland to work as a nurse in England before the 1916 Rising; in 1918, she returned and helped James found the Workers' Union of Ireland.

Larkin, James (1876–1947). Mercurial socialist and labour organiser who founded the Irish Transport and General Workers' Union in 1908. He led the workers during the 1913 Lockout, leaving for the USA soon after. On his return to Ireland in 1923, he found himself at odds with the ITGWU leadership and founded the Irish Worker League, which became the Workers' Union of Ireland.

L'Estrange Malone, Cecil (1890–1965). Born in Yorkshire, he was a second cousin and brother-in-law of Markievicz; his sister Mary ('Molly') married Josslyn Gore-Booth. Although he was elected as a Liberal MP in 1918, he joined the Communist Party after a visit to Russia, so becoming Britain's first communist MP. He spent six months in jail after a fiery speech at the Royal Albert Hall in late 1920. In 1922, he abandoned communism for the Labour Party and later served in government. His wife Leah Kay (1886–1951) was also a politician.

Litvinoff, Maxim (1876–1951). Russian revolutionary and writer; later a diplomat. His book *The Bolshevik Revolution: its Rise and Meaning* was published in 1918.

Lowe, Major-General William Henry Muir (1861–1944). British army officer who commanded the British forces in Dublin during the 1916 Rising.

Lynch, Arthur (1861–1934). A colourful character born in Australia of an Irish father, he fought on the Boer side during the Boer War. For this he was sentenced to death for treason but later pardoned. In the early twentieth century, he was elected as an Irish Parliamentary Party MP to Westminster. He stood as a Labour candidate for Battersea South in the 1918 general election, finishing second to a unionist. After he abandoned politics, he took up practice as a medical doctor. A polymath, he published a large number of books on a variety of topics.

Lynch (later Kelly), Elizabeth, 'Bessie' (1895–1975). An Irish Citizen Army member who was Markievicz's housekeeper at Surrey House. She fought with the City Hall group in 1916 and was held in Richmond Barracks and later Kilmainham Jail.

Lynch, Patricia (1898–1972). In 1916, Lynch was sent to Dublin by Sylvia Pankhurst to report on the Easter Rising for *The Workers' Dreadnought*. She became friends with Constance around that time and supported her during her stretch in Holloway. After marrying the author R. M. Fox in 1922, she settled in Dublin and became a renowned writer of children's fiction.

Lynn, Kathleen (1874–1955). A distant relative of Constance, Lynn graduated as a doctor in 1899 and worked in a number of Dublin hospitals before establishing a private practice in Rathmines. She supported the workers during the 1913 Lockout and was chief medical officer during the 1916 Rising. After independence, she founded St Ultan's Children's Hospital. She was elected a Sinn Féin TD in 1923, but abandoned politics in 1927.

Macardle, Dorothy (1889–1958). Born in Dundalk to a wealthy brewing family, Macardle took the anti-Treaty side after the War of Independence and was jailed during the Civil War. Her pro-de Valera history, *The Irish Republic*, was published in 1937. She acquired the prison letters written by Constance to her sister Eva after Esther Roper's death and presented these to the National Library of Ireland in 1951.

MacDonagh, Joseph (1883–1922). An Irish Republican and anti-Treaty Sinn Féin TD, Joseph was a brother of the executed 1916 leader Thomas MacDonagh. In 1920, he masterminded a boycott of goods from Northern Ireland despite the opposition of Markievicz.

MacDonagh, Thomas (1878–1916). Poet, teacher and political activist. One of the seven signatories of the 1916 Proclamation and later executed. He was married to Muriel Gifford.

MacDonnell, Anthony, 1st Baron (1844–1925). Irish civil servant from Co. Mayo, a liberal and a Catholic. From 1902 to 1908, he was Under-Secretary of State for Ireland; it was during this time that the Markieviczs returned from France to live in Dublin.

Maclean, John (1879–1923). Scottish socialist opposed to the First World War who was arrested for sedition in April 1918 and made a celebrated speech from the dock. He had undertaken a speaking tour of Ireland in 1907 but, as a pacifist, he was opposed to the 1916 Rising.

MacMahon, Seán (1893–1955). A Member of the Irish Volunteers who fought at Bolands Mills during the 1916 Rising. He was interned in Frongach prison camp, north Wales, along with his future brothers-in-law, Leo, Thomas and James Fitzgerald. He married Lucinda Fitzgerald in 1919. MacMahon later became a general in the National Army of the Irish Fee State.

MacNeill, Eoin (1867–1945). Irish scholar and Sinn Féin politician, who established the Irish Volunteers in 1913 and served as chief of staff up to 1916. Despite this, he knew nothing of the proposed Easter Rising until the last minute and famously attempted to call it off.

MacSwiney, Mary (1872–1942). Founder member of Cumann na mBan in 1914. Her brother Terence MacSwiney died on hunger strike in 1920. An 'advanced' republican, she made a three-hour anti-Treaty speech in the Dáil in 1922 and went on hunger strike when interned at Mountjoy Prison in November of that year. In 1927, she became leader of Sinn Féin when Éamon de Valera resigned from the party.

Mallin, Michael (1874–1916). Leader of the Irish Citizen Army garrison in St Stephen's Green, where Markievicz was one of his deputies. He left a wife, Agnes, and four children, with a fifth on the way when he died. Constance did her best to support the family, which was left destitute after his death; his posthumously-born daughter was named after her.

Maunsel and Company. A publishing house established at 96 Abbey Street, Dublin, by Joseph Maunsel Hone supported by Stephen Gwynn. Their offices were burned down during the 1916 Rising. General manager was George Roberts (1873–1953); the company was re-named Maunsel and Roberts in 1920.

Maxwell, General Sir John Grenfell (1859–1929). British army officer sent to Ireland with 'plenary powers' in the wake of the 1916 Rising; best known for ordering the execution of its leaders. In all, he had 3,400 people arrested and 90 sentenced to death. Fifteen were shot between 3 and 12 May before Prime Minister H.H. Asquith called a halt.

McDermott, Seán (1883–1916). Also known as Seán Mac Diarmada. One of the seven signatories of the 1916 Proclamation executed after the Rising.

McGarrity, Joseph (1874–1940). Irish-American leader of Clan na Gael, an American organisation dedicated to supporting the cause of Irish independence financially. He developed close links with de Valera during his eighteen-month USA visit of 1919 and 1920. He visited Ireland during the Treaty election campaign and met Markievicz on her 1922 tour of the USA.

McGarry, Seán (1886–1958). Senior member of the Irish Republican Brotherhood who was sent to Frongach internment camp in Wales after the 1916 Rising. In 1918, he was arrested for involvement in 'German Plot'; he escaped from Lincoln Jail in February 1919 with de Valera and Seán Milroy. In 1922, he supported the Anglo-Irish Treaty.

McGrath, Joseph (1888–1966). Fought in 1916 Rising and was jailed afterwards in England. He was elected to the First Dáil of 1918 as a Sinn Féin candidate. In the Irish Civil War, he was pro-Treaty. In 1930, he founded the Irish Hospitals' Sweepstake, which made him a wealthy man.

McHugh, Frank (?–?). Irish republican based in Glasgow with links to Na Fianna.

McPherson, Ian (1880–1937). Chief Secretary for Ireland, 1919–20. From 1916 to 1918, he was Britain's Under-Secretary for War.

Mellows, Liam (1892–1922). Member of Na Fianna, who was highly regarded by Markievicz and James Connolly. He was anti-Treaty and in December 1922 was executed by a Free State firing squad.

Meynell, Alice (1847–1922). Writer, suffragist and poet. Mother of Viola. Her sister was the artist Lady Elizabeth Butler.

Michelham, Herbert Stern, 1st Baron (1851–1919). Wealthy British banker. On his death-bed, his wife forced him to sign an agreement settling a fortune on his younger son's fiancée, bypassing the older son. The case became a *cause célèbre*.

Milligan, Alice (1865–1953). Influential nationalist poet and writer. A member of the Gaelic League.

Mitchel, John (1815–1875). Irish nationalist, author and political journalist. Mitchel was transported to Van Diemen's Land, Australia, for his activities with Young Ireland. After he escaped, he lived in the USA, supporting the Confederate States during the American Civil War and becoming an advocate for slavery. His *Jail Journal* is one of the pivotal texts of Irish republicanism.

Mitchell, Susan (1866–1926). A distant relative of the Gore-Booths. Worked as the subeditor of *The Irish Homestead*, edited by George 'Æ' Russell, and produced several collections of poetry. With Eva, she visited Surrey House and, with Violet Russell (Æ's wife), helped to clear it out after Markievicz was jailed in 1916.

Molony, Helena 'Emer' (1883–1967). Introduced Markievicz to Inghinidhe na hÉireann (Daughters of Ireland) and in 1908 became editor of their monthly magazine *Bean na hÉireann* (Woman of Ireland), for which Markievicz designed the cover. She helped organise Na Fianna after 1909. During the 1913 Lockout, she opened a shirt factory in Liberty Hall for women who had lost their jobs. In 1916, she fought at Dublin Castle with the Irish Citizen Army; she was interned at Aylesbury Prison until 24 December 1916.

Moorehead, Ethel (1869–1955). A militant suffragette and Modernist artist of Irish extraction who lived in Scotland and attempted to blow up the Burns Cottage in Alloway among other escapades. Later, with the writer Ernest Walsh, she published a quarterly arts journal.

Morrell, Ottoline, Lady (1880–1938). English society hostess linked with the Bloomsbury set of writers and artists.

Muncaster, Josslyn Francis Pennington, 5th Baron (1834–1917). A British soldier and Conservative Party politician. He was married to Constance L'Estrange, a cousin of Constance's mother, Gaga; L'Estrange may be the 'Wuss' referred to often in the letters. He died in March 1917 followed by his wife just four months later; a double blow for Gaga.

Murray Robertson, Rachel (1858–1931). The widow of Scottish architect John Murray Robertson (1844–1901), one of whose last projects was Glenstal Castle in Co. Limerick, which is now a boarding school.

Nansen, Fridtjof (1861–1930). Norwegian Arctic explorer. He worked as the League of Nations' High Commissioner for Refugees from 1921.

Neild, Helen J. (1870–?) Teacher and suffragist; Esther Roper taught at Neild's Pinehurst School. In 1907, Eva Gore-Booth wrote *The Sorrowful Princess* as a school play for Neild.

Nevinson, Henry (1856–1941). British campaigning journalist and writer. His passionate affair with Nannie Dryhurst brought him frequently to Dublin.

Newbold, Walton (1888–1943). British Marxist intellectual. He wrote several books, including *Capitalism* and *Imperialism*, which were familiar to Markievicz.

Norgrove family. All five members of the family were involved in the 1913 Lockout and 1916 Rising: father George, mother Maria, daughters Emily and Annie and son Fred (aged 12 in 1916).

Noyk, Michael (1884–1966). Dublin solicitor and Irish republican politician. He was election agent for both Markievicz and Seán T. O'Kelly in the 1918 election.

O'Brien, William (1852–1928). Irish nationalist associated with campaigns for land reform; in 1887, he famously refused to wear clothes when jailed after a rent strike that resulted in three deaths. A Home Rule MP, he switched allegiance to Sinn Féin during the anti-conscription crisis of 1918. He retired from politics after the establishment of the Irish Free State.

O'Brien, William X. (1881–1968). Cork socialist and friend of James Connolly; co-founder of the Irish Transport and General Workers' Union. A member of the Irish Neutrality League and the Anti-Conscription Committee, he was interned several times. Elected TD for Dublin South in 1922. His feud with James Larkin caused a long-lasting split in the Labour Party and the Irish trade union movement.

O'Byrne, Moira Kennedy [?–?]. Joined Cumann na mBan after the 1916 Rising. She worked for the Department of Labour when Constance was Minister. When the Civil War started, Constance was staying in the O'Byrne family home at Highfield Road, Rathgar, Dublin.

O'Donovan Rossa, Jeremiah (1831–1915). Irish Fenian leader and Irish Republican Brotherhood member who was jailed in 1858 for plotting a

Fenian rising. He was exiled to the USA after his release in 1870. From there, he organised the first bombing campaign by Irish republicans of British cities. He was married three times and had eighteen children. His 1915 funeral in Dublin is remembered for Patrick Pearse's graveside oration: 'Ireland unfree shall never be at peace.'

O'Growney, Eugene (1863–1899). Irish priest and scholar; founding member of the Gaelic League and author of five textbooks on the Irish language.

O'Hegarty, P.S. (1879–1955). Irish writer and historian. Former member of IRB. Married Wilhemina 'Mina' Smyth in 1915. A good friend to Markievicz when she was in jail.

O'Kelly, J. J., 'Sceilg' (1872–1957). Irish politician, writer and publisher who became president of the Gaelic League and of Sinn Féin. He was based in the USA during Constance's 1922 visit.

O'Shannon, Cathal (1893–1969). A founder of Irish Volunteers in Belfast. When arrested during the 'German Plot', he went on hunger strike and was released after seventeen days. In 1922, he was elected to the Dáil as pro-Treaty TD.

O'Shaughnessy, Arthur (1844–1881). A British poet of Irish descent best known for his 'Ode', which ends 'For each age is a dream that is dying/Or one that is coming to birth.'

Pankhurst, Sylvia (1882–1960). Daughter of Emmeline and sister of Christobel and Adela. Socialist. She met Eva Gore-Booth in Manchester and supported the workers during the 1913 Lockout. For this, she was expelled from the Women's Social and Political Union founded by her mother. In 1915, she founded *Woman's Dreadnought* newspaper, later *The Workers' Dreadnought*, which Markievicz requested from Cork Jail.

Partridge, William (1874–1917). Irish trade unionist and revolutionary socialist. He fought with Constance in the 1916 Rising; after his death a year later, she gave the oration at his funeral.

Pearse, Margaret (1857–1932). Mother of Patrick, 1916 leader, and his brother William. She became involved in public life after her sons were executed in 1916. She was elected to the Dáil in 1921, but lost her seat in 1922. She was anti-Treaty and a founding member of Fianna Fáil. In 1924, aged 70, she travelled to the USA to raise funds for St Enda's School, founded by Patrick in 1908. Her daughter, Mary Margaret (1878–1968), served as a Fianna Fáil TD from 1933 to 1937 and as a senator from 1938 until her death.

Pearse, Patrick (1879–1916). Educationalist, writer and revolutionary. He was commander-in-chief of the forces of the nascent Irish Republic during the 1916 Rising. Like the other leaders, he was executed after the Rising.

Perolz, Marie (1874–1950). Known invariably by her surname, she was a founder member of Inghinidhe na hÉireann in 1900 and a member of both Cumann na mBan and the Irish Citizen Army. She substituted for the banned Markievicz at the Fianna Éireann festival in Tralee a month before Easter 1916. In June 1917, she travelled to England to meet Markievicz on her release from Aylesbury Prison.

Pigott, Richard (1835–1889). Author of fake letters that attempted to link Charles Stewart Parnell to the murder of Lord Cavendish, the newly appointed Chief Secretary for Ireland, and Thomas Henry Burke, the Permanent Under-Secretary, in Dublin's Phoenix Park on 6 May 1882.

Plunkett, Count George Nobel (1851–1948). Nationalist politician who was created a Papal Count by Pope Leo XIII in 1884. His son Joseph was executed for his role in the 1916 Rising.

Plunkett, Countess Josephine (1858–1944). Wife of Count George Noble Plunkett and mother of 1916 leader Joseph. She was briefly a member of the Sinn Féin executive.

Plunkett, Horace (1854–1932). Pioneer of the co-operative movement and of agricultural education in Ireland through the Irish Agricultural Organisation Society; supporter of Home Rule. He employed George

(Æ) Russell as the editor of the *The Irish Homestead* weekly publication. In 1922, he was appointed senator, but after his Co. Dublin house was burned out by the IRA in 1923, he resigned from the Senate and moved permanently to England.

Reddish, Sarah (1850–1928). British trade unionist and suffragist. A friend of Eva's.

Redmond, John (1856–1918). Leader of the moderate Irish Parliamentary Party at Westminster from 1900 until his death in 1918. The upsurge in republican sympathies after the 1916 Rising wiped out the party.

Reynolds, Augustus Percival, 'Percy' (1895–1983). An original member of Na Fianna and a particular favourite of Markievicz. He was appointed first chairman of Córas Iompair Éireann (CIÉ), the Irish public transport service, when it was founded in 1945. His horse Sol Oriens won the Irish Derby in 1941.

Robinson, Joseph (1887–1955). Belfast-born republican and first treasurer of Na Fianna Éireann in 1909. His family moved to Glasgow, Scotland, where he set up a Fianna branch and also a branch of the Irish Volunteers. When in Dublin, he stayed at Surrey House. He was interned after the 1916 Rising; later, in 1918, he was again jailed.

Robinson, Lennox (1886–1958). Abbey Theatre playwright, producer and director.

Roper, Esther (1868–1938). Lifelong companion of Eva Gore-Booth; regarded as a 'sister' by Constance. She met Eva in 1896 while on a break in Italy. A year later, Eva moved to Manchester to live with Roper and assist her in her pioneeering work for working-class women. In 1913, Eva's delicate health forced a move to London. Esther supported Constance during her stretches in Aylesbury and Holloway prisons. She edited *The Prison Letters of Countess Markievicz* (1934).

Roper, Reginald Edward (?–?). Esther's younger brother, who helped look after Eva in her final illness. A classics graduate, he had trained as a physical educator, working for several years at Mostyn House Boys' School in Chester. His book *Physical Education in Relation to School Life* was published in 1917. He never married.

Russell, Bertrand (1872–1970). British philosopher, mathematician and anti-war activist. A friend of Eva's and a prolific writer. In 1950, he was awarded the Nobel Prize for Literature.

Russell, George 'Æ' (1867–1934). Poet, artist and visionary. From 1897, he worked for the Irish Agricultural Organisation Society, travelling extensively and editing its monthly magazine *The Irish Homestead*; later he edited the *Irish Statesman* weekly journal. Sometime after 1901, he met the Markieviczs at Lissadell House, and suggested that they live in Dublin. It was at Russell's Sunday evening 'At Home' gatherings in Rathgar that Constance met Arthur Griffith, founder of Sinn Féin. His wife Violet was a good friend to the Markieviczs.

Sheehy Skeffington, Johanna (known as Hanna or Joan) (1877–1946). Suffragist and nationalist and founder of the Irish Women's Franchise League. She was married to the pacifist Francis Sheehy Skeffington, who was arrested and later summarily executed on 26 April 1916 when attempting to prevent looting in Dublin's city centre in the early days of the Rising. Hanna brought food to the Volunteers in the GPO and the Roayl College of Surgeons, and in 1919, she was elected a Sinn Féin TD. A staunch friend of Markievicz, she was an executor of her will.

Sigerson Shorter, Dora (1866–1918). Poet and sculptor. A key figure in the Irish literary revival.

'Squidge' (Miss Noel) (?–?). Governess to the Gore-Booth girls at Lissadell from 1882. She accompanied a young Constance on her 'Grand Tour' of Europe in 1886.

Staines, Michael (1885–1955). Fought in the GPO during 1916 and, in 1918, was elected as a Sinn Féin MP. In 1922, he was appointed first commissioner of An Garda Síochána.

Stanhope, Lady Hester (1776–1839). Niece of William Pitt the Younger. Her expedition to Ashkelon, north of Gaza, in 1815 was the first modern excavation of the Holy Land.

Stuart, Francis (1902–2000). Irish author who married Iseult Gonne at the age of 17 and lived with her in Laragh, Co. Wicklow. Their relationship proved stormy.

Sweetman, Fr J. F. OSB (1874–1953). Founder of Mount St Benedict's School in Gorey, Co. Wexford, which was attended by Stanislaus Markievicz and Seán MacBride, son of Maud Gonne. He was accused of harbouring anti-Treaty IRA men in 1925.

Thomas, Jimmy (1874–1949). British union leader at the time of the 1919 national railway strike.

Wallace, Nora (d. 1970). Nora Wallace and her sister Sheila (d. 1944) ran a small newsagents shop on Cork's Augustine Street that was a centre of Republican activity from 1916 on.

Wallas, Graham (1858–1932). British political scientist and author of *Human Nature in Politics*, a book admired by Markievicz. A member of the Fabian Society.

Wyse Power, Jane 'Jennie' (1858–1941). Founder member and later vice-president of Sinn Féin and member of Inghinidhe na hÉireann. In 1899, she opened the Irish Farm Produce Company at 21 Henry Street, Dublin; its restaurant was a meeting place for nationalists. In April 1914, she was elected first president of Cumann na mBan; in 1922, she left to form Cumann na Saoirse, which was pro-Treaty. Her daughter Nancy (1889–1963) was also an activist.

Young, Ella (1867–1956). Irish poet and folklorist, active in the Irish literary revival, and a member of Cumann na mBan. She emigrated to the USA in 1925.

Acknowledgements

Without the support and help of two great institutions – the National Library of Ireland in Dublin and the Public Records Office of Northern Ireland in Belfast – this book would not have been possible. My sincere thanks to the superb staff at both and to Sir Josslyn Gore-Booth for permission to reproduce Gore-Booth family letters held at the PRONI.

The staff at Merrion Press, led by Conor Graham and Fiona Dunne, whipped the disorderly original into a more reader-friendly shape, while David Naughton, my brother, and Jonathan Williams, agent and editor supreme, cast gimlet eyes over the manuscript at critical stages. Thank you all!

Reading the letters in their original state, mostly hand-written and often scribbled in haste, was not always easy and a few 'puzzlers' remain, especially from letters whose originals have either vanished or are held privately.

Identifying the bewildering number of family members and friends was another mammoth task. There were, for instance, more than a few Maeves, Mauds, Janeys and Seans in Markievicz's busy life. If anyone reading these letters can tell us more, we'd love to hear from you.

Lindie Naughton
Dublin, 2018

Index

Académie Julian, 8, 10, 11
Act of Supremacy, 126
Æ (George Russell), 1, 14, 27
Aeriocht, 163
After the Peace (book), 191, 194
airship, 34
Akron, Ohio, 206
Albert Hall, 160, 161
Anaconda, 205
Anglo-Irish Conference, 199
Anglo-Irish Treaty, 4, 200
Annamoe, Co Wicklow, 173
Annesley, Lady Clare, 38, 45, 47, 54, 68, 70, 78, 79, 80, 93, 100, 106,134, 143, 167, 177, 180, 186, 190, 193, 195
Aonach, 45, 153, 154
Arizona, 208
Armenia, 176
Aquitania, RMS, 200, 202
Ashe, Thomas, 62, 63
Ashley, Evelyn, 18
Asquith, Herbert H., 15, 43
Atlantic Monthly, 223
Augustine, Fr, 141
Australia, 149, 179
'Auxiliaries', 162, 170, 171
Aylesbury Prison, 3, 4, 5, 30, 31, 32–61, 62, 67, 74, 77, 99, 100, 185, 232, 234

Baden-Powell, Robert, 182,
Balfour, Arthur, 124, 179
Ballymote, Co Sligo, 212, 219
Barry, Kathleen, 200, 207

Barry, Kevin, 200
Barton, Dulcibella 'Bella', 70, 71, 74, 75, 79, 92, 106, 135, 169, 173
Barton, Johnny, detective, 155
Barton, Robert, 'Bob', 195
Belcamp Park, 15, 16
Benedict XV, Pope, 188
Besant, Annie, 118
Bialowieza (Poland), 225
Bibby, Fr Albert, 50, 54, 55, 58, 122
Billing, Noel Pemberton, 76
bike, 157
'Black and Tans', 102, 162, 191, 227
Blake, William, 52, 53, 55, 60, 87
Blood Money (play), 222
Bloody Sunday, 18, 170
Bohan, Baby, 212, 219
Bolsheviks, Bolshevism, 117, 132, 142, 147, 148, 197
Book of Kells, 152
Botticelli, 189
Bourgeois, Maurice, 164
Bourne, Cardinal, 179–80
Boy Scouts, the, 2, 173, 182
Braddon, Mary Elizabeth, 128
Brailsford, Henry N., 89, 101, 191–2, 194
Brayton, Teresa, 133
Bridewell, 108, 212
British general election 1918, 3, 85, 88, 91
Brodrick, the Hon Albina (Gobnait Ni Bhruadair), 94, 129
Broken Dreams (play), 228–9, 232

Brown Thomas, 222
Bullitt, William Christian, 143
Butte, Montana, 204, 205, 206, 207
Byrne, Molly, 53,

Carney, Winifrid, 48
Carson, Sir Edward, 43, 123, 129, 130,
    132, 141, 150
Carty, Paddy, 206
Cascade Mountains, 208
Cassidy, Thomas, 130
Castellini, Mr and Mrs, 209
Cathleen ni Houlihan (Play), 38, 91
Catholic Church, 116, 149, 172; and
    Catholic emancipation, 116;
    and flowers for church, 81; and
    Markievicz conversion 62; and
    Markievicz wedding 14; and the vote,
    219
Cavanagh MacDowell, Maeve (Mebhdh)
    37, 46
Ceannt, Áine (Anne Kent), 191
Celtic Twilight, the, 181
'Ceppi', 39
Chesterton, G.K., 115, 116
Childers, Erskine, 203, 210
Children's Court, the, 160
Christ, life of, 217, Eva book on, 231
Christianity, 178
Churchill, Winston, 14
Cincinnati, 205, 208, 209
Clare by-election, 127
Clarke, Austin, 187
Clarke, Daly, 113, 137
Clarke, Kathleen, 103; in Holloway
    Prison, 3, 5, 67–97, 227; letters to,
    107, 112–13, 118–19, 121–2, 137–8;
    and 'flu 104; and house 104, 118;
    president of Children's Court, 160;
    raid on house, 153
Clarke, Thomas, 114
Cleveland, 205
Coffey, Jane, 81, 101, 188

Coghlan, May, 200, 211
Cole, G.D.H., 89
Coleman, Richard, 89, 90
Collins, Beatrice, 46
Collins, Michael, 106, 170–1, 199–200;
    death, 210
Colum Padraic, 133
Colour (magazine), 71, 93, 100, 120, 130
Connolly Heron, Ina, 60
Connolly, James, 2, 18, 96, 114, 140, 222;
    as orator, 114
Connolly, Lillie, 25, 26, 60
Connolly O'Brien, Nora, 131, 133, 136,
    173, 223; letter from Constance to,
    110–12; visit to Russia, 173,
Connolly, Seán 'Shawn', 54
Conquest of Peru (book), 178
Conrad, Joseph, 226
co-operative movement and co-ops, 1,
    20, 37, 50, 141, 148, 194
copper mine visit, 207
Cork, jail, 4, 106–52, 177, 227; release
    from, 153
Cork, 259; lecture in, 64; fire, 171, 176
Corporation (Dublin), 160, 218
Cosgrave, William T, 210, 211
Court of Conscience, 160
Crofts, Margaret, 161
Croke Park massacre, 170–1
Cromwell, Oliver, 149
Cromwell, Thomas, 149
Cumann na mBan, 2, 18, 102, 125, 131,
    195, 200, 228
Cumann na nGaedheal, 211
Cumann an Saoirse, 200
Cunard Line, 200
curfew, 182
Custom House, 188
Czira, Sidney Gifford ('John Brennan'),
    37, 147

Dáil Eireann, 1st Dáil, 3, 4, 90, 102, 105,
    111, 153, 164; 2nd Dáil, 197, 198,

200; 3rd Dáil, 210; 4th Dáil, 211; 5th Dáil, 4
Daily Herald (newspaper), 72, 94, 123, 127, 128, 139, 140, 147, 215
Daily Mail (newspaper), 96
Daly, Madge, 74, 75, 82, 86, 97, 104, 105, 121
D'Annunzio, Gabriele, 182
Danton, Georges, 173, 174
Da Vinci, Leonardo, 71
Davis, Thomas, 114
Defence of the Realm Act (D.O.R.A.) 143, 150
Denikin, Anton, 146
Department of Labour, Dáil Eireann, 62, 164, 198, 211
Derrig, Tom, 214, 218
Detroit, 205, 206
de Valera, Eamon, 'Dev', 3, 4, 96, 98, 105, 106, 111, 122, 136, 161, 179, 202, 212; and Anglo-Irish Treaty, 199–200; Clare by-election, 127; escape from Lincoln jail, 96; and Fianna Fáil, 228; leaves for USA, 106; letters from Constance to, 105, 163; Markievicz funeral oration 238; and 'Oath', 229; 'One man with a dream', 93; president of 2nd Dáil, 197; resigns from Sinn Fein 228; returns from USA, 171; 'straight and honest', 148; 'toleration and sanity', 203
Devlin, Anne, letter from Constance to, 140
Dickenson Sarah, 38
Dissenters, 172
Douglas-Pennant, Violet, 128, 133, 150
Downing, Constable Michael, 153
Dreadnought (magazine), 72, 94, 110
Drogheda, 130
Dryhurst, Hannah Ann ('Nannie'), 45
Dublin Castle, 153, 200, 238
Dublin Repertory Company, 18

Dublin South constituency, 212
Dublin United Tramway Company, 18
Dunne, John Patrick ('J.P.'), 73
Duomo, 165

Easter Rising 1916, 2–3, 22–3, 62; 1916 Proclamation 4
Egyptian Pillar, the, (book), 123
elections, 143, 155, 159, 218, 229,
Elizabeth l, queen, 128, 149, 190
England, 1, 3, 29, 30, 39, 70, 76, 98, 115, 116, 120, 122, 123, 125, 131, 134, 139, 143, 146, 154, 178, 179, 184, 230; and Anglo-Irish nobles, 123; 'awful lookout', 184; and Bolshevism 117, 147; and Catholic emancipation 116; and the 'Common People' 122; and divorce, 93; and education, 175; and English barons 123; 'gaily riding to ruin', 131; and the Georges, 115; 'gutter rats of England' 42–3; and miners, 230; over populated, 192; and Plain English, 117; and Pope 116, 149; and slavery, 114; 'the English enemie', 146; trip of 1923, 211
English labour, 134, 139, 143, 146, 148, 149, 151, 181
Ennis, Peter, 25
Eothen (book) 174
Eriugena, John Scottus, 194

'fags' (cigarettes), 85, 108
Fenians, 26
ffrench-Mullen, Madeleine, 27, 39, 45, 76,
Fianna Eireann, 2, 15, 60, 163, 171, 180, 225, 226
Fianna Fail, 4, 228, 236
Figgis, Darrell, 130
First World War, 3, 18, 67, 68, 72, 85; aftermath, 221
Fitzgerald, Theo, 118, 119, 138, 154
Fitzherbert, Mrs, 116

Fitzpatrick, Nora, 15
Flick, John Michael, 204
Florence (Italy), 165, 166, 167, 169, 189
'flu pandemic, 86, 90, 93, 97, 104, 138,
    167; 'great plague', 84
Foran, Thomas, 37, 111
Forbes-Robertson, Janina, 9, 12
force-feeding, 62
Four Courts, 210
Fox, Charles James, 116
Fox, R.M., 223
Fox, Dr S.F., 42
Freeman's Journal, the (newspaper), 18,
    88, 184
France, 102, 172
French language, 193, 223
French Revolution, the, 172
French Terror, 176
French, the, 8, 172, 192, 194, 198
Frankenstein, Dr, and his monster, 92
Frankfort House, 222, 225, 226, 228, 231,
    232, 233, 234
Frankfort Terrace, 200, 211, 217
Frognal Gardens, Hampstead, 215, 234,
    236
Fry, Roger, 124, 135

Gaelic League 2
Gavan Duffy, Charles, 195
Gavan Duffy, George, 43
general election (December 1918), 3, 85,
    86, 87, 88, 89, 90, 96, 98, 120; 'rigged',
    91
general election (May 1921), 188
general election (June 1922), 200, 210
general election (August 1923), 211,
    218
general election, British (December
    1923) 215
general election (July 1927), 236
George V, King, 15, 17, 73, 74
German grammar, 190, 192
'German Plot', 67, 69, 70, 74

Germany, 18, 20, 85, 87, 94, 98, 114,
    115, 154, 180, and Kaiser, 115, and
    England, 115, and philosophers, 194
Gifford Donnelly, Nellie, 27, 109, 119,
    123
Gifford Czira, Sidney, 'John Brennan', 37,
    147
Ginnell, Laurence, 62, 129,
Glasgow, 213, 219, 225
Glasnevin Cemetery, 238
Glendalough, 79, 135, 173
Glenveigh evictions, 115
Goff, (Gough), Bridie, 5, 25, 27
Gonne, Iseult, 161
Gonne MacBride, Maud, 2, 3, 5, 45,
    71, 76, 86, 103, 161, 170, 227; in
    Holloway, 67, 80, 85; and Inghinidhe
    na hÉireann, 2; letter from Constance
    to, 167
Gore-Booth, Augusta (aunt), 12
Gore-Booth, Eva (sister), 1, 4, 5, 14,
    16, 23, 26, 28–9, 39–40, 41; and
    health, 63, 79, 82, 130, 131, 135,
    150, 151, 155, 228; and landlord
    Roger Fry, 124, 151; and Manchester
    North by-election, 14; and Maunsel
    and Company, 119, 122–3, 133;
    and pacifism, 75, 77, 89, 130, 133;
    and poetry, 75, 121, 130, 187; and
    writing, 183; as trustee, 26, *Broken
    Glory*, 123; letter to Constance, 233;
    on Riviera, 168, 172; *the Egyptian
    Pillar*, 123; *The Triumph of Maeve*, 48
Gore-Booth, Evelyn (sister-in-law), 46
Gore-Booth, Henry (father), 8
Gore-Booth, Josslyn (brother), 1, 5, 6,
    18, 103, 169; and borough election
    of 1919, 103; and Casimir, 39, 103;
    and IRA raid, 165; and Markievicz
    marriage, 8–13; as Markievicz's
    administrator, 26, 28–9, 39, 62, 169,
    184, 185; and Markievicz money
    problems, 19–20, 39, 64–5; and

mother 234; and Staskou, 19–20; and
  St Mary's 169, 235
Gore-Booth, Lady Georgina Mary 'Gaga'
  (mother), 6, 27, 39, 46, 53, 56, 77,
  83, 101, 107, 114, 118, 120, 124, 129,
  130, 190, 195, 219, 227, 234–5; death,
  236; and Grand Tour, 77, 78, 129;
  letter from Constance to, 175; letters
  to Joss, 28–9, 41; on Con and Eva, 41
Gore-Booth, Mabel (sister), 1, 8, 10, 35,
  38; and Staskou, 204
Gore-Booth, Mary 'Molly' (née
  L'Estrange Malone; sister-in-law) 35,
  46, 108, 165, 185; cheque for Staskou,
  20–1
Gore-Booth, Mordaunt (brother), 1, 35,
  46
Gore-Booth, Robert (grandfather), 1
Government of Ireland Act 1920, 18,
  171
Grafton Street, Dublin, 199, 222
'Grand Tour', the, 39, 77, 78, 129
Grangegorman, 212
Greece, 69, 74, 176, 187
Grey, Edward, 154
Griffith, Arthur, 171, 199, 201, 210

Hales, Sean, 210
Hanover, House of, 115
Harding, Gertrude, 195
Harding, William G., 179
Harmsworth, Harold, 140, 146
Henderson, Arthur, 140
Henry VIII,126
Herald, see *Daily Herald*
History of Ireland (book), 113
Hobhouse, Stephen, 77
Hobson, John A., 89, 91, 94, 96, 97
Holloway Prison, 3, 4, 5, 67–101, 102,
  129, 138, 155, 170, 174, 215, 227
Home Office, 45
Home Rule, 2, 15, 17, 129
horoscopes, 52, 109

House of Commons, 3, 90
Howth gun-running, 18
Humphreys, Nell, 102, 103
hunger strike, 15, 30, 62, 63, 76, 165,
  212, 213, 214, 216, 218, 227; and
  Thomas Ashe, 63
Hyde, Douglas, 2

imperialism, 94, 179
Inchicore Hall, 110
India, 177, 179
Industrial Workers of the World (I.W.W.,
  or 'Wobblies'), 207
Inghinidhe na hEireann (Daughters of
  Eireann), 2, 14
IRA, 63, 108, 170, 188, 195, 210
International Women's Congress
  (Women's International League for
  Peace and Freedom congress, Dublin
  1926), 233
'In Tir na nOg', 150
Invincible Mother, The (Play), 222, 238
Irish Citizen, the (newspaper), 134
Irish Citizen Army, the, 3, 18, 22
Irish Free State, 200, 209, 210, 211, 222,
  223, 227, 229
Irish Independent (newspaper), 75, 89,
  125, 131
Irish Labour Party and Trade Union
  Congress, the, 130
Irish Parliamentary Party, the, 103
Irish Race Conference, the, 200
Irish Republican Brotherhood (IRB), 2
Irish Times, The (newspaper), 75, 173,
  180
Irish Transport and General Workers
  Union, 2, 23, 35, 37, 96, 132, 222
Irish Volunteers, the, 2, 18, 201
Irish Women's Franchise League, 15
Irish Women Workers' Union, 103
'Irregulars', 210
Italy, 79,168, 187; politics, 139, 172, 175,
  176, 182

'James Connolly's Policy and Catholic Doctrine' (pamphlet) 222
Japan, 178, 179
Julian, Rodolphe, 8, 10, 11

Kathleen ni Houlihan (play) 38, 91
Kavanagh, Ernest, 46
Kelly, Thomas, Alderman, 153, 158
Kent (Ceannt), Ronan, 48
Kickham, Charles J., 115
Kilmainham Jail, 22
Kilmacannon, 206
'King Billy' (William of Orange), 113, 116
Knocknagow (book), 115
Kolchak, Alexander, 148

Labour, Department of, 3, 62, 105, 164, 197, 198, 200, 211
Labour Party, Irish, 130, and Labour paper, 95; and Sinn Fein 132, 133
Labour Party, English, 29,70, 115, 125, 127, 129, 134–5, 136, 140, 142, 215, 219; and labour papers, 70, 101; and Swansea by-election, 125
labour, 4, 15, 139, 143, 146, 149, 151, 180, 181, 184, 194
Lalor, James Fintan, 114, 195
Lancaster (née Dyer), Annie, 100
Lane, Hugh, 14
Lang, Andrew, 181
Lansbury, George, 139
Larkin, Delia, 18
Larkin, James, 2, 204; leaves for USA, 18; split with ITGWU, 222
Law, Andrew Bonar, 43
League of Augsburg, 116
League of Nations, the, 68, 177, 204
Leinster Road, 19, 20, 63, 64
Lenin (Vladimir Ilyich Ulyanov), 114, 146, 171, 173
L'Estrange, Rhoda, 96
L'Estrange Malone, Cecil, 14, 124, 127, 129, 141, 154, 169, 170, 176, 192, 194

Liberty Hall, 2, 18, 25, 37, 48, 50, 54, 63, 103, 136. 139, 158, 164
Limerick 63, 74, 92, 104; May 1924 by-election, 219
Lincoln Jail, 96
Lincoln Place, Dublin, 213
Lissadell House, 1, 5, 8, 11, 14, 136, 162, 215
Litvinoff (Litvinov), Maxim, 72
Lloyd-George, David, 43, 105, 117, 127, 131, 146, 158, 180, 184, 199
Lockout 1913, 2, 18
'Loan', the, 158
local elections of 1920, 158
London, 1, 10, 45, 67, 68, 74, 110, 112, 115, 125, 127, 130, 131, 135, 148, 149, 151, 152, 162, 179, 199, 211, 218, 222, 223, 227, 230, 231
Los Angeles, 205, 208
Louis XIV, 116
Lowe, William H. M., Major-General, 64
Lumley Hay, Ivan, 120, 124
Lynch, Arthur, 134
Lynch, Bessie, 23, 24, 25, 26, 27
Lynch, Patricia, 70, 79, 83, 84, 223
Lynn, Dr Kathleen, 3, 22, 45, 58, 60, 63, 236

Macardle, Dorothy, 5, 229
MacBride, Séan (Seaghán, Shawn), 87, 159, 164, 167, 188
Mac Diarmada, Séan (Séan McDermott), 114
MacDonagh, Joseph, 164
MacDonnell, Anthony 1st Baron, 50
Maclean, John, 87
MacNeill, Eoin, 18, 152
Macready, Sir Neville, 162
MacSwiney, Mary, 109, 200
Madison Square Garden, 208
Mallin, Agnes, 5, 25, 26, 36, 50
Mallin, Michael, 2–3, 5, 22
Mallow, 107, 108, 109–10,

Manchester, 37, 86, 142, 178; 1908 by-election, 14, 38
Markievicz, Count Casimir Dunin de, 1–2, 8, 11, 12, 14, 15, 16, 18, 28, 30, 36, 40, 43, 44, 65, 72, 118, 142, 146, 153, 197, 204, 236; and 'Bloody Sunday', 18; and Dublin Repertory Company, 18; as playwright, 2; financial problems, 19, 20, 24, 27, 39, 40, 64; and fine ideas, 142; and Russia, 12, 28, 72, 142; goes to Albania, 18; Imperial Guard, 11; in Kiev, 72, 142; in Warsaw, 103–4, 197; letter from Constance to, 198–9; letter from Mary O'Carroll to, 237; visit to Ireland (1924), 221
Markievicz, Countess Constance de, and 1918 election, 3, 85, 86, 88, 89, 90, 96, 98, 120, 121; as an 'alien', 8, 153; and anarchy, 60; and the Anglo-Irish Treaty, 4, 200, 201, 210, 212, 227; and art, 93; and bike, 157; and Bolshevism, 171–2; and censor, 5, 30, 33, 45, 48, 49, 50, 54, 57, 68, 69, 71, 72, 73, 74, 75, 77, 81, 88, 89, 90, 93, 95, 100, 101, 125, 132, 134, 140, 145, 191, 216; and child labour, 143; and civil war, 4, 209; and conscription in Ireland, 72; and conversion to Catholicism, 162; and decentralisation, 152, 172; and education, 93, 117, 127, 171, 175; and economic depression, 184; and English Protestant Church, 115; and 'English Man-Pack', 16; and exhibiting, 99; and face in mirror, 33; and 'fags' 85, 108; and family, 30, 33, 35, 46, 103, 124, 170, 175, 227–8, 236; and the Fianna, 2, 15, 60,163, 171, 180, 225, 226; and Fianna Fail, 4, 228, 236; and financial problems, 19–20, 39, 64–5; and 'flu, 225; and food, 26, 32, 67, 72, 74, 99, 107, 112, 174, 213; and Ford 'Tin Lizzie' car, 224, 235; and 'Free State', 209, 222, 227, 229; and French Revolution, 172; and gardening, 6, 14, 15, 16, 20, 26, 34, 57, 77, 88, 105, 107, 112, 122, 127, 130, 138, 190, 192, 194, 224, 225, 230, 237; and German Kaiser 115; and hunger strike, 30, 63, 165, 212, 214, 216, 218, 227; and imperialism, 179; and Irish Citizen Army, 2, 3, 22; and Irish economy, 73, 127, 132; and Irish studies, 167, 170, 173.183, 187, 190, 192, 193, 194, 238; and 'lie' about policeman in 1916, 130; and mad world, 84, and marriage, 1, 9–13; and music, 9,183; and Northern Ireland, 152; and oath, 200, 212, 229, 230, 236; and old age pensions, 115, 200; and organised religion, 217; and parliaments, 59; and pictures, 10, 23, 34, 58, 104, 199; and Plain English, 117; and plays, 48–9, 53, 123, 126–7, 199, 217, 222, 228–9; and poetry, 27, 42, 52, 53, 71, 75, 124, 198; and police, 16–17, 18, 23, 27, 40, 43, 65, 102, 106, 107, 108, 109, 110–11, 119, 120, 129; and prison visits 83, and raid on Clarke household, 153; and reading, 5, 55, 141, 151; and Republican Players' Dramatic Society, 221; and restrictions on writing, 48, 76; and the Rising, 2, 3, 18, 22, 62, 64; and suffering, 179; and teeth, 27, 31, 33, 213; and trade unions, 18, 42, 117, 130, 132, 174; and typing, 219, 224; and visit of George V, 15, 16–17; and vote, 81; and wars, 136; and women's suffrage, 15; and words 44; and writing, 4, 33, 34, 35, 39, 40, 48, 49, 60, 64, 76, 100, 113, 117, 183, 219, 221, 223, 228, 232; as Dáil Minister for Labour, 3–4, 105, 164; cuts hair,

227; death and funeral, 4, 238; 'death notice' threat, 162; final illness, 236; 'how one longs for peace', 177; 'hurry-scurry life', 44; 'I don't believe in leaders', 94; 'I sit and dream..', 174; jail poems, 34, 51–2; on the English and England, 1, 3, 42, 70, 76, 98, 115, 120, 122, 123, 125, 131, 134, 146, 154, 178, 179, 184, 192, 206; on English Law, 145; on military raids, 155; on political prisoners, 42, 150; 'on the run', 3, 5, 100, 102, 153, 154, 156, 157, 158, 182, 190, 212, 230; on strikes, 125,139, 148, 192; rosary beads, 188; Suffrage Bill, 59; 'taxes are awful', 220; 'that pestilential harridan', 153; visit to the USA, 202–9; War of Independence, 4, 102, 171, 197; weight in prison, 32

Markievicz, Maeve (Meadhbh) Alys (daughter), 1, 6, 14, 117, 227, 230, 234, 236; and music, 120, 230

Markievicz, Stanislas (Staskou) (stepson), 1, 6, 14, 18, 19, 20, 43, 77, 106, 142, 149, 150, 159, 160, 162, 188, 197, 199, 236; held prisoner 197, 204; joins father, 18; letters from Constance to, 203–5, 210–1 220–1, 222–5, 226–7; school, 188; wife, 150, 159, 197, 199, 204, 224–5; with Russian Volunteer Fleet, 77

martial law, 162, 210

Marreco, Anne, 6

Maunsel and Company (publishers), 119, 122, 123, 133

Maxwell, General Sir John Grenfell, 64

McCormack, Katie, 141

McGarrity, Joseph, letter from Constance to, 156

McGarry, Séan, 103, 113

McGarry, Tomasina, 'Tommy', 113, 160

McGrath, Joseph, 102, 164

McGuinness, Father, 190

McHugh, Frank, letter from Constance to 225

McMahon, Sean, 154

McPherson, Ian, 154, 158

Mellows, Barney, 119

Mellows, Liam, 210, 225

Mercier d'Erme, Camille de, 198

Meynell, Alice, 47, 49

Michelham, Herbert Stern, 1st Baron, 128, 133

Millgate Monthly, 233

Milligan, Alice, 57

Minneapolis, 205

Mississippi, 203, 206

Mitchel, John, 114, 115; and rhetoric, 116, 195; and slavery, 114

Mitchell, Susan, 5, 23, 24, 26, 27, 28, 29, 35, 36, 45, 53, 57, 58, 75, 123

Molony, Helena ('Emer'), 4, 48, 76, 140–1; and acting 141; arrest 16

Morice, Sir John, 123

Morrell, Lady Ottoline, 35, 38

motor permit, 155, 164

Mountjoy Prison, 4, 22, 23, 34, 42, 164–96, 197, 227; prisoners' hunger strike, 62, 63, 212; strike, 150, rescues from, 225

Mount St Benedict, school, 188

Muncaster, Josslyn Francis Pennington, 5th Baron, 56, 146, 195

Murray Robertson, Rachel, 45

My Life in Two Hemispheres (book), 195

Nansen, Fridtjof, 204

Napoleonic Wars, 184

Neild, Helen J., 127

Nevinson, Henry, 170

New Age (British literary magazine), 132

Newbold, Walton, 131, 148, 219

New Grange, 136

New Ireland (magazine), 125

New York, 203, 204, 205

Ni Bhrudair, Gobnait (Lady Albina
    Brodrick), 94, 129, 141
Norgrove, Annie (also George, Maria,
    Emily, Fred), 50, 56
North Dublin Union, 212–16, 227;
    hunger strike, 214
Northcliffe, Alfred Harmsworth, 1st
    Viscount, 140
Noyk, Michael, 104, 169, 185

oath to King, 200, 212, 229, 230, 236
O'Brien, dentist, 213
O'Brien, George, 122
O'Brien, William X., 37
O'Byrne, Moira Kennedy, 195, 237
O'Brennan, Lily, 177
O'Carroll, Carroll, 213, 238
O'Carroll, Mary, family, 162; letters from
    Constance to, 212, 213; letter to
    Casimir, 237
O'Connell Fitz-Simons, Daniel, 27
O'Connor, Rory, 210
O'Growney, Father Eugene, 190
O'Daly, the blind poet of Lissadil, 152
O'Donovan Rossa, Jeremiah: daughter,
    21; funeral, 18
O'Hegarty, Mina, 108
O'Hegarty, P.S, 84, 104, 112, 156
Oireachtas, 121
O'Kelly, J.J, 'Sceilg', 207,
Ó Maille, Pádraic, 210
O'Neill, Molly, 88, 93, 99, 109, 112, 135
Orange Lodges, 219
O'Shannon, Cathal, 62
O'Shaughnessy, Arthur, 82, 93
Ossian, 152, 156

pacifism, 75, 89, 130, 133, 155, 158; Eva's
    pacifist novel, 77
Pankhurst, Sylvia, 94, 109, 168, 184, 195
Paris, 1, 8–13, 14, 200, 209
Paris Peace Conference, 65, 68, 69
Parnell, Charles Stewart, 90, 195

Pearse, Margaret, 48, 120,
Pearse, Patrick, 114, 115; and the Fianna,
    2; as an orator, 114; play, 188
'Peelers' (police), 108, 110, 111
Pelmanism, 124–5, 127
Percy Place, Dublin, 213
Perolz, Marie, 36, 37, 40, 140
'Petrol Oil Co', 20
Philadelphia, 205
Pigott, Richard, 90
Pigott (music shop), 25
Piles building, 25
Plunkett, Count George Noble, 145
Plunkett, Countess Josephine, letter from
    Constance to, 144–5
Poland, 14, 187, 211, 221
Police ('Peelers') strike, 80
Pope, the, 113, 116, 126, 190; Benedict
    XV, 188; English plot, 149
Poppet ('Mr P'; dog), 25, 37, 45, 47, 70,
    92, 106, 136,
Prescott, William H, 178
prison, 23; and reform, 42, 107, 171;
    prison food, 32, 67,107,112
Proclamation of the Republic 1916, 4
proportional representation (P.R.), 121,
    155, 158
Public Health Board, 160
Public Records Office of Northern
    Ireland, 5
Public Safety Act, 210

railway strike, 129, 150
Rathgar, 2, 14, 200, 211, 217, 222
Rathmines, 2, 15, 24, 76, 222, 235
Rathmines and Rathgar Urban District
    Council, 222
Reddish, Sarah, 38
Redmond, John, 18, 118; and Volunteer
    split, 18; 'Redmondites', 132
Rembrandt, 52
Republican Players Dramatic Society,
    221

Reynolds, 'Percy', 28
RMS Aquitania, 200, 202
Robinson, Joe, 127, 148, 152
Robinson, Lennox, 127, 133
robberies in Dublin, 154–5
Robespierre, Maximilien, 177
Roberts, (Dublin shop), 222
Roberts, George, 122,
Rockies, 204, 207
Romantic (novel) 226
Rome, 61, the catacombs, 60
Roper, Esther, 54, 211, 215; lecturing,
    176; letters from Constance to,
    231–14; letter from Esther to Hanna
    Sheehy-Skeffington 236–7; and
    prison visits to Markievicz, 23, 30,
    47, 50, 61; and publication of *Prison
    Letters*, 5
Roper, Reginald, 37, 46, 54, 72, 87, 135,
    147, 198, 237; and Pearse play, 188
Rosary beads, 58, 188,189
Royal College of Surgeons in Ireland, 3,
    22
Russell, Bertrand, 97, 258
Russell, George (AE), 1, 14, 27
Russell, Violet, 36
Russia, 28, 72, 77, 98, 115, 123, 136, 139,
    142, 146, 148, 173, 176

Salisbury, Lord, 69
Sandyford cottage, 14, 27
San Francisco, 205, 208
San Miniato, 165, 167
Seddon, J.A., 29
Selfridge, 222
separation allowance women, 66
Scotland, 148, 152, 211
Sheehy Skeffington, Francis, 21
Sheehy Skeffington, Hanna, 5, 98,
    159, 212; and Irish Women's
    Franchise League, 15; co-executor
    of Constance's will, 5; could have
    been an M.P., 95; election campaign

(1918), 89; election to Sinn Fein
    board, 135; 'knocked about', 134;
    letters from Constance to Hanna, 21,
    89–90, 134–5, 144, 177; letter from
    Esther Roper to Hanna, 236–7; letter
    from Hanna to Constance, 76; sister
    Katherine, 118; visit to USA, 76
Sidney, Philip, 149
Sigerson Shorter, Dora, 58
Sinn Féin, 2, 14, 62, 76, 88, 111, 121,
    124,125, 127, 133, 161, 222; and
    labour,132; and Bolshevism, 132;
    Aonach, 45; de Valera resigns from,
    228; general election (1918), 3, 85,
    90; general election (1921), 188;
    'German Plot', 67; Harcourt Street
    HQ, 135; in Sligo, 103; local elections
    (1920), 158; 'outrages', 155
Sir Patrick Dun's Hospital, 236
Sligo, 1,8, 40, 48, 53, 206, 212, 227, 228,
    229, 230; 1919 borough election, 103
Southampton, 200
Springfield, Massachusetts, 205, 208
'Squidge' (Miss Noel), 55, 58, 81, 165,
    189
Staines, Michael, 'Mick', 97, 102, 161
Stanhope, Lady Hester, 175
St Benedict's School, 188
St Brigid, 152
St Enda's School, 48, 96,
St Francis, 55, 58, 60,
St Malachy's Prophecy, 91
St Mary's (house), 2, 14, 15, 19, 24, 27,
    39, 40, 169, 175, 235
St Patrick's pilgrimage, 81
St Patrick's Ward, Dublin, 3, 85,103, 121,
    160
St Paul, Minnesota, 203, 205
Strindberg, August, 135
St Stephen's Green, 3, 22
Stuart, Francis, 161, 259
Store Street Police Barracks, 161
Suffragettes, in Dublin, 15

Surrey House, 5, 15, 23, 27
Susquehanna, river, 205
Swansea by-election, 125
Sweetman, Fr J.F, 188, 189
Swift, Dean Jonathan, 107
Switzerland, 8
Switzer's (shop), 222

taxes, 220, 223
Taylor, Dr William, 236
Thackeray, William Makepeace, 124
Third Home Rule Bill (1913), 15, 17
Thomas, Jimmy, 148, 180
Tolstoy, Leo, 174
Tramway Company (Dublin), 18
Treason Felony Act of 1848, 129
typewriting, 15, 224

Ukraine, the, 18, 72, 146
Ulster Unionists, 17, 43
Ulster Volunteers, 2
United Arts Club, 14
United States of America (USA), 101,
    106, 179; 1922 visit, 200–9; and
    Hanna Sheehy Skeffington, 76; and
    First World War, 54, copper mine in
    Butte, 207; houses, 206
Usk, 89, 90, 103

Vatican, the, 179–80
Versailles, 68

Wallace, Nora, 108, 111
Wallas, Graham, 136
War of Independence, 4, 102, 171; truce
    188, 197, 198, 201

Webb, James, 36
Welt-Politik, 94
Wexford, 188, 226
When Winter Comes (novel), 226
White, Captain Jack, 18, 161
White Russians, 146; Kolchak (leader)
    148
Wilde, Oscar, 117
Wilhelm, Kaiser, 74
'Women, Ideals and the Nation' (lecture),
    15
Workers'Dreadnought (newspaper), 72,
    94, 110
women elected to 2nd Dail, 188
women and local elections, 158, 159, 160
women's peace congress (Dublin 1926),
    233
women's rights, 1, 2, 3, 90, 135; and 1916
    Proclamation, 4; and Cumann na
    mBan, 125; in Ireland, 172, 182
women and vote, 3, 15, 85, 200, 201, 211
Woodrow Wilson, Thomas, 68, 91,148,
    156
'Wuss', 116, 120, 147, 195
Wyse Power, Jenny, 5, 76, 97, 100,121,
    160, 177, 200; letters from Constance
    to, 141–2,166
Wyse Power, Nancy, 142, 166

Yeats, W.B., 38, 91, 181
Young, Ella, 44

Zeppelin, 34
Zywotowka, 199, 204, 227